JERUSALEM

Directed and Designed by Hans Hoefer
Written by Norman Atkins
Photography by Richard Nowitz

APA PUBLICATIONS

THE INSIGHT GUIDES SERIES RECEIVED SPECIAL AWARDS FOR EXCELLENCE FROM THE PACIFIC AREA TRAVEL ASSOCIATION.

JERUSALEM

First Edition

© 1988 APA PUBLICATIONS (HK) LTD
Printed in Singapore by Apa Press Pte. Ltd.
Colour Separation in Singapore by Colourscan Pte Ltd

APA PUBLICATIONS

Publisher: Hans Johannes Hoefer
General Manager: Henry Lee
Marketing Director: Aileen Lau
Editorial Director: Geoffrey Eu
Editorial Manager: Vivien Kim
Editorial Consultants: Adam Liptak (North America)
Brian Bell (Europe)
Heinz Vestner (German Editions)

Project Editors

Helen Abbott, Diana Ackland, Mohamed Amin, Ravindralal Anthonis, Roy Bailet, Louisa Cambell, Jon Carroll, Hillary Cunningham, John Eames, Janie Freeburg, Bikram Grewal, Virginia Hopkins, Samuel Israel, Jay Itzkowitz, Phil Jaratt, Tracy Johnson, Ben Kalb, Wilhelm Klein, Eric Oey, Daniel P. Reid, Kim Robinson, Ronn Ronck, Robert Seidenberg, Rolf Steinberg, Sriyani Tidball, Lisa Van Gruisen, Merin Wexler.

Contributing Writers

A.D. Aird, Ruth Armstrong, T. Terence Barrow, F. Lisa Beebe, Bruce Berger, Dor Bahadur Bista, Clinton V. Black, Star Black, Frena Bloomfield, John Borthwick, Roger Boschman, Tom Brosnahan, Jerry Carroll, Tom Chaffin, Nedra Chung, Tom Cole, Orman Day, Kunda Dixit, Richard Erdoes, Guillermo Gar-Oropeza, Ted Giannoulas, Barbara Gloudon, Harka Gurung, Sharifah Hamzah, Willard A. Hanna, Elizabeth Hawley, Sir Edmund Hillary, Tony Hillerman, Jerry Hopkins, Peter Hutton, Neil Jameson, Michael King, Michele Kort, Thomas Lucey, Leonard Lueras, Michael E. Macmillan, Derek Maitland, Buddy Mays, Craig McGregor, Reinhold Messner, Julie Michaels, M.R. Priya Rangsit, Al Read, Elizabeth V. Reyes, Victor Stafford Reid, Harry Rolnick, E.R. Sarachandra, Uli Schmetzer, Ilsa Sharp, Norman Sibley, Peter Spiro, Harold Stephens, Keith Stevens, Michael Stone, Desmond Tate, Colin Taylor, Deanna L. Thompson, Randy Udall, James Wade, Mallika Wanigasundara, William Warren, Cynthia Wee, Tony Wheeler, Linda White, H. Taft Wireback, Alfred A. Yuson, Paul Zach.

Contributing Photographers

Carole Allen, Ping Amarand, Tony Arruza, Marcello Bertinetti, Alberto Cassio, Pat Canova, Alain Compost, Ray Cranbourne, Alain Evrard, Ricardo Ferro, Lee Foster, Manfred Gottschalk, Werner Hahn, Dallas and John Heaton, Brent Hesselyn, Hans Hoefer, Luca Invernizzi, Ingo Jezierski, Whilhelm Klein, Dennis Lane, Max Lawrence, Lyle Lawson, Philip Little, Guy Marche, Antonio Martinelli, David Messent, Ben Nakayama, Vautier de Nanxe, Kal Müller, Günter Pfannmuller, Van Philips, Ronni Pinsler, Fitz Prenzel, G.P. Reichelt, Dan Rocovits, David Ryan, Frank Salmoiraghi, Thomas Schollhammer, Blair Seitz, David Stahl, Bill Wassman, Rendo Yap, Hisham Youssef.
While contributions to Insight Guides are very welcome, the publisher cannot assume responsibility for the care and return of unsolicited manuscripts or photographs. Return postage and/or a self-addressed envelope must accompany unsolicited material if it is to be returned. Please address all editorial contributions to Apa Photo Agency P.O. Box 219, Orchard Point Post Office, Singapore 9123.

Distributors:

Australia and New Zealand: Prentice Hall of Australia, 7 Grosvenor Place, Brookvale, NSW 2100, Australia. **Benelux:** Uitgeverij Cambium, Naarderstraat 11, 1251 AW Laren, The Netherlands. **Brazil and Portugal:** Cedibra Editora Brasileira Lueras, Rua Leonidia, 2-Rio de Janeiro, Brazil. **Denmark:** Copenhagen Book Centre Aps, Roskildevej 338, DK-2630 Tastrup, Denmark. **Germany:** RV Reise-und Verkehrsuerlag Gmbh, Neumarkter Strasse 18, 8000 Munchen 80, West Germany. **Hawaii:** Pacific Trade Group Inc., P.O. Box 1227, Kailua, Oahu, Hawaii 96734, U.S.A. **Hong Kong:** Far East Media Ltd., Vita Tower, 7th Floor, Block B, 29 Wong Chuk Hang Road, Hong Kong. **India and Nepal:** India Book Distributors, 107/108 Arcadia Building, 195 Narima Point, Bombay-400-021, India. **Indonesia:** Java Books, Box 55 J.K.C.P., Jakarta, Indonesia. **Israel:** Steimatzky Ltd., P.O. Box 628, Tel Aviv 61000, Israel (Israel title only). **Italy:** Zanfi Editori SRL. Via Ganaceto 121, 41100 Modena, Italy. **Jamaica:** Novelty Trading Co., P.O. Box 80, 53 Hanover Street, Kingston, Jamaica. **Japan:** Charles E. Tuttle Co. Inc., 2-6 Suido 1-Chome, Bunkyo-ku, Tokyo 112, Japan. **Kenya:** Camerapix Publishers International Ltd., P.O. Box 45048, Nairobi, Kenya. **Korea:** Kyobo Book Centre Co., Ltd., P.O. Box Kwang Hwa Moon 1 658, Seoul, Korea. **Philippines:** National Book Store, 701 Rizal Avenue, Manila, Philippines. **Singapore:** MPH Distributors (S) Pte. Ltd., 601 Sims Drive #03-21 Pan-I Warehouse and Office Complex, S'pore 1438, Singapore. **Switzerland:** M.P.A. Agencies-Import SA, CH. du Croset 9, CH-1024, Ecublens, Switzerland. **Taiwan:** Caves Books Ltd., 103 Chungshan N. Road, Sec. 2, Taipei, Taiwan, Republic of China. **Thailand:** Asia Books Ltd., 5 Sukhumvit Road Soi 61, P.O. Box 11-40, Bangkok 10110, Thailand. **United Kingdom, Ireland and Europe (others):** Harrap Ltd., 19-23 Ludgate Hill, London EC4M 7PD, England, United Kingdom. **Mainland United States and Canada:** Graphic Arts Center Publishing, 3019 N.W. Yeon, P.O. Box 10306, Portland OR 97210, U.S.A. (The Pacific Northwest title only); Prentice Hall Press, Gulf & Western Building, One Gulf & Western Plaza, New York, NY 10023, U.S.A. (all other titles).

French editions: Editions Gallimard, 5 rue Sébastien-Bottin, F-75007 Paris, France. **German editions:** Nelles Verlag GmbH, Schleissheirner Str. 371b, 8000 Munich 45, West Germany **Italian editions:** Zanfi Editori SLR. Via Ganaceto 121 41100 Modena, Italy. **Portuguese editions:** Cedibra Editora Brasileira Ltda, Rua Leonidia, 2-Rio de Janeiro, Brazil.

This book was researched during the relatively calm summer of 1987, and was written and compiled during the Palestinian uprisings, a time of great anguish and fear in Jerusalem and Israel. While it's common for some people to speak about Jerusalem in apocalyptic terms, one must remember that the city has been through far worse over the past 3,000 years than the current political troubles. This volume, while necessarily acknowledging the present tensions, also recognizes that Jerusalem is an eternal city that will draw visitors and pilgrims long after the present headlines have faded.

Hoefer

Atkins   Eu

Cityguide: Jerusalem is primarily the inspiration of **Hans Hoefer**, publisher and founding father of APA Publications, who started the *Insight Guides* back in 1970. The first title released was Bali and its extreme success launched APA. In the years since, Hoefer has employed his innovative approach towards travel and graphic design by directing the expansion of the series to include every continent on the earth.

His latest brain-child is the *Cityguide* series. Hoefer wanted to create a practical book that the visitor could walk with down the street and one that would also provide current and vital information that covers the major tourist attractions and some interesting nooks and crannies which are all too often overlooked in other travel guides. As a result, the *Cityguide* series was born, with an initial 14 titles going to press in 1988.

With most other APA guidebooks, a destination is generally covered by a team of writers who are put together by a project editor. However, in the case of *Cityguide: Jerusalem*, writer **Norman Atkins** elected to do the job on his own. The result is a book which presents a very unique perspective on Jerusalem and stands out among others in a very competitive market.

Atkins, a 26 year-old Chicago-born, New York-based freelance journalist, has written on culture and politics for the *Village Voice* and *Rolling Stone,* and his work has appeared in *The Washington Post, The Boston Globe, Manhattan, Inc., In These Times,* and *The Birmingham News,* among a variety of other publications. He also served as the editor and president of the *Brown Daily Herald* at Brown University, where he received a B.A. in History. Upon graduation in 1984, he spent a year traveling around Morocco, the Western Sahara, and Europe.

One day in Spain, something inspired him to fly to Israel, a place for which he never had any real interest, but to which he found himself suddenly drawn. Within a week there, he was studying 12 hours a day at a Jerusalem *yeshivah*, and stayed on nearly four months. Although he did not become what one would consider *frum* (Orthodox), he emerged with profound respect for the tradition and the guru-rabbis who are its curators; his only promise was that he would continue to learn.

With this in mind, it was not too difficult for APA's Editorial Director **Geoffrey Eu** to persuade Atkins to put together a book on Jerusalem. As it happened, Atkins was already headed back to the city for the summer of 1987 with his Zionist girlfriend, **Angie Kritz**, who was in the process of organizing her Israeli jewelry import business, Angie Olami.

Having made several trips to Israel since 1983, she had held several jobs in Jerusalem and worked in the chicken coops at Kibbutz Menara. After graduating *cum laude* from Yale University in 1985 with a degree in English Literature and then studying at the

University of Leningrad, she brought her fluent Hebrew and Russian back to Jerusalem to work for the Soviet Jewry Education and Information Center. She helped write, research, and copy-edit the guidebook.

During the course of this book's production, Atkins and Kritz were married and had a baby son. They named him Zohar, which is Hebrew for splendor, or spiritual light. They currently live in Bearsville, New York, a small village in the Catskill Mountains, and hope to live in Jerusalem in the not-too-distant future.

One of the outstanding features of the *Insight Guides* series is the striking photography, and the offerings of the two professionals represented in this volume are no exception. They show Jerusalem to be an exceedingly photogenic place.

Providing most of the photography in this book is **Richard Nowitz**, whose 12 years experience working and living in Jerusalem have put him among the ranks of the nation's top photographers. Originally from America, Nowitz was a high school teacher and a pharmacist before moving to Israel and becoming a professional photographer. His credits include work for *Time* and *Life* magazines, Time-Life books, the *New York Times, Hadassah* magazine, and commendation in the Nikon International Photo Contest. He also worked on the APA guides to Israel and London.

Another photographer, **Werner Braun**, was born in Nuremburg, Germany and emigrated to Palestine in the mid-1940s.

 *Nowitz*  *Braun*

Braun has gained wide renown as one of the country's leading photographers in the decades since. He has worked for a spectrum of publishers including *Time, Life, Look, Newsweek, Fortune, Reader's Digest, World Book, Encyclopedia Brittanica,* and Weidenfeld & Nicoloson Press (for whom he photographed a guide to the Negev &

Sinai), to name only a few, and he has had numerous exhibitions around the world. Braun specializes in aerial and underwater photography.

The extensive Travel Tips section in the back of the book is a product of the work **George Melrod** did for APA's Israel guide, along with assistance from **Phyllis Glazer**

Melrod   *Kim*   *Maschmeyer*

and **Asher Weill**.

Back at APA headquarters in Singapore, editor **Gloria J. Maschmeyer** edited the final copy, finalized the layout and helped to monitor the book through the production phases.

Maschmeyer, a graduate in journalism, is an American freelance writer and photographer. She has lived in Singapore for two years, becoming widely published in the Pacific Asian region. In addition, she is the Asian correspondent for *Passages*, a U.S.-based travel magazine.

Overseeing various aspects of the project in Singapore were Editorial Director Geoffrey Eu and Editorial Manager **Vivien Kim**. The project editor wishes to thank them both for their unending support and perseverance.

Some initial help in setting the book in motion was provided by APA Executive Editor **Adam Liptak** in New York.

In Singapore, freelancer **Evelyn Chan** provided her invaluable expertise and expedience to assembling the Travel Tips section into final form.

In Jerusalem, the following people provided assistance, suggestions, support, and knowledge: **Yehudit Baruch**, **Evelyn Baruch**, **Avi Katzman**, **Motti Stein**, **Jeremy** and **Susan Kagan**, **Yitzhak Feldman**, and **Fayek Bilbiesi**.

—APA PUBLICATIONS

TABLE OF CONTENTS

TABLE OF CONTENTS

OTHER INSIGHT GUIDES TITLES

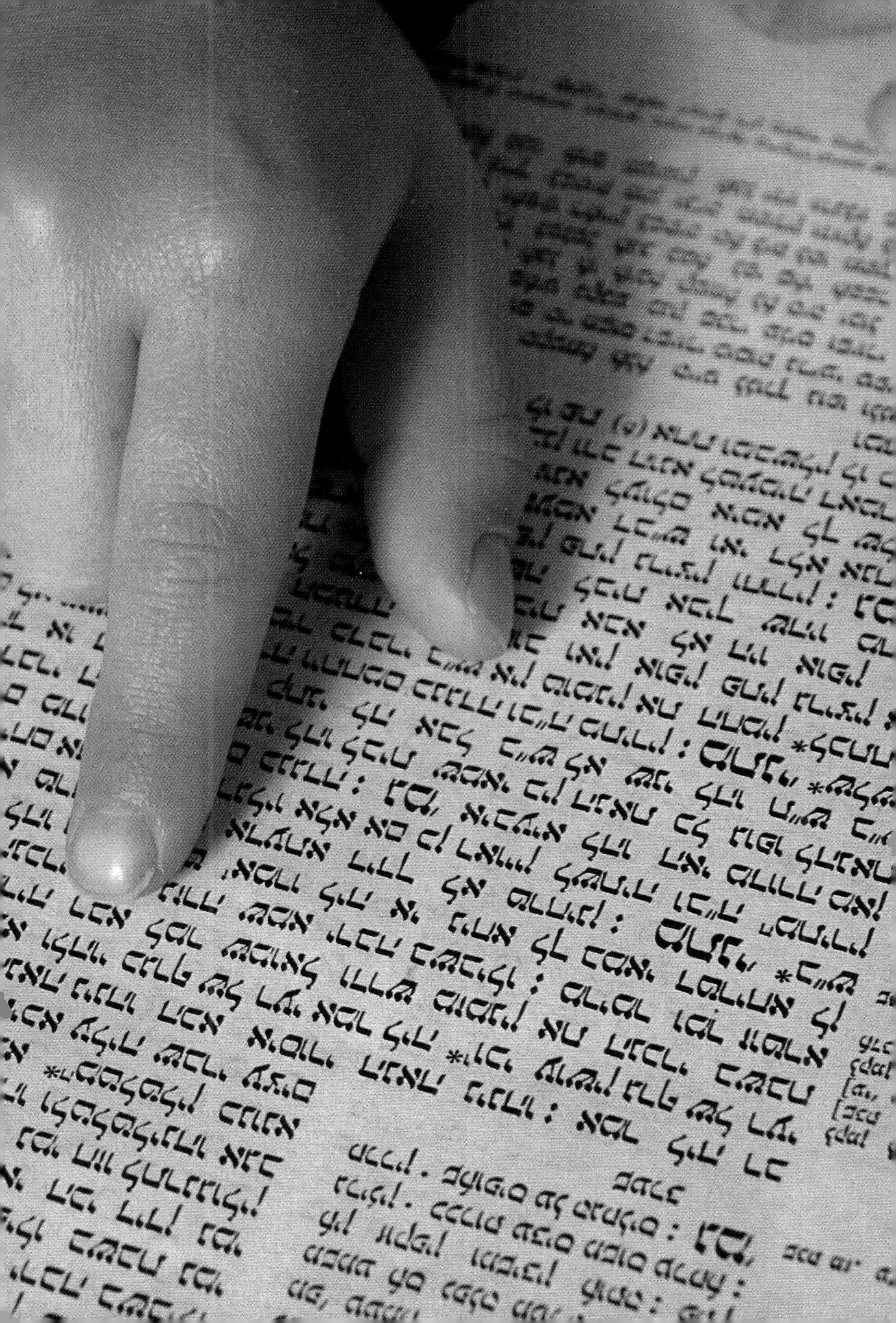

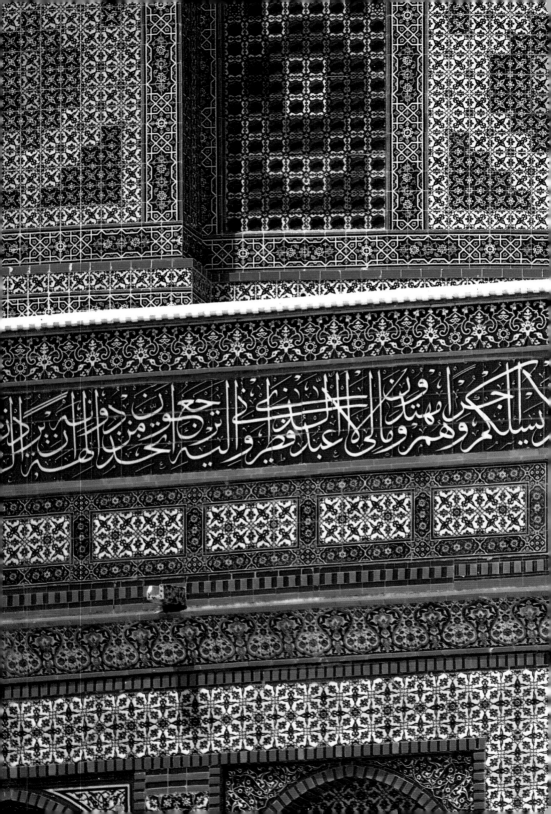

THE CHALLENGE OF JERUSALEM

Have you ever come across Paul Fussell's distinction among the three types of journeys? Fussell is fairly well known for having written quite a bit on the enchantments of foreign places, and in a slim, but wise volume called *Abroad*, he lays down this declension of trip-making: first comes adventure, then travel, and finally tourism. Sad to say for those of us trapped in the 20th century, there is precious little land or sea in the world left unexplored, and thus adventure stands on the verge of virtual extinction. Indeed, most trips today are lucky enough to be considered even travel, and normally end up as mere tourism. Such is especially true when one ventures to the obvious places (London, Paris, Berlin, etc.), and over the course of history, none has been more obvious or attracted more tourists than the city of Jerusalem.

That has become clear once again in recent times. Ever since the Israeli army vanquished Jordan in 1967 and reunited the city, visitors have flocked here from every corner of the earth. For the modern secularist, Jerusalem is the stuff of legends, a place that was once considered the geographic center of the world. For Moslems, Jerusalem (after Mecca and Medina) is the third most important pilgrimage site, and during the Islamic festival of *Ramadan*, they crowd the famed shrines, the Dome of the Rock and the Al-Aksa Mosque. For Christians, Jerusalem is *the* mecca, the single most important place of worship, and many would not think of dying before visiting the "Holy Sites" of Jesus. The Talmud (which comprises all of Jewish oral law) says that when 10 measures of beauty came upon the world, "nine were

taken by Jerusalem—and one by the rest of the world." For the Jews, there is a commandment not merely to visit the city, but if at all possible to settle there and an increasing number have made that commitment since 1967. In that time the Israeli government has labored to make the city hospitable to these and still other visitors and residents, with no small financial rewards accruing to the state's booming tourist industry, the bulwark of an otherwise unstable economy.

Having said all this, what is so astonishing is that unlike Rome, Athens, or other such ancient capitals, Jerusalem is *not* a tourist town. It is not cute, quaint, or easy. To be sure, you will find swinging sidewalk cafes, shopping stores and swimming pools on roofs or overpriced hotels (in abundance). But this city is not about any of those things. No matter what your intentions may be in embarking upon your journey, once you have arrived, Jerusalem will show you that rare bird, an adventure. It will not let you get away with simply clicking snapshots from tour bus windows.

Preceding pages: A Yemenite Jewish woman in traditional dress; a youngster tries his hand at Talmud; detail from the Dome of the Rock; view from the Dominus Flevit Church. Left, acrobat teeters over the Valley of Hinnom. Right, an Orthodox Jew prays at the wall.

"You see that arch from the Roman period?" writes the city's poet laureate Yehudah Amichai. "It is not important but next to it...there sits a man who bought fruit and vegetables for his family." Amichai has captured the city's ethos. For it liberates you from strictly sightseeing and lets you squeeze the vegetables and get to know that man and his family. Everyone you meet here, from the bus driver to the mayor, seems to have lived a thousand lives and can fill your ears with stories that defy the imagination. Moreover, they're constantly asking *you* questions: What are your politics? Do you believe in God? Where are you *really*

The city is a challenge, even getting there can be an adventure. By air, you arrive at Ben Gurion airport near Tel Aviv, or perhaps you come overland from Jordan, across the Allenby Bridge. But by whichever port of entry, you are instantly struck by the tight security that greets you, the way your bags are rifled, your passport photo scrutinized for an extra minute, or your Swiss army knife confiscated.

Visitors are often irritated (and the Palestinians bitter) by such inconvenience, not to mention the rudeness that the Israeli soldiers almost invariably display. But the Israelis themselves are actually comforted by the

from? If you permit yourself, Jerusalem will engage you, force you to marvel at the sweep of all human history, and prod you to confront your own identity, whatever it may be.

In a passage of his book *To Jerusalem And Back*, Nobel Prize-winning Jewish writer Saul Bellow has written about this inexplicable mystical grip: "The air, the very air, is thought nourishing in Jerusalem, the Sages themselves said so...The universe interprets itself before your eyes in the openness of the rock-jumbled valley ending in dead water. Elsewhere you die and disintegrate. Here you die and mingle."

trouble. They figure it's a small price to pay for safety.

Jerusalem, you must remember, is geographically situated at the fulcrum between Asia and Africa, in the heart of Israel, a tiny nation itself in the heart of the Middle East, a disturbed, fractured, increasingly fanatic, and increasingly powerful region. The city is prized, the object of much resentment and longing. The Palestine Liberation Organization (PLO) of Yasser Arafat would like to establish an independent state and make this city its capital. The Pope wants it to be an international city. And the Israelis in defiance of the United Nations and the world community declared it their capital. At no time since they gained control of the entire city in the 1967 war, have they given any signs that they plan to retreat a solitary inch. The politics of Jerusalem are a nightmare. You will soon see there are more "on the other hands" than any individual has hands.

One cannot easily even understand what people are saying in the midst of this heated discourse, so strange is the melange of languages. Indeed, it is easy to imagine that every language that has ever been spoken is spoken on any average day in Jerusalem. The city itself has the character of each part of the world from which these languages sprang—Russian ghetto, Armenian village, Fez souk. Passing from one neighborhood to the next can feel like being spirited from one universe to another. Amos Oz, the famed Israeli novelist who was born in the city, wrote in his celebrated book *My Micheal* about the strange admixture of fire, angles, and light that characterize the place:

"Jerusalem is a burning city. But a closer glance reveals an immeasurable weightiness. The overpowering arbitrariness of the intertwining alleys. A labyrinth of temporary dwellings, huts and sheds leaning in smouldering anger against the gray stone that takes on now a blue, now a reddish tinge. Rusting gutters. Ruined walls. A harsh and silent struggle between the stonework and the stubborn vegetation. Waste-plots of rubble and thistles. And, above all, the wanton tricks of light: if a stray cloud comes for a moment between the twilight and the city, immediately Jerusalem is different."

Take this landscape and throw into it the oddest and most diverse collection of geniuses, exiles, dreamers, and freaks on the face of the earth. A city with so many joyously pious or genuinely spiritual pilgrims is also a magnet for its fair share of charlatans, faith healers, and false messiahs patroling the streets for newcomers. It is not always easy to distinguish one from the other, but to be too cautious about whom you talk to or

whose dinner invitation you accept is to deny yourself the city's richest resource.

Perhaps, for example, you will find yourself in the forbidding neighborhood of Mea Sharim, face to face with a bearded, dandruff-infested Hassidic Jew, whose family came from some Russian ghetto somewhere in the Pale of Settlement. Perhaps, if you are lucky, he will talk to you. Perhaps, if you are luckier still, he will tell you a story such as this one, which has for the Jerusalem visitor, a special significance.

"The founder of Hassidism was the Baal Shem Tov. It is said that when he saw misfortune threatening his people, he would find a special place in the forest where he would meditate, light a fire, say a prayer, and the misfortune would be avoided. Some time after, one of his disciples found that special place, but he did not know how to start a fire; so he said the prayer and again the danger was averted. Later still, another disciple, who could neither light a fire, nor say the prayer, saved his people because at least he could find the special place in the forest. After many years, yet another disciple said to God, 'I do not know how to light the fire. I do not know how to say the prayer. I cannot even find the place in the forest. All I can do is tell the story, and this must suffice.' And, you know something, it did suffice because, so it is related, God made human beings because He loves stories."

Jerusalem may be a mystical place, but the people who reside there are so far removed from the lives of Abraham, David, Mohammed, Jesus, and the other historical and prophetic personages who made the city what it is. Jerusalemites today only have the stories, and even that is a miracle. For the modern visitor, the challenge of any trip to Jerusalem is not to see the greatest number of shrines and monuments, many of which are described herein. The challenge is to open oneself to meeting the disciples, of whichever faith and no matter how many generations removed, and hear the stories of how the city—and all the world—came to be what it is. Whether one goes away convinced that one, several, or no stories are the truth hardly matters. For, as the Hassidic tale says, God loves stories.

Left, instamatic tour bus experience: the wrong way to travel around Jerusalem.

23

ΑΓΙΑΠΟΛΙCΙΕΡΟΥCΑΛ

Some 4,000 years ago Abraham (so the Bible tells us) ventured 2,000 miles from his native Ur to the Land of Canaan. Thereupon this sheikesque Chaldean shepherd emerged as a prosperous trader, a skillful warrior, and the undisputed leader of his family clan.

At a time when idolatry was "in," and polytheism was the rage, Abraham was smashing his father's idols. Abraham swore fealty to *one* God.

So fervently did he worship God that one day he journeyed to Mt. Moriah and prepared to sacrifice his son simply because the Lord willed it. When Abraham had bound Isaac and laid him across the altar, however, God intervened. "Do not raise your hand against the boy," said an angel of the Lord. "For now I know that you fear God, since you have not withheld your son, your favored one, from me."

Thus did Abraham emerge as the patriarch of the Jewish people and the progenitor of monotheism, a prophet venerated by Christians, Moslems and even modern philosophers. In the context of the history of Jerusalem, this particular revelation resulted in the city's origin as the world's great spiritual center. A belief that has transcended time.

In the time of Abraham, the town was a small Canaanite city-state settled in the middle of the Bronze Age, perhaps 2500 BCE. The town was ruled by the Amorites, Hittites, and Jebusites. The former supposedly followed a lord named "Shalem," from which the city ("yerah") got its name "Yerushalayim." Shalem (or "Shalom") also means peace, and hence Jerusalem is more commonly called "The City of Peace," an encomium not wanting in irony.

One may wonder why so many wars have been fought in the past 3,000 years over an area which the city's historians delight in

cataloging its inadequacies: Jerusalem sits at the head of no generous river or harbor; no vital trade route or highway cuts though it; it's hurting for mineral riches; and it has never represented a crucial domino in the sport of empire conquest. In short, the city has no more military, topographic, or economic value than any other average Bedouin base camp.

No wonder Abraham's descendants, the Jews, upon escaping from Egypt and sweep-

ing into Canaan didn't bother to conquer Jerusalem. Even after settling the land around it, they left the city to the Jebusites perhaps because these 12 tribes of Israel were preoccupied with their own civil wars until the time of King David.

Now David was a stunningly handsome farmer who had become fairly famous while still a lad, so the legend goes, by defeating the enormous Philistine champion Goliath in combat. The southern tribes of Israel, known as Judah, gathered around David, and he ascended to the throne in the capital of Hebron. As he grew in power, the weaker northern tribes came to Hebron and recognized David, anointing him their monarch as well in about 1000 BCE.

King David is remembered for destroying the Philistine armies and finally securing the borders of the land that God had promised the children of Abraham. But he is remembered best of all for his decision to conquer and take as his new capital Jerusalem.

This was not as foolish as it may have seemed. In terms of the land apportioned to the 12 tribes, Jerusalem was centrally located. Since no tribe in particular held any historical claim to it, all could be brought together under its aegis without inspiring the

normal amount of rivalry.

As the conquest and achievement of King David, Jerusalem came to symbolize the new monarch ("The City of David") and unified the nation. Given all that, the city was strategically well positioned for defending itself against foreign foes, mountains fortifying it on three sides. Although lacking the ideal water supply, it was conveniently located near the spring of Gihon, a surprising water source in the otherwise barren, soil-poor Judean hills. Those hills may have looked nasty, but the Jews learned to make the best of a bad situation and subsequently pioneered mountain agriculture and reared sheep and goats.

To Jerusalem David brought the Ark of the Covenant. It was reputed to be the mobile shrine that the Jews built during 40 years of wandering to hold the tablets of law which God gave Moses and all of Abraham's descendants on Mt. Sinai. Once in Jerusalem, David built a tabernacle to cover the shrine, and went in search of land upon which a permanent home could be established. To this end he purchased for 50 shekels of silver the threshing floor of Araunah the Jebusite on a hill just outside the settled part of the city.

This very hill brings us back to the story of Abraham. In the oral tradition of the Jews, David did not select this spot arbitrarily, God showed it to him. The Lord is to have revealed it as Mt. Moriah, the very place where Abraham offered his son Isaac in sacrifice. This meant that Jerusalem was the holiest ground of all.

David may have found the land, but the tradition says he could not build the Temple because he was a warrior, his hands too bloody. Shortly before he died in 960 BCE, David anointed his youngest son Solomon to be his successor. Solomon was known for being both a splendid poet and statesman, both wise and rich. He forged treaties with a number of former adversaries, taking their daughters for wives. He was even linked romantically with fabled queen of Sheba. But the culmination of Solomon's rule was fulfilling the mission set forth by his father, building the Temple. It was dedicated at *Sukkot* (the feast of the tabernacles) in 953 BCE. At that moment, Jerusalem became the religious as well as the political center of the Jewish people.

Upon Solomon's death in 922 BCE, the 10 northern tribes, unhappy with rule from Jerusalem, seceded to establish their own state, the Kingdom of Israel. The southern two tribes — Benjamin and Judah — continued to follow the House of David and formed

Left, replica of an ancient mosaic of Chanukah menorah. Right, model of Herod's Temple.

31

the Kingdom of Judah, with the capital remaining in Jerusalem. There followed over the next two centuries an on-again-off-again civil war between these two kingdoms. For the city, the war with the northern tribes meant a loss of trade and taxes.

In 722 BCE, King Sargon II of then powerful Assyria conquered Samaria, where the northern tribes had their capital. He exiled them to the furthest reaches of the empire, where many presumably assimilated. Thus they are called the Ten Lost Tribes of Israel. By all logic, the other two tribes should have met the same destiny and would have were it not for Judah's King Hezekiah, the unsung

side it for very long without water.

When King Hezekiah died in 687 BCE, he had done much to save the city. His son Manasseh, who succeeded him, proceeded to undo much of that work, making Judah the virtual vassal of Assyria, adopting idol-worship, and regularly permitting the sacrifice of children in the valley of Hinnom, customarily regarded ever since as the geographic site of Hell. Manasseh's grandson, King Josiah (640-609 BCE) was considered considerably more righteous, and during his rule child sacrifices were abolished and a religious revival took place under the influence of the prophet Jeremiah. During this

hero of Jewish history.

He prepared the city for siege first by rallying the previously doomsayers' populace. With the support of the prophet Isaiah, he repaired the temple, destroyed all idols, and outlawed pagan-worship.

Then he mobilized the Jews to build a massive wall around the city and a 1600-foot (500-meter) tunnel through which water could be drawn from the Gihon Spring to the Siloam pool just inside the city walls. In 701 BCE, Assyrian King Sennacherib came with his armies to Jerusalem. His forces could neither penetrate the wall, nor survive out-

period, the cycle of three yearly pilgrimages to Jerusalem began.

Although Josiah was able to annex the northern territories, by 602 BCE the Kingdom of Judah was torn asunder in the midst of war between Babylon and Egypt. At first Josiah's son, a treacherous ruler named Zedekiah, ruled Jerusalem as a Babylonian puppet. When he finally tried to resist and forge an alliance with Egypt, Babylonian King Nebuchadnezzar came to Jerusalem and turned away the Egyptians. Although the Jews barricaded themselves inside the city for many months, even as they were on the verge of starvation in 587 BCE the city walls were breached.

Zedekiah fled to Jericho, but was soon captured, forced to watch his family butchered before his own eyes were ripped out and he was carried off to Babylon in chains. No kinder fate awaited the rest of the Jews. By 586 BCE Nebuchadnezzar toppled the city, burned down the Temple, killed off part of the population, and hauled the rest of the people off into exile.

Fifty years later, the Persian king Cyrus reduced Babylon and allowed the exiles to return. A benevolent dictator, Cyrus even donated money from the royal coffers for

King Ataxerxes I to make him governor of the land and he immediately returned to a home he had never seen.

Nehemiah led the third and decisively important wave of returning exiles in 440 BCE. It is said that under his guidance, the walls of the city were built in 52 days, the Temple significantly refurbished. Meanwhile, Ezra the Scribe led a group of priestly types from Babylon to Jerusalem to revitalize the study of Jewish law. The community in exile had practised a far more rigid observance of the tradition than the community of returnees. Ezra is remembered best of all for compiling the cannon of Jewish Torah (or

reconstruction of the Temple, which was finished in 515 BCE. Despite this good fortune, many Jews had remained in Babylon, where they had become well established in business and in the Persian administration. One such high-ranking official was Nehemiah. And when a delegation of Jews from Jerusalem visited him and told of the terrible conditions of their city, he persuaded

Left, medieval view of King Solomon and the Queen of Sheba. Above, ruins of the steps leading to the Temple.

Bible), which has been followed ever since.

The Persians continued to control Jerusalem until 333 BCE when the young and indominatable general Alexander the Great annexed it to the Greek empire. At first, the Greek Ptolemies of Egypt did not dicker with the established Judean theocracy and the city prospered. They did, however, haul off a substantial number of Jewish prisoners to the Egyptian city of Alexandria, which hence became an important early center of diaspora Jewry.

The Greeks of Egypt were finally ousted by the Greeks of Syria, the Seleucids, in 198

BCE. If they were benevolent initially, by 175 BCE Seleucid King Antiochus IV, whose chief goal was to transform Jerusalem into a Greek city, made observance of Judaism punishable by death. He built a Hellenistic fortress on the Temple mount, rededicated the Temple itself to Zeus, and sacrificed swine across its altars.

In a recurring pattern throughout their history, many Jews accepted idol worship and assimilated to Hellenism. Others passively resisted, continuing their Jewish prayers and observance in private. Others still preferred death. By 167 BCE, the Jews began a National War of Resistance against the Greeks. It was led by five brothers from the House of Hasmon, the eldest of whom was called Judah the Maccabee because he was as powerful as a hammer.

The Hasmoneans fought a guerilla war from the Judean mountains, culminating in the reconquest of the Temple mount in 164 BCE. When they reached the Temple, it was terribly befouled and (so the Talmud tells us), there was only enough pure oil to last one day. But (by the miracle of God) it lasted eight days until a new supply of oil became available. That is why on the yearly Jewish celebration of Chanukah, which commemorates the Maccabbean victory, the Jews light eight candles.

Within a few years, from the Temple Mount base, the Hasmoneans beat back the Seleucids and controlled Jerusalem once again. Judah the Maccabee died in 160 BCE, but he was succeeded first by his righteous brothers Jonathan and Simon and finally by his fascistic nephew John Hyrcanus, who ruled from 135 to 104 BCE.

Not happy with mere independence, Hyrcanus dreamed of building a Jewish kingdom and — in an act thoroughly out of sync with Jewish law or tradition — he forcibly circumcised and converted a conquered people called the Idumeans.

Opposed to Hyrcanus was an ideological faction of Jews called the Pharisees. They cared more about the Torah than the kingdom and were more concerned with religious observance than imperial conquests. The Sadducees, a competing faction representing the priestly and monied caste, supported the combined political and religious leadership of Hyrcanus. The rift between these two groups coupled with shoddy leadership from the heirs to Hyrcanus left Jerusalem ripe for the picking when the Rome's conquering hero Pompey arrived in 63 BCE.

Within 25 years, Roman control was firmly grounded with the appointment of Herod as king of Judea. Herod descended from the aforementioned Idumeans. He reigned for 35 years, during which time the city prospered and underwent massive repairs.

Rome considered him an ally, but Herod disturbed many of his so-called subjects the way he flaunted the latest foreign styles and fashions. In Jerusalem itself, for instance, he constructed a Greek Hippodrome near the Temple mount.

Herod was so paranoid a ruler that he had his own wife and two sons killed because he feared they would destroy him. This, along with his disregard for Jewish dietary law, prompted one of the king's admirers, Emperor Augustus Caesar to quip: "I would rather be Herod's pig than Herod's son."

It's impossible to say, however, whether the Jews could have mistrusted Herod as much as he imagined. In any event, he decided to try to ingratiate himself by leading the reconstruction of the Temple. According to the historian Josephus, Herod's Temple was built by 10,000 workmen and 1,000 priests. It took eight years to complete the courtyard and another couple of years for the Temple itself. When it was finished, it was widely regarded as one of the wonders of the world. The Talmud says that one who had not seen Herod's Temple had not seen a beautiful building.

Herod came to a bloody end in 4 BCE, upon which a Jewish revolt was put down by Roman legions, and soon Judah was annexed by Rome and ruled by procurators. It was into this chaotic world and time that a certain child named Jeshua, or Jesus, was born, and that world, as they say, has never been the same.

Right, David playing the harp, as depicted by Marc Chagall for the Knesset.

Now the Jews believe there is a man in every generation who has the potential to be the Messiah, and since these times seemed to call urgently for divine intervention, there were repeated claims around town that one or another zealous type was, in fact, the Messiah who had come to save the Jews from the Romans. It is probably true that such a claim was made on behalf of Jesus as much or more than any other man of his time.

When Jesus was born in Nazareth not so far away, the population of Jerusalem was nearly a quarter of a million and it swelled to about a million during festival times. Pilgrims would come from all across the land and the Diaspora to make sacrifices and worship at the Temple for the three festivals: *Pesach* (Passover), which marked the celebration of the Jews' exodus from Egypt; *Shavuoth* (Feast of Weeks), the wheat harvest festival; and *Sukkot* (Feast of the Tabernacle), in which the Jews give thanks for God's bountiful nature.

Jesus' parents, Joseph and Mary (so we learn from Luke), were in the habit of making this pilgrimage from their native Galilee on *Pesach* every year. When Jesus was 12 years old, they brought him along. On their way home after the festival, however, they lost track of the boy and had to search for him for days. They went back to Jerusalem and finally found him still inside the Temple, completely absorbed with the teachings of Pharisee rabbis, engaged in a dialogue that greatly impressed his elders.

Like the Pharisees, Jesus was contemptuous of Roman authority and scorned the priestly administrators of the Temple, the way they privileged ceremony over spiritual substance. He was bothered by the materialism of the wealthy Jerusalemites and the fact that they exploited the poor. He denounced the rampant hate that had spread across the

Left, Crusader crosses in the Church of the Holy Sepulchre. Right, the 1683 floorplan of the church.

town, and expounded upon the Gold Rule of Rabbi Hillel: "Don't do unto your neighbors that which you find offensive."

As Jesus got older, it was apparent he wasn't the typical yeshivah *bucher* (student). It would be said later about him that he was indeed the Messiah, a direct descendant of the House of David, that he had performed certain miracles, and that he had thrown off the formalistic religious observance of the Pharisees. Still, in terms of his criticism of

the Roman rule and the decadence of his contemporaries, his concerns were shared by a growing number in Jerusalem.

Because of this widespread discontent, the Roman Procurator Pontius Pilate (26-36 CE) attempted to diminish the significance of the city by shifting the capital to Caesaria on the Mediterranean coast. But Pilate was so deeply concerned about the rumblings in Jerusalem that he came to watch at festival time just to make sure the vast influx of pilgrims were not roused to revolt. It was in this spirit Pilate arrived on the eve of Passover in the year 33 CE.

Jesus and his disciples had also come from the Galilee to celebrate the festival. A large *Pesach* meal (a *seder*) was prepared for them on Mt. Zion, and they drank the customary four full cups of wine. Then they crossed the Kidron Valley to the Mount of Olives, and to the garden of Gethsemane. If Jesus sensed he was in danger, his disciples were of little help, falling asleep from all the wine. It is said that Jesus wept that night when he beheld the city because he presaged its ultimate destruction and the fall of the great Temple. Shortly thereafter, he was arrested, and brought before a Jewish court and then before Pilate himself. Jesus was found guilty

his own image carved into the Temple, he helped instigate the ultimate revolt, which came in 66 A.D. The war of the Jews Against the Romans, as it was called, lasted five years. At first, the Jewish zealots seized Massada, Herod's old fortress, and eventually triumphed in Jerusalem, to which the Romans responded by butchering the entire Jewish population of Caesaria.

Emperor Vespasian set out to restore Roman rule in Jerusalem, dispatching his son Titus to quash the insurrection. In 70 A.D., Titus routed the Jews, though the Temple remained a last holdout a month longer. Finally, Titus' armies broke through

of some trumped up charges of crimes against the state and the procurator sentenced him to the death penalty, customarily carried out by crucifixation in those times. After suffering on the cross, he was given a proper Jewish burial, and though his disciples went into deep mourning, with the exception of this small cadre of followers, his death was scarcely noticed for the next two centuries or so.

The Romans may have executed so-called revolutionary leaders like Jesus, but Jewish resistance was building. When the lunatic Roman Emperor Caligula attempted to have

and burned the Temple to the ground. This happened, hauntingly enough, on the 9th day of the Hebrew month of Av, on the very anniversary of the day the First Temple was destroyed by the Babylonians. It is worth noting that the Talmud does not say that the Temple fell because the Romans were better armed or stronger than the Jews, but because of causeless hate among the Jews themselves. Interestingly enough, Jesus, among other zealots of his time, had dedicated their lives to preaching causeless love.

After the destruction of the Temple, the Jews worshipped on its ruins. Emperor

Hadrian saw in the rubble a Jewish nationalism that frightened him. So he outlawed the observance of the Sabbath, circumcision, and resolved to turn Jerusalem into a Roman city, replete with a temple to Jupiter on the old Temple mount. This touched off yet another rebellion and, improbably enough, the Jews actually won their city back for three years, 132-135 A.D.

They were led by the brilliant general Simmon Bar Kochba, whom Rabbi Akiva, one of the great sages of all Jewish history, thought to be the Messiah. In this rare case, the rabbi was gravely mistaken and the Jews lost a grip on Jerusalem, Akiva himself cru-

of this decree that followers of Jesus made a certain decision. Up until this time, they were considered a small Jewish sect, who followed all Jewish laws and customs, except that they believed Jesus was the Messiah and were awaiting a second coming. Now, however, to distinguish themselves from the Jews, and gain admittance to Jerusalem, they would change certain traditions—for instance, starting to observe the Sabbath on Sunday instead of Saturday.

In the Greek town of Antioch, this group of followers acquired the derogatory name "Christians" because they believed Jesus was Christos, the anointed one. Still this was

elly murdered in front of his community.

Hadrian intended to wipe out any trace of the former Jewish city and he renamed it Aelia Capitolina, built the temple to Jupiter, and placed an equestrian statue of himself in front of it. He further decreed that, upon penalty of death, no Jew could enter the city except on the 9th of Av, the anniversary of the Temple's destruction. It was in the wake

Left, original pavement showing ancient Roman dicing game. Above, Byzantine carving from the door of the Holy Sepulchre Church, now in the Rockefeller Museum.

such an obscure group that Jesus would certainly have faded from memory were it not for Saul of Tarsus, a tentmaker, rabbinic student, and zealously observant follower of Jewish law. Of Saul, the historian Cecil Roth has written: "Few Jews have ever influenced the world to the same extent." Saul scoffed at the Messianic claims made by Jesus' followers until one day, as he was approaching the city of Damascus, it hit him in a flash that they were right.

At first, he set about proselytizing in Jewish circles, at synagogues throughout Diaspora, but he wasn't too successful.

Some say he was embittered by the experience and began throwing off Jewish traditions altogether. Others say that he realized that Christianity wouldn't go over too well so long as it clung to the adherence of so many rigorous rules, including the rite of circumcision. Whichever the case, when Saul began his wide-ranging missions in the non-Jewish world, Christianity began spreading like wildfire and the words of Apostle Paul—as Saul became known—were widely quoted.

Of those who had been profoundly influenced by Paul's teachings, by far the most important was Constantine the Great (288-

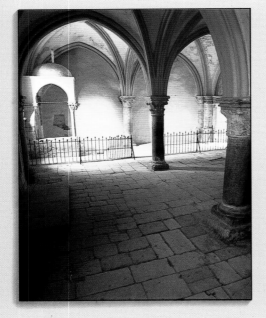

337 A.D.). Constantine by this time ruled the Roman empire, a good chunk of the world that included Jerusalem, from his capital of Byzantine. Soon Christianity became the official faith of the empire and Constantine dispatched his enthusiastic mother, Queen Helena, on a mission to Jerusalem to locate the: "Holy Places"—where Jesus tarried and where he'd been buried. Escorted around town by Jerusalem's Bishop Micarius, Queen Helena had one stroke of good fortune after another. When she found a Roman temple to Venus, she determined it was the place where Jesus had actually been cruci-

fied. Hadrian built it there, she surmised, to wipe out any memory of the Jewish martyr Jesus. Constantine replaced it with the fabulous Church of the Holy Sepulchre, an earlier version of the very one you find in Jerusalem today.

Under Constantine, Christianity gained many adherents. Jerusalem emerged as a holy city for a whole new and larger group of people, and pilgrims flocked there from all over the world. Monasteries, hospices, churches were built across the city, and the Christians comprised a majority of the population. Meanwhile, Judaism was regarded as a dangerous rival to Christianity. So much so that marrying a Jew at this time could get one the death penalty. And under Emperor Theodosius II (408-50 A.D.)—"the first Christian Inquisitor"—anti-Jewish discrimination became part of the fabric of the European attitude and jurisprudence. In 610 A.D., Emperor Heraclius went so far as to order that all Jews be baptized.

So when the majestic Byzantine Jerusalem was sacked by the Persian armies in 614 A.D., it is not surprising that the Jews of Galilee jumped to their assistance. The city was taken in 20 days, and the Jews expected that Jerusalem would henceforth be given back to them. But this was a mere pipe dream. The situation worsened when in 629 A.D. Heraclius turned back the Persians and reconquered Jerusalem. Predisposed to despise the Jews, Heraclius was especially incited against them by charges that they had beaten and killed Christians during Persian rule. He, in turn, permitted a new wave of Jew killing. Those who survived the massacres were banished and forced to live at least five km outside the city limits.

Heraclius' own days were numbered, the Byzantine reconquest short-lived. For within ten years, the Arabian army of Caliph Omar, inspired by a new religion called Islam, besieged Jerusalem until the Byzantines threw out the white flag. Once a Jewish city, then a Christian city, Jerusalem now became a center of the Moslem religion.

Left, the Cenacle, where Jesus ate the Last Supper. Right, pilgrims flock to Jerusalem from all over the world.

CITY OF ISLAM

With the dispersion of the Jews and the spread of Christianity, Jerusalem's religions reached many a far-flung land. In Arabia, a young religious student named Mohammed studied with a group of banifs, teachers of both brands of worship. It is said that one night, on a spiritual quest of his own, this Mohammed walked into a cave, and when he finally emerged, he was reciting an Arabic literature such as none before had ever heard. (*The Koran*, which is the written version of Mohammed's message, literally means recital.) Mohammed had placed himself squarely on Abraham's shoulders, his principal idea simply expressed in a new and more widely spoken language: *La-Al-lah-il-Allah* ! ("The only God is God!"). Mohammed did far more than Abraham to bring monotheism to the masses. So it was not altogether inappropriate for his followers to add, *Mohammed rasoula*! ("And Mohammed is His prophet!")

Like the Apostle Paul, Mohammed first hoped his message would attract many Jews, especially with his emphasis on the rite of circumcision and the strict Jewish dietary laws. For a year and a half, he even instructed worshippers to face Jerusalem during their prayers. But the stiff-necked Jews turned away from the new prophet and the Moslems, a situation which has created tension between the two groups to this very day.

None of this would have touched the history of Jerusalem quite the way it has were it not for the Islamic tradition of Mohammed's "Night Journey." Mohammed had a legendary wonder horse named el-Burak, which had wings, a woman's face, and the tail of a peacock. It was upon this trusty steed that the prophet (so the *Koran* tells us) rode one night from Mecca to "The Farthest Mosque." He met there the Angel Gabriel, and was accompanied through the seven heavens, where he

prayed with all the old Jewish and Christian prophets and finally with God Himself. The Moslems identified "The Farthest Mosque" with a heavenly place, but later said that it was on the Temple Mount of Jerusalem, which they called *el Quds* ("The Holy").

It's doubtful whether Mohammed's successor, Caliph Omar, had any of this in mind when he led the invasion on the Byzantine and Persian empires not long after the prophet himself died. Omar conquered Jerusalem in 638 A.D., greatly assisted by Jewish armies. He believed he came to power because of his relationship with the Jews, and he allowed them to return to Jerusalem, even granting them permission to rebuild the Temple on the mount.

Shortly thereafter, the Caliph must have changed his mind. According to Moslem tradition, he was so disgusted by the way the Byzantines befouled the Temple Mount, he forced the Christian Patriarch to crawl on his hands and knees through the dung heaps. Then he poured his purse full of gold and silver on the mounds of garbage as reward to

Left, 1898 portrait of a Palestinian Arab. Right, the Al Aksa Mosque, where every Islamic ruler of Jerusalem has come to worship.

43

the poor for cleaning it up. The Temple Mount, called by the Arabs *Haram esh-Sharif* ("Noble Sanctuary"), was rededicated as a place of Moslem worship.

The fabulous shrine known as the Dome of the Rock was built by a later Caliph, Abd al-Malik in 691 A.D. on the site where the Temples of Solomon and Herod once stood. The Moslems, agreeing with the Jewish tradition, said this Rock (*as Sakhra*) was the one upon which Abraham prepared his son for sacrifice. They also believe it is the precise spot from which Mohammed rose to the heavens during his "Night Journey".

Abd al-Malik, however, may not have

erected the magnificent edifice only for spiritual reasons. As the ruler of the Umayyad Dynasty in nearby Damascus, he may have felt it necessary to put up something that could compete with Mecca and thus keep local pilgrims from patronizing the rival caliph there. Also he may have wanted to outdo the Christian shrine of the Holy Sepulchre, and it is ironic that he relied on Byzantine architects to help him accomplish the task.

In the early part of the eigth-century, Al-Malik's son, Al-Walid built the Al-Aksa Mosque on the southern end of the Temple Mount. It was subsequently said about this mosque: "One prayer in Mecca is equal to ten thousand (anywhere else); one prayer in Medina equals one thousand; and one prayer in Jerusalem equals five hundred." It was thus that Jerusalem came to be known as the third city of Islam.

The city never served as the capital of the Umayyad Dynasty, but during this time it underwent great restoration and revival. After the Baghdad-based Abbasid Dynasty seized control of Jerusalem in 750 A.D., the city declined in importance over the next two centuries, with most Moslems making pilgrimages to Mecca. The Jewish and Christian populations maintained communities without interference from the distant rulers and the Abbasids still found pilgrimages profitable. One ruler actually permitted Charlemagne to endow and maintain a center for European pilgrims.

All that changed with the rise of the Fatimid Dynasty. The Fatimids had stormed through Mecca, Medina, Egypt, Palestine, and Syria, assisted by the Bedouins. When they conquered Jerusalem, the Egyptian-based "Mad Caliph" Al-Hakim had all synagogues and churches destroyed. It was said that he more than any other figure during Moslem rule, paved the way for the coming Crusaders. What was especially tragic about this episode was that it was widely rumored back in Europe that the Jews instigated the Caliph's fanaticism, and there followed in Christian towns across the northern continent the massacre of Jews.

The Fatimids lost a grip on Jerusalem when in 1071 the Seljuks — Asian slaves-cum-Moslem converts — overtook Syria and Palestine. The Seljuks wildly went about vandalizing Jerusalem and persecuting both Jews and Christians, the latter of whom were sufficiently riled to prepare an invasion of their own from the north. The Fatimids reconquered Jerusalem before the turn of the century, but as they were doing so, the Crusader armies were on their way.

Left, idyllic 18th-century Jerusalem. Right, the Dome of the Rock, where Mohammed rose to heaven.

PERPETUAL CONQUEST

By the second half of the 11th century, pilgrims returned from Jerusalem to Christian Europe with horror stories about the way the Moslems were treating the Holy Places. Pope Urban II finally exhorted the Christians to recover control of the Holy Land. The campaign culminated in 1097 when Godfrey de Bouillon led combined forces of the German and French Knights (the Crusaders, as they were called), into Jerusalem. The streets of the city, it is said, ran with blood, nearly every one of the 40,000 inhabitants (Jews and Moslems) killed. Any Jew who survived was either sold into bondage or ransomed to the Jewish community in Alexandria. By 1099, the Crusaders' newly established Latin Kingdom declared that Jerusalem was its capital.

Subsequently, as many as 10,000 Christian pilgrims journeyed to Jerusalem each year. Churches and monasteries were built like crazy, each in some way connected to the life of Jesus and his disciples. Christian Arabs were brought in from the East to settle the Jewish Quarter, and the Syrian and Armenian Quarters were firmly established.

All told, the city was greatly fortified, which made the Crusader defeat by the Egypt-based sultan Saladin all the more impressive in 1187. Saladin did not seek retribution against the Christian population for the massacre of the Moslems. In fact, he encouraged Eastern Christians, as well as Jews, to settle in Jerusalem, especially if they would assist the ongoing war against the Crusaders.

The Crusaders, however, retook Jerusalem through the back door in 1241. After Saladin died, his sons divided up the empire and then went into battle against each other. To outmatch the Damascus heir, the Egyptian heir brokered a deal with Frederick II of Germany. In exchange for an alliance, the Crusader emperor could have all of Jerusa-

lem except the Temple Mount (which remained in Moslem hands). The Pope, meanwhile, withheld his blessing since he believed one must battle Moslems, not bargain with them.

After three years, the Crusaders were expelled once more, this time by an army of nomad Turks, who were the paid mercenaries of the new Egyptian Sultan. And shortly thereafter in 1258, the Mamelukes seized power from Saladin's successors. The

Mamelukes ruled from Cairo, where they had been brought originally to serve as a special guard of the sultans. They eventually rebelled against their masters and established an empire of their own.

During their rule, Jerusalem was relegated to minor importance, serving primarily as the Siberia of its time, a place of exile for dangerous or disgraced government officials. The Mamelukes levied heavy taxes on the local populations, which proved hellish for the economy. Despite this, they did bring to the city an exotic and beautiful style of architecture that (though not showcased)

Left, every conqueror has maintained control of the Old City from the Citadel of David. Right, a Mameluke fountain.

can be seen in the city to this very day.

Eventually the Mameluke Empire disintegrated, and the powerful Ottoman Empire succeeded it in 1516. Within a year, Jerusalem was in Turkish hands. The first ruler, Selim I, was responsible for imposing yet another stiff tax on all non-Moslems. Selim's son, Suleiman the Magnificent, who ruled from 1520-66, is generally considered a brilliant and benevolent ruler.

Suleiman brought to Jerusalem a new era of prosperity and took as his mission rebuilding the walls of the city, which are the very ones you see today. He also reconstructed, with much flourish, the Damascus

Gate and fortified the Tower of David.

After Suleiman's death and for the following three centuries, the city fell to pieces. The rulers from Constantinople cared not a whit about the place. They made themselves scarce and their custodians were corrupt. They extracted bribes from each of the Christian sects squabbling for the right to control various Holy Places.

Toward the Jews the Turks were just as arbitrary. They proved particularly capricious in 1799 after Napoleon had beseeched the Jews of Africa and Asia to follow him to Jerusalem and rebuild the city. Of course the Emperor never made good on his whim, but the Turks, riled by the putative connection between Napoleon and the Jews, allowed thieves to run rampant looting and destroying Jewish homes.

In 1831, the Jews and Christians received a temporary respite during the fabulous and surprising rule of the Egyptian army officer Mohammed Ali. Ali assumed control of Egypt and expelled the Ottoman Empire from Jerusalem and all of Palestine. He embodied the modern ruler and was largely responsible for initiating a series of economic and governmental reforms in the city.

Ali's greatness was also recognized by the European powers. In 1840, when Ali tried to attack Istanbul, the European states assisted the Turks in turning him back.

Ottoman control resumed, but each sultan thereafter was reduced to obsequiousness before European leaders. When the Sultan's guest, the German Kaiser Wilhelm, made his grand entrance through the city walls at the turn of the 20th century, it was as if he were conquering the place.

The British also made their presence known in Palestine. Fighting both the Germans and the Turks in World War I, the British General Edmund Allenby waltzed into Jerusalem on December 11, 1917, and inaugurated a 41-year rule by yet another imperial power.

British rule was both positive and negative. The British Mandate has been credited with overseeing Jerusalem's economic renewal and at the same time preserving the city's special historical character through a rigorous set of architectural planning guidelines. However, the Mandate's legacy is also known for sewing the seeds of the Arab-Israeli conflict. In 1917, even before the start of the Mandate, a British lord named Balfour signed a declaration that the Jewish Zionists subsequently regarded as their Magna Carta: "His Majesty's Government view with favor the establishment in Palestine of a National Home for the Jewish people."

Left, Jaffa road awaits the visit of Kaiser Wilhelm II in 1898. Right, the present city walls, built by Suleiman the Magnificent in the 16th century.

49

ZIONISM AND THE ARAB-ISRAELI CONFLICT

Even with the Balfour Declaration, who could have imagined the Jewish rise to statehood from the ashes of destruction and exile? Ever since the Second Temple was destroyed, Jews in exile the world over have cried out in messianic hope: "Next year in Jerusalem!" And yet throughout this Diaspora, many have maintained that the Messiah would not come until the Jews stopped waiting on Him and instead returned to Jerusalem and began rebuilding the city.

Though small, there has been a continuous presence of this community in Jerusalem ever since the Crusaders were turned back in the 13th century. At that time, Rabbi Mocco ben Nachman (Nachmanides) led the return of Spanish Jews. Upon reaching the city, Nachmanides wrote to his family: "What shall I say of this land? Great is its desolation. The more holy the place, the greater the desolation. Jerusalem is the most desolate of all...The only Jewish residents are two brothers, dyers by trade. The city has no master and he that wishes may take possession of the ruins. May you, my son and your

brothers, and the whole of our family, see the salvation of Jerusalem."

By the early 19th century, the city was not so bleak as when Nachmanides lived there, but still most of its precious sites lay in shambles. Two thousand Jews or one fifth of Jerusalem's population were crammed into the filthy, disease-ridden Jewish Quarter. Most were elderly, poor and religious. It was not until the second half of the century, with the advent of Zionism, that Jews began to actively resettle Jerusalem.

Zionism comes from the Hebrew word *tzion*, a Biblical name for at times Jerusalem (site of Mt. Zion) and the entire land of Israel. It developed as a decidedly secular, nationalist movement, advocating the rebuilding Jerusalem and not to hasten the coming of the Messiah. Zionism was an attempt to give the Jewish people a home, making them a nation like all others.

The early movement: The idea first came up in a 1862 book *Rome and Jerusalem*, by Moses Hess, the father of German Social Democracy. He advocated the establishment of a truly socialist nation-state in Palestine. The argument, however, failed to gain credence until another book, *Auto-Emancipation* by the Russian Jew Leo Pinsker, was published in 1882. Pinsker, arguing that Jews were vulnerable to anti-Semitism precisely because they lacked a nation of their own, had enormous influence. He inspired the formation of young Zionist clubs all over the Russia, where pogroms against Jews were becoming commonplace.

It's doubtful, however, that Zionism based solely on the enthusiasm of Russian Jewish youth would have endured. What gave the movement structure and popularity was the tireless work of a Viennese journalist named Theodore Herzl. Herzl, a thoroughly assimilated, liberally educated and

Left, Israel's soldiers see the Wailing Wall for the first time in 1967's Six-Day War. Right, Theodore Herzl, one of Zionism's founding fathers.

affluent Jew, was an archetypal product of the European Enlightenment. It was not until he witnessed the rampant anti-Semitism in France while covering the Dreyfus Affair that he realized that Enlightenment was a false promise— Jew-hate was deep-seated and ineradicable.

Herzl popularized Pinsker, wrote books of his own, met with Jewish and foreign leaders, and convened the first International Zionist Congress in Switzerland in 1897. He didn't care about preserving Jewish culture, much less religion. His goal was to find a place where Jews could gather.

By the time of Herzl's death in 1904, there

Nations—the British set up its administrative capital there and rapidly modernized the city. Jerusalem's infrastructure was vastly improved and in the beginning the British helped the Jewish Agency with immigration and land purchases.

Britain's first civilian governor, Sir Herbert Samuel, himself a Jewish Zionist, attempted to gain acceptance from Arabs as well as Jews. He even appointed a young, radical Arab nationalist, Hajj Amin al-Husayni, to be mufti (chief Moslem legal officer) of Jerusalem. The mufti, extreme though he might have been, gave full expression to the mainstream and burgeoning Pal-

was no Zion, though Zionism was catching on: Jews were leaving behind the pogroms of Russia and moving to Palestine. The population in and around Jerusalem reached nearly 60,000, with more than 60 percent Jews. In the ten years following the failed Russian revolution of 1905, there was another huge influx of Jews on the shores of Palestine.

The British presence: Jerusalem's development was slower than some of the new towns on the Mediterranean coast. But after World War I—the Palestine Mandate having been approved by the newly-formed League of

estinian consciousness. He later became such an influential leader that the British deported him in 1937, and he signed on with Hitler's propaganda machine.

Samuel encouraged Jews and Arabs to establish their own institutions, which the former did with a fervor (the inauguration of Hebrew University on Mt. Scopus in 1925 was considered a landmark in Zionist development) and the latter did hardly at all.

For a time during the administrative rule of Samuel it appeared the Jews and Arabs might live in peace. The number of Jewish settlers shrank; from 1926 to 1928 as many

52

Jews were leaving Jerusalem as entering it. Some say there was even a symbiotic relationship developing between the two people—Jewish capital and Arab labor, and Jewish technical expertise and Arab knowledge of the land.

That flickering hope of peaceful coexistence was put out forever in 1929 when a turf war between Arabs and Jews over access to the holy sites at the Temple Mount erupted into violence and spread from Jerusalem to the rest of the country, leaving more than 200 dead. Although most of them were Jews, a British White Paper blamed the systematic Jewish land purchases from Arab peasants

Arabs naturally began to wonder when they would become a small minority.

In 1936, al-Husayni, the Jerusalem mufti, took control of the Arab Higher Committee, which represented almost all Palestinian Moslems and Christians in the land. He then called for a large Arab strike *cum* rebellion which lasted three years. In response, the British government dispatched the Peel Commission to Palestine to study the causes and nature of the conflict. The commission's report first spelled out the idea of partitioning the land. The Jews would gain a small patch of land in the north and the Arabs the rest, except for an enclave in and around

for creating the tinderbox of tensions that had been sparked.

By the early 1930s, with the rise of Hitler, the worldwide depression and the strict immigration quotas in America, more and more Jews sought refuge in Palestine. In Jerusalem the large number of immigrants strained the limits set by the British and the

Left, Israel's revolving prime ministers—Shimon Peres (left) and Yatzik Shamir. Above, Soviet dissident Natan Sharansky and mother were finally allowed to make aliya to Jerusalem.

Jerusalem, of which the British would retain control over. Meanwhile, Jewish immigration would be drastically restricted.

The policy adopted by the British was virulently anti-Zionist and tensions between Jews and Arabs increased. The Jews of the Old City lived exclusively in the Jewish Quarter. The Jewish underground and Zionist defense force, the Haganah, engaged in terrorist acts. Some Arabs hoped the Germans would liberate Palestine from the Jews, however the Jews supported a ceasefire during World War II and joined the allied forces to fight Hitler.

Arab conflicts: With the world war over, the civil war resumed in Palestine. In Jerusalem, the Zionist underground Irgun, led by future Prime Minister Menachem Begin, blew up part of the King David Hotel, where the British administration and army had set up offices. The next year, in 1947, the British beseeched the United Nations to resolve the problem. The United Nations voted to partition Palestine and to make Jerusalem itself a separate international municipality.

For the Jews, the proposed borders were bad from a military and political point of view, but they accepted them as the first step to statehood. The Arabs, however, refused

them altogether. During the next half year, the Jewish underground and Arab partisans fought. Jerusalem became a battle zone—a city in siege. In April 1948, the Irgun massacred a peaceful Arab village called Dir Yasin on the outskirts of Jerusalem, killing more than 200 and an Arab terrorist group ambushed a Jewish bus on its way to Mt. Scopus to the Hadassah Hospital, killing 75 professors, doctors, and nurses. The British stood by idly and finally evacuated Jerusalem on May 15, 1948.

The Jews immediately took over the British administration buildings and the State of Israel was declared. The Zionists called on Arab inhabitants "to preserve the ways of peace" and asked the surrounding Arab nations to cooperate with their rule. Whether this was a sincere plea or diplomatic propaganda, one could hardly expect the Palestinian Arabs to trust the Zionists. Many fled their homes during the early fighting and looked to the Arab nations for assistance.

The next day, five Arab states sent troops to Palestine to fight Israel. Forces from Iraq and Egypt easily reached the Jerusalem border and on May 28, after weeks of furious fighting, the Jewish Quarter of the Old City finally fell to the Jordanian Legion. For the first time in its history, Jerusalem was now divided. The Jews controlled West Jerusalem and the Jordanians controlled East Jerusalem, including the Old City.

Because West Jerusalem was virtually surrounded by hostile Arab territory, Israel initially established its capital in Tel Aviv. When the United Nations proposed to internationalize the city, in utter defiance, Israel moved its capital to Jerusalem. While West Jerusalem underwent continued urbanization, East Jerusalem was neglected by its Jordanian caretakers.

For the next 19 years, a border of minefields and barbed wire ran through city. In June 1967, Jordan's King Hussein ignored Israel's pleas not to interfere in the war with Egypt. Some say the King wanted to join Arab forces and push Israel into the Mediterranean; some say he purposely sought to relinquish the burden of Jerusalem. Whichever the case, in response to his advances, the Israelis moved swiftly inside the Old City and captured it.

So moved by the fact that Jerusalem was now in Israeli hands, the soldiers instinctively rushed to pray at the Wailing Wall. The territories that Israel controlled after the Six Day War, were placed under military rule and regarded as temporarily "occupied territories." East Jerusalem was officially annexed on June 28, 1967.

Left, the Israeli flag shows the Jewish Star of David. Right, the menorah in front of the Knesset was a gift from Great Britain.

JERUSALEM TODAY

In the irreconcilable Arab-Israeli conflict, Jerusalem is the ultimate prize. Shortly after the Israelis vanquished Jordan in 1967, they began polishing it up. One morning after the war, they bulldozed every barricade, crushed every checkpost, snipped open every barbed-wire fence and toppled all the shanties in front of the Wailing Wall. In the two decades since, the city has undergone a renaissance which has been credited mainly to the leadership of the city's indefatigable Mayor Teddy Kollek.

When Kollek's own government wouldn't pay for all the new museums, parks, neighborhoods, roads, sports stadiums and community centers, he established his own Jerusalem Foundation and made rebuilding the city a project for International Jewry. During his two decades of administrative leadership, the Jewish Quarter in the Old City has been entirely refurbished and, in the process, archaeologists have turned up a wealth of historic ruins that have become part of the city's fabric and myth. Meanwhile, new Jewish neighborhoods started sprouting up. And in such a way as to make any future partition of the city impossible.

Yet, East and West Jerusalem—with their own business centers, transportation systems and electricity grids—remain two cities in one. "Jerusalem," wrote a *Washington Post* reporter in 1987, is "Belfast without the bombs, Berlin without the wall, Beirut without the bullets."

When the Jews annexed East Jerusalem, they gave the Arab residents an opportunity to apply for Israeli citizenship, but only a thousand or so did. Instead of East Jerusalem becoming integrated with the rest of the city, it has become the unofficial capital of a Palestinian national movement. Such was apparent in late 1987 and early 1988 when Palestinian riots against Israeli military

forces in the occupied territories spilled over in the streets of Jerusalem.

Christian and Moslem Arabs make up about one third of the city's 475,000 population. Aside from small enclaves of Armenians and European Christians, the other two thirds of its residents are divided between secular and Orthodox Jews. Some believe that it is the internal conflict among the Jews themselves, rather than the one between Jews and Arabs, that poses the greatest threat

to the survival of Jerusalem.

This conflict, in short, is over the future of the city. While only a few bizarre groups advocate reconvening the Sanhedrin (the ancient body of sage-judges) or rebuilding the Temple, the Orthodox would like to see the city organized in accordance with *halacha,* the Jewish law derived from Torah. The secular Jews, on the other hand, prefer a rollicking, modern, more epicurean city.

This struggle is not uniquie. It is the same one that has gripped Jerusalem during the Hasmonean dynasty and throughout Jewish history—that is, between strict observance

Left, young women serve in the military. Right, study time at Hebrew University.

of Torah law and the pull of Hellenism.

At the heart of the current dispute is the issue of how the city observes Shabbat. Even though no restaurants are open and no buses run on Shabbat, some Orthodox Jews have protested that the spirit of their holy day is upset by such things as unnecessary traffic and theaters showing movies. Meanwhile, some secular Jews have purposely driven their cars through municipal barricades closing off religious neighborhoods on Shabbat simply to provoke the *chareidim,* as the devoutly Orthodox are sometimes called. This, in turn, has led some Orthodox Jews to throw rocks at the cars. When the city gov-

ernment sold advertising space in Jerusalem's bus shelters for billboards featuring scantily-clad women, the Orthodox (to whom modesty isn't merely a virtue, but a law) set many billboards ablaze.

As the religious Jews have gained more power and numbers in the city, resentment has grown in the secular community. Some have fled to Tel Aviv, a considerably more laid back city. Jerusalem's reputation as a somber and rigid place have prompted the municipal government in 1987 to launch an advertising campaign, trying to sell Israelis on the idea that it is really a good-time town:

"Jerusalem," the catch phrase went, "is not what you imagine!"

For that matter, young secular Jews in Jerusalem have a decidedly hedonistic streak. When John Gregory Dunne, the lapsed Catholic American writer visited Jerusalem in 1987, he wrote, with some bemusement, that the whole country was full of "an overwhelming charge of sexual energy," probably because the garrison state throws the sexes together at such an early age. With both men and women facing mandatory military conscription at the age of 18, a roll in the feathers seemed small enough allowance for children who would soon enough be standing on the thin red line."

The sense of a city always on the brink of battle is apparent everywhere. Some have remarked that with so many Jerusalemites wielding guns, the city is reminiscent of the old American Wild West. The truth is that Jerusalem suffers from far less crime than most European and American cities.

What unites the Jerusalemites on the Jewish side is neither politics, nor religion, but some intangible sense of believing with confidence that they are on the center stage of the historical monument. Such can be seen when, for example, Soviet Jewish dissident Natan Scharansky was freed from a Siberian prison and arrived at the Wailing Wall in Jerusalem welcomed by the songs of a people with one voice.

Jerusalem's future depends on the ability of Mayor Kollek's successor to put together a coalition of religious and secular Jews and Arabs to keep them from killing each other. The problem is that Jerusalem has to do this under watchful eye of the world press. There are some 350 news organizations represented in Jerusalem and Tel Aviv, and 1,000 reporters visit Israel each year on special assignment. There are more journalists per square inch here than anywhere else on the globe. Certainly no city on earth faces such scrutiny. But that's the way it's always been.

Left, the bustle of Ben Yehudah mall. Right, Israeli-born people are called "Sabras," tough on the outside, tender on the inside.

ALIYA: A CONSTANT RENEWAL

In the days before the great Temple was destroyed, long before Zionism, Jews spoke of making *aliya*, literally meaning "going up." By this they meant ascending the hills of Judea to Jerusalem and climbing the stairs of the Temple to offer a sacrifice at festival time. In the Diaspora, *aliya* always signified a return to Jerusalem, and thus it was only natural for Zionists to so name immigration to the Land of Israel.

The "First Aliya" came from Russia in the 1880s. Inspired by the publication of Leo Pinsker's Zionist manifesto, *Auto-Emancipation*, a Russian Jewish federation called *Chovevai Tzion* ("Lovers of Zion") began sending Jewish students to Palestine. Within two decades, some 40 new settlements were established in the land; many of the new *olim* ("ascenders") came to Jerusalem, where they began building the first neighborhoods outside the Old City.

The "Second Aliya" represented an even larger emigration of Jews from Russia following the aborted 1905 revolution there. Most of these Jews migrated to the United States, lured by the belief that the roads were paved with gold. A small minority headed to Jerusalem and Palestine, an altogether more idealistic and adventurous lot.

The *olim* who arrived between 1905 and 1914 are largely credited as the founding fathers and mothers of the State of Israel, establishing many of its important education, business, and political institutions. By the outbreak of World War I in 1914, there were nearly twice as many Jews living outside the Old City as those residing within it. As a result of the Jewish *aliya*, an increasing number of Arabs were sent up to Jerusalem, attracted by the city's increasing prosperity and modernity.

Some 35,000 Jews from Eastern Europe accounted for the "Third Aliya" (1919-1924). Many were grievously disappointed by the failures of the Bolshevik Revolution and placed their hope in a Jewish state. Such

hope was fueled by the Balfour Declaration and its ratification by the League of Nations. The Zionist dream had actually been ratified by international law.

Fleeing the anti-Semitic repression in Poland, 68,000 Jews comprised the "Fourth Aliya" (1924-29). Over one third of them left shortly after their arrival. In the mid-1920s, an equilibrium was reached between the number of Jew leaving Jerusalem and the number coming in.

The "Fifth Aliya" (1930-39) coincided with the rise of Hitler. Given the British restrictions on Jewish immigration during and after World War II, it is common to speak of those who came in up until the creation of the state in 1948 as the "Aliya Bet" (illegal immigration).

All along the Zionists had hoped Israel would provide a home for displaced Jews. In 1950, the Israeli parliament, the *Knesset*, unanimously passed the Law of Return, which said that every Jew in the world had a right to settle in Israel. In the next 14 years, there was a mass *aliya*, the vast majority were Jews from Arabic countries: Iraq (126,000), Morocco (120,000), Egypt (75,000), Tunisia (30,000), Libya (35,000) and Syria (26,000). In a project called "Operation Magic Carpet," the entire Jewish population of Yemen (nearly 50,000) boarded Israeli airplanes and flew to a home they'd never seen.

After struggling in temporary "relocation centers," many of the new *olim* started villages around the country. Very few affluent and assimilated Jews make up the *olim*. However some American and Western European Jews made *aliya* to Israel in the Zionist fervor that surrounded the successful 1967 war and reunification of Jerusalem.

Since 1967, the *aliya* movement has concentrated on fighting for the rights of oppressed Jews to emigrate, such as those in the Soviet Union. The entire nation was inspired when in late 1984 the Israeli government helped thousands of Ethiopian Jews escape poverty and tyranny and settle in Israel.

ARCHAEOLOGY

Jerusalem is an excavation-mad town. "Archaeology in Israel," writes Amos Elon, in his brilliant book *The Israelis*, "is almost a national sport. Not a passive spectator sport but the thrilling, active pastime of many thousands of people, as perhaps fishing in the Canadian lake country or hunting in the French Massif Central."

The first to systemically excavate Jerusalem was a stern, adventurous British man named Charles Warren, who was sponsored by the Palestine Exploration Fund in London in the 19th century. The British have proceeded with some important excavations ever since, most recently under the leadership of Dame Kathleen Kenyon in the 1960s. When the city was "reunified" in 1967, the Israeli archaeology establishment, saddened at the way the Jordanians carelessly let the Old City go to waste, had the whole area made a protected antiquities landmark.

A detailed study of the Old City was prepared in 1968, and 300 separate sites of historical, religious, or architectural significance were identified. The law in the Old City of Jerusalem now is that before you're allowed to build up, you must first dig down. As a result, many development projects have been stalled for years, if not indefinitely, while archaeologists sift through countless layers of time lying beneath the city. Walk through the Jewish Quarters today and you can see new pieces of the historical jigsaw puzzle fit together before your eyes.

The most prominent find in the Old City was the Cardo, the ancient Roman/Byzantine commercial thoroughfare that crossed Jerusalem, and which stands out on the 6th-century Madaba Map. A huge section of the street has been restored—remains of the actual stone road as well as a row of ancient columns. In 1985, the City of David, which is perched on a ridge below the southeast corner of the Old City, was opened to the public. It highlights a structure from the 10th

century BCE, perhaps built by King David himself. During the excavation in the late 1970s, a small group of ultra-Orthodox Jews attempted to halt the dig, arguing that sacred and ancient graves were being desecrated. Although the archaeologists won that particular fight, demonstrating that this was not a grave site, in many other cases in Israel, religious protesters have prevailed.

For religious Jews, the Torah provides a sufficient sense of history and ties to Jerusalem and Israel. But for the young and secular state, archaeology is the means by which a history justifies Jewish claims to the land and a mythology weaves a national story well beyond the current politics. As Amos Elon writes: "There are undoubtedly deep psychological reasons that lend Israeli archaeology its distinctive political, even chauvinistic air...It is possible to observe in the pursuit of patriotic archaeology, as of faith or Freudian analysis, the achievement of a kind of cure; men overcome their doubts and fears and feel rejuvenated though the exposure of real, or assumed, but always hidden origins."

Some of the most spectacular archaeological digs have taken place at Massada and the Qumram caves, the latter of which is where the Dead Sea Scrolls were found. In all this work, Israel has produced some of the world's greatest archaeologists—Eliezer Sukenik and his son Yigael Yadin, for example. At the same time, young Jews and archaeology buffs from around the world have come to Jerusalem and Israel to volunteer their services for these landmark digs. These digs seem to have aroused passion in Jewish youth that even Judaism itself has not always been able to inspire.

As Elon points out in his book, Israelis customarily describe the national attitude toward archaeology as a *bulmus*, which is actually an ancient Talmudic phrase. "It denotes a ravenous hunger," says Elon, "a faintness resulting from prolonged fasting, an exaggerated eagerness, a fit, a rage, a mania."

Left, excavations and reconstruction at the Cardo in the Jewish Quarter of the Old City.

JERUSALEM CULTURE

In the Diaspora, Jews were always known as the "People of the Book" for the way in which they cleaved to the Torah. For religious Jews today, cultural life still centers around the *yeshivah*, where the Torah is passed down from one generation to the next. Although secular Israelis read Hebrew too, the Book has been replaced by books in general.

Jerusalemites especially are voracious

castle of literature on thin air, most famous among them, S.Y. Agnon, the 1966 winner of the Nobel Prize and Chaim Bialik, the nation's first poet laureate.

Today, the Jerusalemite poet Yehudah Amichai best captures the nation's pathos—the sense of loss and war, the passion and the unflagging sense of humor. The best-read novelist is Jerusalem-born Amos Oz, who writes foreboding novels (such as *My*

readers, and as one can see from walking into any Stiematzky's book store, they have a wealth of Hebrew literature to choose from.

The revival of Hebrew as a modern language was, astoundingly enough, accomplished by one man, Eliezer Ben-Yehudah, an Eastern European Jew who came to Jerusalem in 1881. Compiling the modern Hebrew dictionary, Ben-Yehudah was a kind of Tower of Babel in reverse, presenting an exiled people of so many foreign tongues the language of their forefathers.

What is even more amazing is how the writers who came after Ben Yehudah built a

Michael) about the city and the land in the shadow of the Arab-Israeli conflict. Many of these writers are of Ashkenazi origin, writing in Yiddish rhythms.

In the last 15 years, a group of Sephardic writers, such as A.B. Yehoushua and Amnon Shamosh, have brought to the language a distinctly Arabic flavor. Perhaps the book that represented the greatest triumph for Hebrew literature, however, was written by a Christian Arab, *Arabesque*, published in 1985 by Anton Shams. Said Oz, "If the Hebrew language is becoming attractive enough for a non-Jewish Israeli to write in it, then we have arrived."

If an Arab has put Hebrew to the service of his story, Jews have long been setting Hebrew lyrics to Arabic melodies in their popular music. Israeli music has undergone a considerable change since the mid-1970s, when the scene was dominated by Ashkenazi intellectuals, such as David Broza and Arik Einstein, belting out folk songs in the manner of Bob Dylan.

Most older Jerusalemites—especially those from European countries —are avid classical music fans. In Jerusalem, one can hear the Jerusalem Symphony Orchestra play at the Henry Crown Symphony Hall or (even better) drive to Tel Aviv and catch the world renowned Israeli Philharmonic under the direction of Zubin Mehta.

Jacobo Timmerman once wrote that while Israelis seems very coarse on the outside,

The Arabic-influence music made by Sephardic Jews was once referred to pejoratively around Jerusalem as "bus station music" for the milieu in which it was most often heard. Now it has become part of the mainstream culture in the work of Yehudah Poliker, Yehudit Ravitz and others.

Left, the Jerusalem Symphony plays at the Citadel of David. Above, a dance performance at the Rubin Academy of Performing Arts.

one can only appreciate their sensitivity and emotions by watching them sing. For music is perhaps the only media in which they truly feel comfortable. Every Shabbat the streets of Jerusalem fill with the songs—*nigguns*— of that inner spirit.

Each spring Jerusalem hosts a range of international festivals that transform the city into a bustling cultural center. The annual Israel Festival is a showcase of opera, symphony, and chamber music, theater and dance from around the world. Each December there is a liturgical music festival— Liturgica.

POINTS OF DEPARTURE

Jerusalem rests at the edge of the Judean desert, and is roiling hot during the summer days—the *Chamsin* (fifty days), as the Palestinians call it. During this time of year, it's best to do your touring in the morning and evening. The nights, even in the summer, are always crisp and pleasant. That's because the city is in the mountains and is itself surrounded by mountains. The Old City of Jerusalem is shaped like a cradle between the Kidron and Tyroppean Valleys and Valley of Hinnom.

Outlined on the following pages are suggested tours routes which include all of the traditional tourist attractions and some additional nooks and crannies which might otherwise be overlooked. However, Jerusalem is, above all, not a linear place and visitors are best advised to wander by instinct, to be willing to get lost. Given a short visit it's best to check out the historical sites in the Old City by day and hit the restaurants and cafes of the New City at night.

The first suggested route starts at the Jaffa Gate in the Old City and winds through the four quarters: Armenian, Jewish, Moslem, and Christian. After which, it doubles back across the Kidron Valley to Palestinian East Jerusalem, before visiting the New City.

Preceding pages: The deep, dark eyes of a Yemenite Jew; Christians and Jews both believe the Messiah will come to Jerusalem, opening the Golden Gate, or Gate of Mercy; Damascus Gate at Festival time. Below, detail from Lion's Gate.

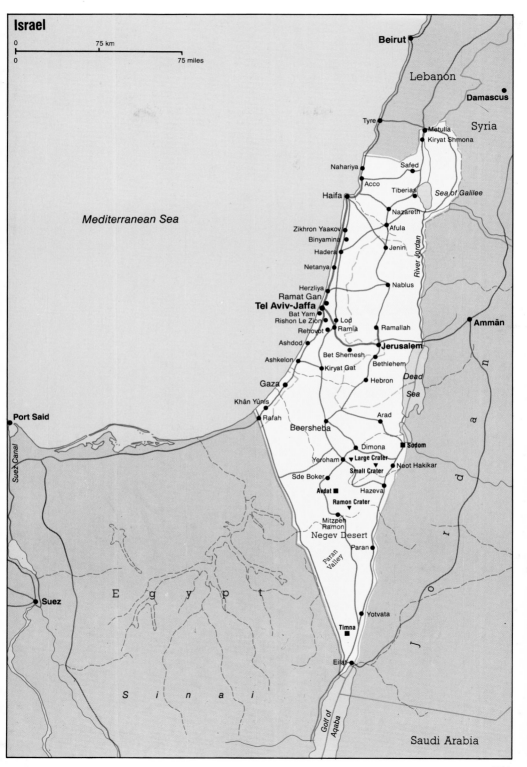

Israel

| 0 | 75 km |
| 0 | 75 miles |

Beirut

Lebanon

Damascus

Tyre
Metulla
Kiryat Shmona

Syria

Nahariya
Safed

Acco
Tiberias

Haifa
Sea of Galilee

Nazareth

Zikhron Yaakov
Afula

Binyamina
Jenin

Hadera

Netanya

Nablus

River Jordan

Herzliya

Ramat Gan

Tel Aviv-Jaffa
Bat Yam

Rishon Le Zion
Lod

Rehovot
Ramla

Ashdod
Ramallah

Amman

Bet Shemesh
Jerusalem

Ashkelon
Bethlehem

Kiryat Gat
Dead

Gaza
Hebron
Sea

Khān Yūnis

Rafah
Arad

Mediterranean Sea

Port Said

Beersheba

Dimona
Sodom

Yeroham
Large Crater

Small Crater
Neot Hakikar

Sde Boker

Avdat
Hazeva

Ramon Crater

Mitzpeh
Ramon

Negev Desert
Paran

Suez Canal

E g y p t

Paran Valley

J o r d a n

Suez

Yotvata

Timna

S i n a i

Eilat

Golf of Aqaba

Saudi Arabia

72A

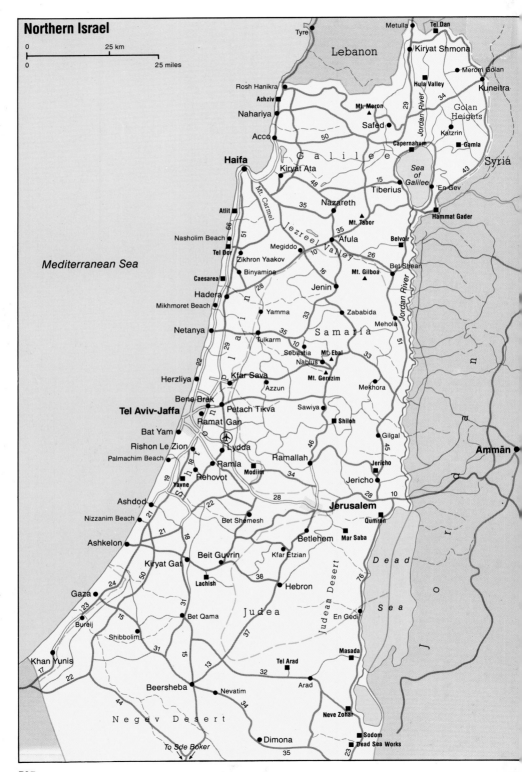

Northern Israel

0 — 25 km
0 — 25 miles

Lebanon

Tyre
Metulla
Tel Dan
Kiryat Shmona
Rosh Hanikra
Merom Golan
Hula Valley
Kuneitra
Achziv
Mt. Meron
Golan
Heights
Nahariya
Safed
Katzrin
Acco
Capernahum
Gamla
29
34
Syria
50
Galilee
Haifa
Kiryat Ata
Sea
of
Galilee
'En Gev
48
15
Tiberius
43
Nazareth
Mt. Tabor
Hammat Gader
35
Atlit
Mt. Carmel
Jezreel Valley
35
Afula
Belvoir
Nasholim Beach
51
Megiddo
26
Tel Dor
10
Bet Shean
Zikhron Yaakov
Mt. Gilboa
66
Caesarea
Binyamina
16
Jenin
Hadera
28
Mikhmoret Beach
Yamma
33
Zababida
Netanya
Mehola
35
Samaria
Tulkarm
29
10
51
22
Sebastia
Mt. Ebal
33
Herzliya
Kfar Sava
Nablus
Azzun
Mt. Gerezim
Mekhora
Bene Brak
Tel Aviv-Jaffa
Petach Tikva
Sawiya
Ramat Gan
Shiloh
Bat Yam
Gilgal
Rishon Le Zion
Lydda
46
45
Ammān
Palmachim Beach
Ramallah
Jericho
19
Ramla
Jericho
Rehovot
Modiim
34
Yavne
28
28
10
Ashdod
22
Jerusalem
21
Nizzanim Beach
Bet Shemesh
Qumran
Ashkelon
Betlehem
Mar Saba
18
Beit Guvrin
Kfar Etzian
Dead
Kiryat Gat
50
Lachish
38
Judean Desert
Sea
Gaza
24
Hebron
76
23
31
15
Bureij
Bet Qama
Judea
En Gedi
Shibbolim
37
31
15
Khan Yunis
13
Masada
17
22
Tel Arad
32
Beersheba
Nevatim
Arad
34
44
Neve Zohar
Negev Desert
Sodom
Dimona
Dead Sea Works
35
23
To Sde Boker

Mediterranean Sea

Jordan River

Jordan River

72B

Jerusalem

500 m

To Nablus, Ramallah

Hadassah Hospital

Tombs of the Sanhedrin

Mount Scopus

Sanhedria

Shmuel Hanavi

Sderot Eshkol

Ammunition Hill

Derekh Shekhem

Hebrew University

Sheikh Jarrah

Biblical Zoo

Yirmeyahu

Bukharian Quarter

Tomb of Simon the Just

American Colony

American Colony Hotel

Tombs of the Kings

Wadi El Joz

Geulla

Bet Yisrael

Malkhe Yisrael

Mandelbaum Gate

St. George

Saladin

Rockefeller Museum

Mount of Olives

Romema

Mea Shearim

Garden Tomb

Church of the Assumption

Church of Pater Noster

To Tel Aviv

Central Bus Station

Jaffa

Nahar Strauss

Shivte Yisrael

Tourjeman Post

Prophets

Nablus

East Jerusalem Bus Station

Suleiman

Derekh Jericho

Church of All Nations

Binyene HaUmma

Agrippas

Mahane Yehuda

Anna Ticho House

Zion Square

Russian Cathedral

Notre Dame de France

Paratroopers

The Old City

Mary Magdalene Church

Hilton

Bezalel

Jerusalem Tower

Ben Yehuda

Hillel

Queen Shlomzion

Jaffa

Central Post Office

Absalom's Pillar

Tomb of Zachariah

Yad LaBanim (Soldiers Memorial)

Ussishkin

Italian Synagogue

Bet Agron

Independence Park

Mamillah

Tomb of Hezir

Intercontinental

Sacker Park

King George

Mamillah Pool

Gershon Agron

City of David

Gihon Spring

Rose Park

Kiryat Ben-Gurion

Bezalel Academy of Art

Plaza

Arts & Crafts Lane

King David Hotel

YMCA

Yemin Moshe

Hezekiah's Tunnel

Ruppin

The Knesset

Hechal Shlomo & Great Synagogue

Kings

Keren Hayessod

King David

Herods Family Tomb

Moriah

Pool of Siloam

Silwan

Ramban

Azza

Terra Sancta College

Sheraton

King Solomon

Plumer Square

Montefiore Windmill

Cinemateque

Mount Zion

Valley of Hinnom

Kidron Valley

Shrine of the Book

Sderot Shazar

Rehavia

Van Leer Foundation

President's House

Jabotinsky

German Colony

Church of St. Andrew

Liberty Bell Park

Khan Theater

Israel Museum

Monestary of the Cross

Jerusalem Theater

Chopin

Railroad Station

Hebrew University

Neve Granot

L.A. Mayer Museum of Islamic Art

Natural History Museum

Peace Forest

Sderot Herzog

Hapalmach

Katamon

Emek Refaim

Gonen

Emek Refaim

Derekh Bethlehem

Derekh Hebron

To Mount Herzl, Yad Vashem, Ein Kerem

Talpiot

UN Headquarters

Haas Promenade

Pierre Konig

Yad Harutzim

Holyland ✓ Model of Ancient Jerusalem

Diplomat

72C

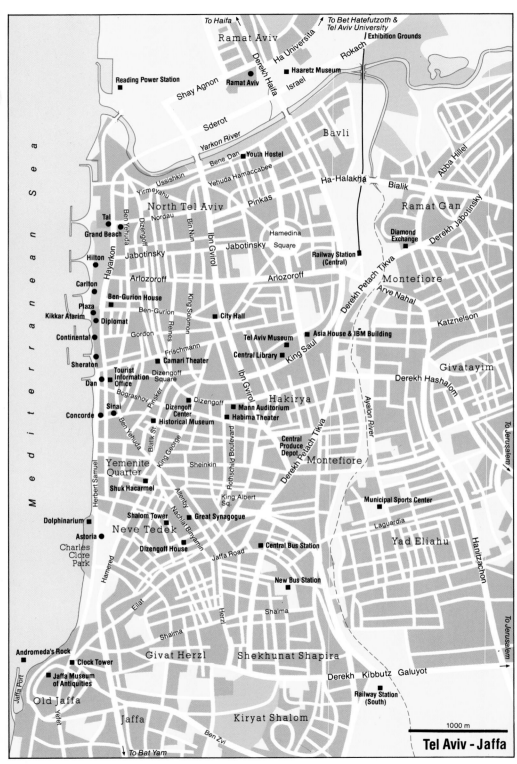

Mediterranean Sea

To Haifa

Ramat Aviv

To Bet Hatefutzoth &
Tel Aviv University

Exhibition Grounds

Ha Universita

Derekh Haifa

Rokach

Reading Power Station

Haaretz Museum

Shay Agnon

Ramat Aviv

Israel

Sderot

Bavli

Yarkon River

Ha-Halakha

Bialik

Bene Dan

Youth Hostel

Yehuda Hamaccabee

Ramat Gan

Abba Hillel

Yirmeyahu

North Tel Aviv

Pinkas

Derekh Jabotinsky

Ussishkin

Nordau

Bin Nun

Ibn Gvirol

Jabotinsky

Hamedina
Square

Diamond
Exchange

Tal

Ben Yehuda

Dizengoff

Jabotinsky

Railway Station
(Central)

Montefiore

Arve Nahal

Grand Beach

Hayarkon

Arlozoroff

Arlozoroff

Derekh Petach Tikva

Hilton

Katznelson

Carlton

King Solomon

Ben-Gurion House

City Hall

Plaza

Ben-Gurion

Reines

Tel Aviv Museum

Asia House & IBM Building

Givatayim

Kikkar Atarim

Diplomat

Gordon

Central Library

King Saul

Derekh Hashalom

Continental

Frischmann

Camari Theater

Sheraton

Dizengoff
Square

Tourist
Information
Office

Ibn Gvirol

Hakirya

Dan

Bograshov

Dizengoff

Mann Auditorium

Ben Yehuda

Pinsker

Dizengoff
Center

Habima Theater

Avalon River

To Jerusalem

Concorde

Sinai

Historical Museum

Derekh Petach Tikva

Bialik St.

King George

Central
Produce
Depot.

Montefiore

Yemenite
Quarter

Sheinkin

Rothschild Boulevard

Shuk Hacarmel

King Albert
Sq.

Allenby

Nachalat Binyamin

Municipal Sports Center

Herbert Samuel

Dolphinarium

Shalom Tower

Great Synagogue

Laguardia

Astoria

Neve Tedek

Dizengoff House

Central Bus Station

Yad Eliahu

Hanitzachon

Charles
Clore
Park

Jaffa Road

New Bus Station

Hamered

Eilat

Shalma

Herzl

Shalma

Andromeda's Rock

Givat Herzl

Shekhunat Shapira

Derekh Kibbutz Galuyot

To Jerusalem

Clock Tower

Jaffa Museum
of Antiquities

Railway Station
(South)

Jaffa Port

Old Jaffa

Yefet

Jaffa

Kiryat Shalom

Ben Zvi

To Bat Yam

1000 m

Tel Aviv - Jaffa

72D

Before the city was reunified in 1967, the Israelis controlled only West Jerusalem, which today is considered the New City. The tour of the New City begins with its oldest neighborhoods, those established in the 19th century. Next, the route zigzags about the downtown area from Zion Square across the cafe-spotted Ben Yehudah Mall, where the nightlife really gets cracking. It continues down some of the major thoroughfares, Jaffa Road and King George Street with the latter leading towards the tree-lined streets of Rehavia and the German Colony.

Crossing the city, the tour resumes at Zahal Square in downtown. From here, it leads through the Russian Compound, around the Street of the Prophets, and into two intriguing neighborhoods: ultra-Orthodox Mea She'arim and the century-old Bukharin Quarter.

After surveying the northern rim of the city, the route moves west into the Valley of the Cross, where the national parliament and the Israel Museum are located. Finally it ascends two more peaks that hover the city—the Hill of Evil Council to the southeast and Mt. Scopus to the northeast.

Many people who come to Israel for a short visit spend most of their time in Jerusalem and give a day or two to Tel Aviv and the rest of the country. Day Trips concludes the itinerary with some of the most popular excursions from Jerusalem. None of which are more than an hour and a half away, such as Bethlehem, the Dead Sea, Herodian, and Massada.

Below, menorah from third century CE synagogue.

OLD CITY SITES

Imagine the absurdity: in 1987, Kyoto, Japan hosted a "World Conference of Historical Cities," and although relatively prepubescent towns like Boston, Kiev, and Montreal attended, Jerusalem, the most wizened and immortal polis of all, was conspicuously uninvited. They might as well have gathered the planets in the solar system and told Earth it didn't belong.

For as you stand here in the Old City of Jerusalem you realize almost immediately that it simply cannot get any more historical than this. If anything, the place suffers from being *too* historical. In the babble of tour guides ticking off dates and names, first-time visitors often contract epochal vertigo. Tarry here long enough and you'll likely to imagine Mohammed, Jesus and Abraham engaged in a constant theological brawl over Turkish coffee at the corner falafel stand.

The history doesn't come in a nice, neat package and if you expect to retain any of it, you must be careful—especially during a short visit—not to try to absorb too much at once.

The Israeli capital could not be included in the historical cities conference the organizers said, because it was "the subject of political controversies." This is an understatement. It means quite simply that unlike other so-called "historical" cities, Jerusalem's history is not finished, written or fossilized. You are not about to enter a mausoleum, but a *living* museum. Precisely because of these political controversies (and philosophical, archaeological and military ones) a historical drama is being played out every day. Adding to the amusement, the characters themselves look and act as if they'd just stepped out of the previous millennium or two.

Before entering this maze, you can orient yourself by climbing the stairs at

any one of the main gates and follow a **Ramparts Walk** around the Old City walls. These were built by the Ottoman Emperor Suleiman from 1537-41 and are four km (2.5 miles) all the way around.

You can "walk entirely around the city in an hour," Mark Twain once said. "I do not know how else to make one understand how small it is." It is hard to believe that such a small place has come to be the most contested thatch of land since the beginning of time.

Entering the Old City: The **Jaffa Gate** marks the end of the road from the ancient port of Jaffa to Jerusalem, and like the hard-core pilgrims from centuries before them, most Western travelers today still step into the spiritual labyrinth of the Old City through this very entrance.

To the right of the gate, the only real break in the city walls is visible, a paved 39 feet (12 meters) opening. The rampart here was destroyed and the moat filled in 1898 to prepare for the osten-tatious entrance of German Kaiser Wilhelm II—an important political guest of the Turkish Sultan—who didn't care to dismount his white horse on cruising into town.

Inside the gate to the left is the **Government Tourist Office**, which organizes a host of inexpensive, solid tours that depart near the Jaffa Gate. It's also a decent repository of maps and information, as is the **Christian Information Center**, which is located on the first right just before the start of the boisterous Arab market.

Next door, in the **Anglican Compound**, is the **Christ Church**, the first such Protestant edifice in all of Palestine. Built by stone masons brought in specially from Malta in the 1840s, the church became the locus of a budding Protestant Quarter, serving missionaries and British explorers.

Opposite the church is the famed **Citadel**, strategic high ground that has been controlled and fortified by virtually all of Jerusalem's conquerors. The

Preceding pages: Aerial view of the Jewish Quarter. Left, Citadel of David.

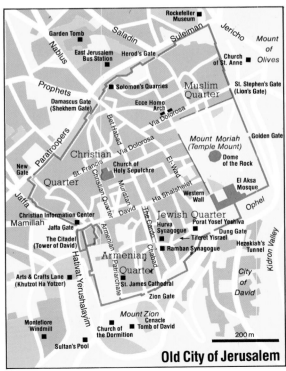

Old City of Jerusalem

Tower of David, despite its name, has nothing to do with King David, but is believed to be a remnant of King Herod's palace, placed on this site 2,000 years ago.

A case study in paranoia, Herod probably set up his home here on the edge of town because he felt more vulnerable to attack by his fellow Jews inside the city than the Romans outside.

In 1967, the Israelis turned the Citadel area into a **Museum of the History of Jerusalem**, and from the ruins inside you begin to get a sense of the layers of time here: a **Herodian mikvah** (ritual bath), for instance, served later as a Roman king's pool and then a Byzantine quarry. It's also worth checking out the **Model of Jerusalem**, another useful tool for getting your bearings. In addition, there's a regular slide presentation and in the evenings a schmaltzy sound and light show is offered in many different languages

Armenian Quarter: As you leave the Citadel, on the right is the Israeli Police Station, which served as the Jordanian Police Headquarters before 1967. Just beyond it you will enter the **Armenian Quarter**. Home to 2,000 Armenians and representing about one-sixth of the area of the Old City, it is definitely the most tranquil quarter inside its walls.

Though the quarter may seem an inhospitable place for curious travelers, spend some time here and discover a proud and friendly people more than willing to show visitors around and tell a story of their nation.

Located in what is today the Soviet Union and Turkey, Armenia boasts that it was the first nation to convert to Christianity—about 300 years after the birth of Christ. Well before the Emperor Constantine's conversion and Queen Helena's discovery of the "holy places," Armenian pilgrims were already flocking to Jerusalem.

Armenians have traditionally stayed as apolitical as possible here, and that, perhaps, accounts for their relative success in making their way among

Armenian Easter celebration.

much larger and more powerful factions. For merely six weeks, in 1300, when the king of Armenia conquered Jerusalem, did the Armenians wield any considerable power.

Between 1915 and 1918, when the Turks exterminated one and a half million Armenians, as many as 10,000 sought temporary refuge here, and the quarter was bursting at its seams. Today, the Armenians run a large monastery. Behind the monastery, the southwestern corner of the city is a giant garbage dump, one of the few patches of completely undeveloped land within city walls.

Across from the monastery is a simple portal leading to the **St. James Cathedral**, one of the most important and beautiful Christian sites in the Old City. This is believed to be the place where, in 44 C.E., Mary was sitting when she was brought the head of the martyred apostle St. James. This cranium is supposed to be buried inside the Cathedral.

Through the iron gate is a courtyard, inside of which you see two wooden clappers, reminders of the Turkish rule when bells were forbidden. In the Cathedral itself is the **Throne of St. James the Lesser**, upon which the Armenian Patriarch sits once a year—on the Feast of St. James.

Behind the Cathedral is a very private courtyard, not normally open to tourists, except on request. Here is a fine Armenian school and the **Gulbenkian Public Library**, which was established in 1929 and houses a number of rare books and manuscripts.

There is access to the **Armenian Museum** either through this courtyard or by the main road. The museum displays archaeological findings from the quarter, Armenian art and books, and an exhibit on the genocide.

The Armenian Patriarch Road leads toward the Zion Gate and Mt. Zion, but we'll come to that later. In the meantime, backtrack 50 yards (45 meters) and turn down St. James Road. Tucked

St. James Cathedral in the Armenian Quarter.

away on your right is an Armenian pizza place that's only open Wednesday night and Saturday afternoon, it's an unusual place to grab a meal.

Jewish Quarter: If you continue along this alleyway, the name changes to Or Ha-Hayim Street and you enter the **Jewish Quarter**—without question, the most affluent one in the Old City. After the Six Day War, when the Israelis assumed control of the Old City, Jews returned to this quarter and they've been building it up ever since. Although they've tried to preserve the sense of architectural tradition, space is so tight that they've raised the skyline, putting a third floor on many previously two-story flats.

Despite the physical and political tensions, apartments are in tremendous demand, fetching anywhere between $100,000 and (given a view of the Wailing Wall) $500,000. Security in the Old City is fierce to protect these burgeoning economic interests.

To the left of what is now Or Ha-Hayim Street, is the **Old Yishuv Court Museum**, which preserves relics of life in far less bourgeois times. The *Old Yishuv* refers to the Jewish settlement in Palestine before statehood, when the Jewish Quarter was a dirty, disease-ridden ghetto.

In the museum, you can compare the essential stylistic and aesthetic differences between the *Sephardic* (Spanish and Eastern) and *Ashkenazi* (Eastern European) Jewish settlers.

The museum has also refurbished two simple but elegant synagogues. **Ha-Ari** ("The Lion") is a Sephardic synagogue named after the great 16th-century mystic Isaac Luria, who, according to tradition, was born on this spot. Luria devoted his life to the study of *Kabbalah*, a Jewish mystical tradition passed down orally to a select few from Mt. Sinai. An ascetic and visionary who believed he was in constant contact with the prophet Elijah, Luria founded a Kabbalistic school in the Holy City of Safed. The **Or Ha-Hayim**

Shopping along the Cardo.

Synagogue was founded by a Moroccan rabbi, but later became one of the central synagogues for the Ashkenazim in the old *yishuv*.

If you continue on this street you'll come to Habad Road and the **Habad House**, underneath which begins the Champs Elysées of Roman and Byzantine Jerusalem, the **Cardo**. When the Romans rebuilt Jerusalem as Aelia Capitolina, they laid it out like a traditional Roman city and it is this character that shapes the city today.

For the Crusaders, the Cardo was their main market thoroughfare but after they were expelled the road was eventually buried underneath 13 feet (four meters) of rubble. Historians guessed such a street existed from the famous map, but only in digging up the Jewish Quarter during the early 1980s did archaeologists come upon this magnificent discovery.

It's been beautifully preserved—you can see how wide the street must have been and the pillars that ran along it—but the commercial row these days, including a ridiculous fur shop, raises the tacky quotient one notch too high.

Continuing down Habad Street, you'll reach **Archaeological Seminars**, which organizes the best and most comprehensive tours of Jerusalem at very reasonable prices. Even further still is a set of metal stairs that take you up on the rooftops for a view of the city.

Above the Cardo is the Jewish Quarter Road, where you'll find the **Jewish Quarter Museum**, which gives the history of the area since 1948. A multimedia show here emphasizes the loss of the quarter to the Arab Legion and its recapture by Israeli forces in 1967. Across the way is a **War of Independence Memorial** that highlights on an electronic map the house-by-house battles that took place in 1948.

Just above the memorial is the **Hurvah Synagogue**, a piling on of ruins. In 1701 a one-time believer in the famed false messiah Sabbatai Tsvi, Judah the Hassid came to Jerusalem from Poland

Soldier patrols the Old City wall and right, Hassids in the Jewish Quarter.

with 500 followers, one of the largest single immigrations before modern Zionism. He died five days after he arrived, but his disciples continued to build the synagogue here, borrowing the funds from local Moslems. When they couldn't meet their debts, the synagogue was burned down by their creditors in 1720, reduced to a ruin (*hurvah*).

In 1856 it was rebuilt, and became the centerpiece of the growing Jewish community in the Old City, but in 1948 it was blown up by the Arab Legion, left in a ruin once again.

The arch you see today has been reconstructed in a manner which gives you an idea of its once grand scale. Much talk is spent on how the Hurvah Synagogue should be rebuilt, but not surprisingly the different Jewish theo-political factions in Jerusalem can't seem to reach an agreement.

And below the Hurvah is the **Ramban Synagogue**, the oldest in Jerusalem. The Ramba (Rabbi Moses ben Nachman or Nachmanides), a famed Talmudic exegete essentially exiled from his native Spain after successfully disputing the king, founded the first Jewish settlement in Jerusalem since the Second Temple was destroyed. At first he wanted to establish a synagogue near the Tomb of David on Mt. Zion, but it's said he was scared off by the Bedouins. Instead, he put his house of worship here on ancient ruins. There has been a continued Jewish presence in this city ever since. The Ramban Synagogue has recently been refurbished and is in full use today.

Legend has it that the **mosque** preserved above the synagogue was built by a disaffected Jew from the Ramban congregation who converted to Islam.

In the courtyard adjacent to the Ramban Synagogue, are several Jewish educational institutions, including the **Jewish Heritage Information Center** and the **Aish HaTorah Yeshivah**. Many offer free tours of the quarter, places to sleep, Shabbat meals, and Talmud classes. (See box story.)

Remains of the Hurvah Synagogue.

The *shuls*: Following Hakehuna Street to the right to complex of **Four Sephardi Synagogues**: the **Elijah**, the **Yochanan Ben-Zakkai**, the **Stambouli** and the **Middle**, as they are called. Originally built by Jews expelled from Spain, they served for several centuries as the chief places of worship for Jerusalem's Sephardic community. Note the underground entrance and Islamic architecture, which was perhaps intended to mask the religious significance of the complex to hostile strangers. The *shuls* which were bombed in the 1948 war and used as stables during Jordanian rule, have been beautifully restored.

If you head in the opposite direction from the Ramban Synagogue courtyard down Tiferet Yisrael, you'll come across eight-meter wide collection of stones known as the **Broad Wall**. Discovered only recently, it supplied important archaeological evidence of a major chapter of Jewish history.

King Hezekiah mobilized the entire population to build—in just three months—an enormously thick wall around the city to protect it against the invading armies of Assyrian King Sennacherib in 701 BCE. The Bible says this wall was put up so quickly that it had to run through entire homes, one of which seems to be visible on the present archaeological site.

Head back north up Tiferet Yisrael to the **Burnt House**. An eerie and exciting place, it is literally a frozen moment of history—a time capsule of Jerusalem during the Second Temple period. It is believed to have been burnt when Titus razed Jerusalem in 70 A.D. A regular slide show here helps makes sense of the collected artifacts.

The holiest shrine: Past the Burnt House, down a set of stairs, and through the requisite Israeli security check, you enter a bustling plaza at the end of which is the holiest shrine in all of Jewish civilization, the **Wailing Wall**. Anyone may approach the Wall and lodge paper prayers in its cracks. You

Worshipping at the Wailing Wall.

THE YESHIVA SCENE

It begins this way: A young Diaspora Jew on a two-week tour of Israel visits the Wailing Wall. In short order he is asked by a Hassidic man, *"Do you want to put on tefillin?"* Or perhaps another Orthodox Jew offers to set him up for a Shabbat meal or to give him a free place to sleep as long as he's in the Old City. There follows a series of provocative discussions about the nature of Judaism, and how assimilated Jews of America and elsewhere have lost touch with their roots. Would the young man be interested in pursuing the issues farther? And so it goes on until he is fully ensconced in one of Jerusalem's many **ba'al teshuvah yeshivot**.

Ba'al teshuvah means "master of return," and in the past 20 years a large number (some rabbis put the figure at 20,000) of the assimilated Jews—both male and female—have returned to the religious observance of their ancestors, through the yeshiva experience. The yeshiva is an age-old Jewish school, where students (or *buchers*) pore over the Talmudic laws. The Talmud is comprised of commentaries in Hebrew and Aramaic on the oral law that God gave the Jews along with the written Torah at Mt. Sinai. The yeshiva is based on the idea that the best way to learn these oral laws is by engaging in a constant, hands-on-text discussion of these commentaries.

In the courtyard next to the Ramban and Hurvah Synagogues are several Jewish educational centers, including **Aish HaTorah Yeshiva**. (Another big ba'al teshuvah yeshiva is **Ohr Someyach** outside the Old City.) The **Heritage House** will put you up for a few nights as you begin to enter the yeshiva world. If you decide to partake, be prepared to face considerable (if gradual) pressure to conform to various religious observances.

Being invited to a religious home on Shabbat.

THE WAILING WALL

When the Romans burned and destroyed the great Temple in 70 A.D., all that was left was rubble. That is, except for one remaining wall, which was built—by the poorest of Jews, it is said—to support the western portion of the Herodian Temple Mount. According to traditional Judaism the Temple cannot be rebuilt until the Messiah comes and the Diaspora Jews regard The Wall (or *HaKotel*) as their most sacred shrine.

To pray here has been the abiding dream of observant Jews ever since the beginning of their exile 1,900 years ago. The wall, which is as smooth as the endless stream of tears spilled mourning the destruction of the Temple, has come to be known as the Wailing Wall.

The Wall itself is 50 feet tall, and most of the stones were carved and stacked here during Herod's time, but those at and near the top were put there during restoration by the Mamelukes and Turks. When the Jordanian Legion captured the Old City in 1948, Jews were forbidden—as they had been many times throughout history—to worship at the Wall. So it was with special meaning on June 7, 1967, that Jews everywhere watched TV footage of the Israeli Army retaking the Old City, and the young soldiers praying and weeping at the Wall.

Immediately following the Six Day War, the Arab shanties in the large area in front of the Wall were cleared, and the plaza was made into a place of worship. Traditionally, observant Jews gather here on holidays and days of mourning—especially on Tisha ba'Av, the anniversary of the Temple's destruction. The weekly Torah portion (*parsha*) is read aloud on Monday and Thursday mornings, and on these days there are ceremonies for Jewish boys who come from all over the world to be *bar mitzvahed*.

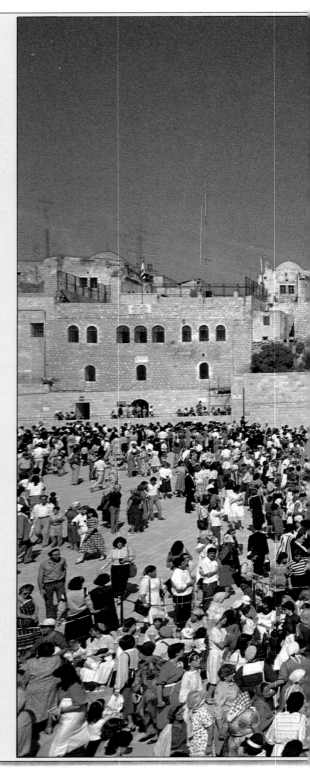

will note that women ("modestly dressed") enter on the left, men (heads covered) on the right. Remember, too, that photos are forbidden on Shabbat.

To the left of the prayer area and leaning on the Wall itself is **Wilson's Arch**, discerned by the 19th-century British surveyor Charles Wilson to be part of the bridge over which ran a road from the Upper City to the Temple Mount. To the right of the prayer area by the southwestern corner of the Temple Mount is **Robinson's Arch** (named for a 19th-century American scholar/adventurer), which was presumably part of a similar bridge.

Below Robinson's Arch and along the southern wall are the **southern excavations**. The slope just outside the city wall below the southeast corner of the Temple Mount is called the **Ophel**, and has been the site of extensive archaeological excavations since 1968. Three tour routes are marked off for your convenience. One of the most impressive finds are remains of the ancient staircase and the Hulda Gate through which pilgrims climbed the Temple compound. Note the stairs are of uneven size, designed so that pilgrims would not casually bound up to the Temple Mount to worship, but would concentrate upon the meaning of their ascent.

Beneath the Ophel are the **City of David** excavations, where it is believed King David laid the foundations for the city of Jerusalem around 1000 BCE. The digs here, which began in 1978, have produced ruins related to the Canaanite settlement of Jerusalem even before King David in the third and second millennium BCE.

If you make the detour this way, follow the hill down to the water source that probably attracted King David to this site, the **Spring of Gihon**. Because the spring was located outside the city walls, in a cave at the bottom of the Kidron Valley, Jerusalem was in danger of having its water supply cut off by Assyrian invaders in 701 BCE. There-

Preceding pages: Jews gather on Sukkot at the Wailing Wall plaza. Below, the 'pinnacle' of the Temple Mount.

fore, the shrewd King Hezekiah had a tunnel built to connect the Gihon spring to the **Siloam pool** inside the city. If you wish to explore Hezekiah's Tunnel—a favorite activity for the kids—bring a candle or flashlight, and prepare to roll up your pants or get wet. An early explorer of this tunnel was the 19th-century British archaeologist Charles Warren. He also discovered an underground well, **Warren's Shaft**, where Jerusalemites could fetch their water in ancient times.

The Temple Mount: Now climb back up to the Old City through the **Dung Gate**, so called for the heaps of rubbish that was left here during Roman and Byzantine times. As you face the Temple Mount, remember that this is reputed to be the place where Abraham prepared to sacrifice Isaac, and where in ancient times a Temple twice the size of the Dome of the Rock stood in its place. The southeastern corner of the Temple Mount is sometimes called the "pinnacle" since legend has it that Sa-

tan brought Jesus to this spot from the place of the Temptation.

When Israel conquered the Old City in the 1967 War, the Israeli government decided to put the Temple Mount under the jurisdiction of the Wakf — the Moslem Religious Trust. Though the Arabs control it today, there have been stirrings in some very right-wing religious circles to retake the mount and rebuild the Jewish Temple. There have been protests and increasing violence on the Temple Mount since the Palestinian strike and uprising of late 1987.

But to the solitary searcher of spiritual light, the Temple Mount still holds itself like the name the Arabs call it, Haram esh-Sharif, or "Noble Sanctuary." And the **Dome of the Rock** is perched like Jerusalem's crown.

There are ten portals leading to the Temple Mount. At the kiosk inside the southeastern **Mughrabi Gate**, so named for the Moroccan and Algierian Islamic pilgrims who settled here, you can purchase a ticket that permits mul-

Praying at the Al Aksa Mosque and right, inside the Dome of the Rock.

DOME OF THE ROCK

Moslems (and many Jews) believe that the Dome of the Rock (or *Haram esh-Sharif*) was placed on the precise spot where the great Temple once stood, and that the rock itself rests on location of the "Holy of Holies," where the Jewish high priest communed with God once a year. The rock was widely believed to be the Stone of Foundation, the very center of the earth.

The Dome is the oldest, one of the most important and probably the most beautiful monument in all of Islam. It is often called the Mosque of Omar, but it is neither a mosque, nor was it built by Omar. It was put up by Caliph Abd al-Malik, the ninth successor of the prophet Mohammed, in 691 A.D. Influenced by the Christian edifice industry of his time, the Caliph commissioned Byzantine architects to do the job, and they constructed it on the exact scale of the Church of the Holy Sepulchre. Caliph Abd al-Malik had his name and the year inscribed inside the dome, but two centuries later the Caliph al-Mamoon had his predecessor's name erased and his own put in its place. In one of the better bloopers in history, however, he forgot to change the date and his fraudulence is here for all to see to this very day. The structure has been renovated throughout history, most notably during the reign of Suleiman the Magnificent, whose mosaic tile work gives the Dome its ornate and rich Eastern flavor.

Inside of the Dome, you can see the holy rock (called, in Arabic, *Kubbet es-Sakhra*) upon which it is said Abraham prepared to sacrifice Isaac and from which Mohammed rose to heaven. Next to the rock there is a box that is said to contain a few hairs from the Islamic prophet's beard. In the underground cave referred to as the **Well of Souls**, the dead congregate for their prayer meetings.

tiple entrance to the Dome of the Rock, the Al-Aksa Mosque, and the Islamic Museum.

Moselm holy place: The silver-domed edifice on the Temple Mount is called the **Al-Aksa Mosque**. Some say it was originally built in the 6th century as a church honoring the Virgin Mary, and that it was converted into an Islamic place of worship, but Moslems scoff at this notion. According to their tradition, the Umayyad caliph had it built in the early 8th century. It has been destroyed and renovated many times since.

Unlike the Dome of the Rock, Al-Aksa is a mosque, and as such, is the most important Moslem place of worship in Jerusalem, one of the most famous in the Islamic world. Non-Moslems are not permitted to enter the mosque during prayer. When you do go in (remember to take your shoes off, according to custom), you have the feeling as though you are walking into an elaborate carpet warehouse. It's actually quite beautiful in its simplicity,

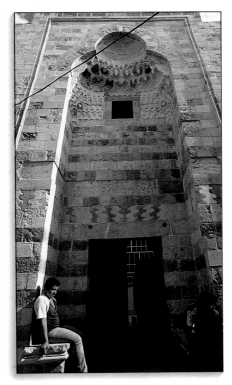

and innovative for its use of six rows of columns set perpendicular to the wall which is customary to face when one prays. Where Jews the world over face Jerusalem when they pray, Moslems face Mecca; in this case that's toward the southern or back wall.

It was in front of Al-Aksa in 1951 that a fanatic Moslem murdered Jordanian King Abdullah in front of his grandson, the current King Hussein. In 1969, another nut, this time an Australian, set the mosque aflame, leading calls for jihad against Israel. When Anwar came to Jerusalem in 1977, he came to pray at Al-Aksa. There are still demonstrations there today, either by Palestinians trying to raise the national flag or by Israeli right-wingers.

When the Crusaders conquered Jerusalem, they transformed Al-Aksa into a royal palace before finally setting up the headquarters of the Order of the Knights of the Temple here—the Templars. Below the mosque, along the southeast corner of the Temple Mount are **Solomon's Stables**, a name given by the Crusaders because that's where they kept their chariots and horses. The **Islamic Museum** across from Al-Aksa is worth a short visit, especially for its large collection of beautifully calligraphied copies of the Koran.

Exactly in the middle of Al-Aksa and the Dome of the Rock is the 14th-century **Fountain of Al Kas** (or "the Cup"), which originally hooked up with an extensive subterranean system of cisterns from Temple times. The Dome of the Rock sits on the Upper Platform of the Temple Mount. The eight staircases leading up topped by stone arcades called the **Mawazzin**. It is said that on Judgment Day only the virtuous souls will be allowed to continue through the Mawazzin. Behind the Dome of the Rock is the **Dome of the Chain**, one third its height, though built in a similar form.

If you leave the "Noble Sanctuary" by way of the **Iron Gate**, turn right through a small alley to the **Small Wall**,

Preceding pages: Ramadan at the Dome of the Rock. Left, the Mameluke architectural style. Right, Arab shopkeeper.

which is actually another section of the sacred Western Wall of the Temple Mount. Some religious anti-Zionists prefer to pray here rather than at what they feel is the circus-like atmosphere at the Wailing Wall.

If you leave the Temple Mount by the **Gate of the Chain**, you may wonder how this gate got its name. In Temple times when a Jewish court met here, the accused were asked to hold a certain chain. Anyone who could hold the chain was considered innocent; if someone grasp at the chain and it disappeared, they were considered guilty.

Mameluk architecture: The Street of the Chain leads to the Moslem Quarter markets, but along the way it has a few examples of Mameluke architecture worth mentioning. *Mamluke* means "owned" in Arabic and in 13th-century Egypt, the Mamelukes were high-class slaves of Turkish origin who overthrew their masters, thereby gaining control of Jerusalem, among other places. In this city, they are remembered best for

the ornate, stylish buildings—a kind of early precursor to Art Deco.

The first building on the left of the gate, with the black and white interlacing stone facade, is the **Madrassa Tankiziyya**. *Madrassas,* of which the Memelukes built many, were Moslem theological seminaries. Further down along the Street of the Chain are some other Mameluke gems, including the tomb of a princess (at number 149) and another *madrassa* (number 106).

Stepping back in time: The Moslem Quarter is the largest, most crowded, and by far the most confusing quarter in the Old City. You don't sightsee here, you wander. And if you get lost in the labrythine alleyways here, that's the whole point. The Moslem Quarter gives one the sense of how Jerusalem looked, smelled, and sounded up until the 20th century.

Many visitors start their adventure just inside either the Damascus or Jaffa Gates, people-watching over Turkish coffee, before wading through the souk.

A Haj door and right, Palestinian girl.

Here you'll find for sale endless rows of mummy bead jewelry, fake antiques, olive wood, Roman glass, Turkish coins, Bedouin carpets, and *keffiyahs* (the popular Arab headcoverings).

Haggling is the native sport, and one must not be put off by the overbearing, hard-sell approach; most shopkeepers speak many languages and have interesting stories to tell if you take the time to chat with them over tea.

The Moslem Quarter isn't a place where you go to have a sit-down meal, but rather to sample the local cuisine. As you walk along, try picking up *houmous* at **Abu-Shukri's** at **El-Wad Street** along the Via Dolorosa. Although it's reputedly the best houmous in Israel, save some room for the goodies on the silver trays at the pastry shops along **Souk Khan**: *baklava, kanaffi,* and other honey-and-nut combos. If a kid approaches you with a huge brass, samovar-like vat, don't be afraid; he's probably trying to sell you a serving of *sachleb*, a sweet, hot, milky, wintertime

drink topped with dried fruit, cinnamon, raisins and nuts. Since West Jerusalem is closed on a Friday night, many gather at the *schleb* stands at the **Damascus Gate** on this night.

Money-changers abound and will offer far better exchange rates than the banks, though official Israeli guides will discourage you with anti-Palestinian propaganda. All Jewish money-changers and official Israeli guides complain about them as well. ("They're undermining the value of the shekel!")

The Damascus Gate, which is the fulcrum of Arab life in the Old City, was built in the 16th century by Suleiman the Magnificent. Underneath it, archaeological excavations have revealed an earlier portal from the Roman period, suggesting that it was the major entryway for Emperor Hadrian's Aelia Capitolina. From here, you can wind your way through the Old City or walk along the outside of the walls to the Lion's Gate for a tour of the Via Dolorosa.

In the alleyways of the Moslem Quarter.

VIA DOLOROSA

Putting aside the crass commercialism of the local merchants hawking Jesus paraphernalia, an excursion down the **Via Dolorosa** (or Way of Sorrows) is one of the most culturally resonant routes in the Western World. This is the fabled path that Jesus was said to have taken to meet his fate of crucifixion.

The Fourteen Stations of the Cross leading to the Calvary in the Church of the Holy Sepulchre (nine were described in the Gospels and five by tradition) were fixed during the time of the Ottoman rule.

Most historians and archaeologists today debunk the authenticity of these particular sites, but suggest that Jesus may have followed a path very similar to it. The controversy doesn't discourage pilgrims from all over the world every year at Easter to gather here to follow Jesus' footsteps, many of them dressing and acting the part of the ancients with considerable flourish.

It's best to start down the Via Dolorosa from the **Lions' Gate**, where a pair of lions (some say panthers) flank both sides of the entrance. According to legend, Suleiman the Magnificent dreamed one night that four lions were ripping him to shreds. The interpretation of the local sages was that the Lion of Judah was enraged because the Holy City was in shambles as no wall had been built around it.

Upon hearing this, Suleiman immediately erected walls—the very ones you see today—and had the four lions carved to commemorate his dream. When the Israeli Army penetrated the Old City during the 1967 War, they entered through the Lions' Gate.

To the Christians, however, it is known as **St. Stephen's Gate** because Stephen the Martyr is said to have been stoned to death at this very site. Just inside the gate, you'll find a **Pilgrim's**

The "Way of Sorrows" in Hebrew, Arabic and Latin.

Reception Plaza, where most guided tours of the Via Dolorosa begin. Opposite the plaza is the **Church of St. Anne**, which was built by Crusaders on the remains of a Byzantine church to commemorate the traditional place where Anne lived when she gave birth to Mary. **Mary's Birthplace** is specifically marked by the crypt underneath the church. The **Bethesda Pool**, where Jesus miraculously gave the water curative power, is in the courtyard.

Turn right as you leave the church, and you will come to the **First Station of the Cross**, where Jesus was sentenced to crucifixion by the Roman Procurator Pontius Pilate. Today this is Umariayah school for Islamic boys, built during the Ottoman Empire on the site of the **Antonia Fortress**, the Roman administrative headquarters in Jesus' time.

From the courtyard is a splendid view of the Temple Mount. Also, this is the point from which the Franciscans lead a procession down the entire Via Dolorosa every Friday afternoon. Good Friday proves to be a veritable mob scene every year.

Continuing along, on your right you will come to the **Second Station**, where Jesus was brutalized by the Romans, a crown of thorns put on his head. The spot is marked on the street, just in front of the **Chapels of the Condemnation and the Flagellation**.

Overhead as you continue is the **Ecce Homo Arch**, named for Pilate's words of scorn: "Behold the man!" After considerable archaeological excavations conducted by the Sisters of Zion, it was determined that the arch did not even exist in Jesus' time.

In the process, this intriguing religious order became expert in the field, and the entire **Convent of the Sisters of Zion**, on your right, is an archaeological museum all its own.

Past the convent, a century-old **Austrian Hospice** is on the right. Then you must follow Jesus' path to the left a short jog on E1 Wad Street. Here on the

Retracing Christ's steps along Via Dolorosa.

left side of the street is a pillar in the wall which marks the **Third Station**, where Jesus first fell under weight of the cross. Immediately after it, you see the **Fourth Station**, where Jesus is said to have met Mary. A sixth century mosaic in the crypt of the **Armenian Catholic Church of Our Lady of the Spasm** here depicts the outline of sandals where Mary putatively stood when Jesus passed by.

Before turning right down a bustling Old City thoroughfare grab a snack at the hummus stand of **Abu-Shukri**, one of the better known and tastier (if not more expensive) tourist haunts along the way.

After turning right, you come to the **Fifth Station**, where the Roman soldiers commanded Simon the Cyrenian, a Jew from North Africa, to carry the cross the rest of the way.

The **Sixth Station** is a short way down on the left. It is also called the **House of Veronica** because this is where St. Veronica dabbed Jesus' brow

with her veil and then miraculously watched his image appear upon it.

At the corner of Via Dolorosa and Souk Kahn er-Zeit Street is the **Seventh Station**, where Jesus fell once again. Also called the **Gate of Judgement**, it is believed this was the site of the gate leading outside the city in Jesus' time. Historically this makes sense to the extent that Jewish law says one cannot be buried inside city walls.

The **Eighth Station**, just outside the Greek Orthodox **Chapel of St. Chralampos** and the **German Lutheran Hospice of St. John**, is where Jesus is said to have addressed the women: "Do not weep for me, weep for Jerusalem." The Via Dolorosa as a street ends here. To reach the **Ninth Station**, retrace your steps and climb the flight of stairs to the **Ethiopian Coptic Church**. There's a pillar inside the entrance that marks where Jesus fell the third time.

Past that pillar, you will come onto one of the most serendipitous sites in Jerusalem. Here is a generous court-

Pilgrims pass the "Holy Fire" on Easter.

yard on the top of the Church of the Holy Sepulchre: the dome you see in the middle of the terrace is actually the roof of the **Chapel of St. Helena**, where it's believed the cross was found. The **Ethiopian Village** up here is literally out of this world—an African village transported to the midst of a bustling metropolis.

The last five stations are inside the **Church of the Holy Sepulchre** itself. As you enter the Church follow the stairs to the right to the rocky hill lock over which this edifice was erected. It is called **Calvary** in the Latin tradition, **Golgotha** in Greek tradition. Golgotha is actually the Hebrew world for skull and this place was so named because of the Christian belief that Adam was buried here and that a drop of Jesus' blood fell upon Adam's skull.

Up here are four stations: in the Catholic room on the right is the **Tenth Station**, a floor mosaic that marks where Jesus was forced to strip off his clothes; behind the altar you will find the **11th Station**, a mosaic that indicates the spot where Jesus was nailed to the cross; in the Greek Orthodox room on the left is the **12th Station**, where the cross was fixed and Jesus died; outside of the room, a statue of Mary wearing a diamond and gold crown represents the **13th Station**, where she took Jesus into her arms.

Down the stairs is the **14th Station**, the **Holy Sepulchre** itself, where Jesus was laid to rest. Inside the rotunda it is the miracle rock that rolled away from the entrance to the tomb. The holes you see in the tomb itself is where the Greek Orthodox Bishop receives the "Holy Fire" from God on Easter every year.

Also underneath the rotunda is the **Angel's Chapel**, so called because when Mary Magdalene came to visit Jesus' grave on Sunday after the crucifixion, she saw no trace of his body, but rather an angel perched on a stone altar.

At the rear of the sepulchre, there is a small, but important chapel that belongs to the Copts, their only "posses-

Olivewood images of Jesus and Mary.

CHURCH OF THE HOLY SEPULCHRE

When in 326 A.D. Constantine's mother Queen Helena started exploring Jerusalem assisted by a bishop (so she said) as her guardian angel, she came upon a Temple of Venus, which was built by Hadrian. The Roman Emperor, she surmised, must have put his pagan edifice on top of a holy one, and when she discovered a crypt and three crosses, she was sure it was where Jesus had been crucified.

The original Church built by her son, Emperor Constantine, must have been truly magnificent for it was twice the size of the church we see today. It was destroyed by the Persians three centuries later. Its replacement was the victim of an earthquake one century later in 746 A.D. The fiercest of about 50 earthquakes that have rocked the place during its history. The church we see today is a Crusader church built in its

place. It is one of the oldest standing buildings in Jerusalem.

For the Western Christian pilgrim coming upon it for the first time, the church has a very definite Eastern, exotic aura, which reflects how little the place has changed in the past 800 years. Such may well have been what made the English General Gordon so uncomfortable during his visit here in the 1840s. General Gordon rejected the church as Jesus' burial place and established the Protestant site as the Garden Tomb near what is today the East Jerusalem bus station.

An amateur historian and archaeologist, General Gordon said that Jewish cemeteries were always outside city walls and this Holy Sepulchre was not. What he did not realize is that in Jesus' time, it may well have been outside the city walls, since the current wall outline was established after the crucifixion.

Of course, when General Gordon made his visit, the Protestants had no "possessions" inside the church, those having been apportioned to the various Christian sects before the Reformation. The church is divided between six such sects, and each believes it should rightfully control the entire complex. This has been the source of an ongoing acrimonious struggle between them, which until a recent rapproachment has caused the church to fall into a terrible disrepair. Who shall dust this archway, who shall fix these steps?

The most fascinating time to visit the Church is during the Greek festival of Easter week. The festival culminates in an extraordinary event. On Easter Eve, the "Holy Fire" descends from heaven in the Chapel of the Sepulchre. Thousands of pilgrims from all over the world gather to light their candles at the flame as it shoots forth from the grave of Christ.

The fire itself is not considered dangerous; the faithful are convinced that it will do them no harm. However, many pilgrims have lost their lives in their struggle to fulfill their faith.

Left, where Christ lay in the Holy Sepulchre. Right, outside the church.

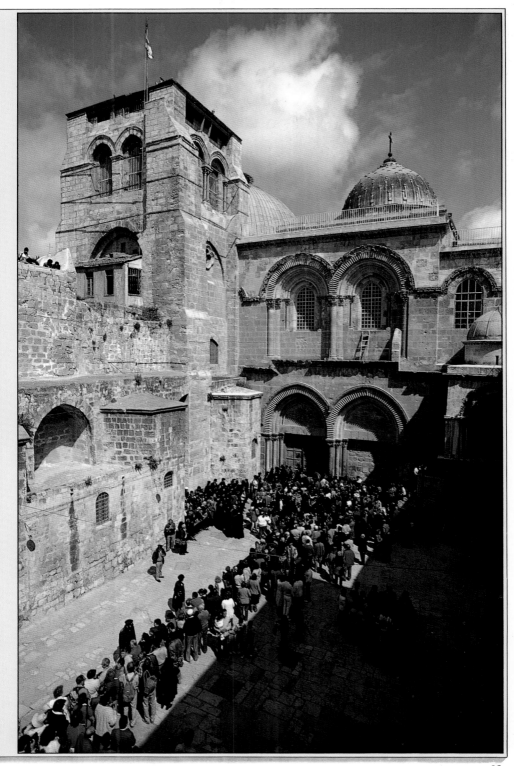

sion" in the Church. On the other side of the sepulchre is a bulky Greek Orthodox cathedral called the **Cathlicon**. The Greeks believe that the chalice on the floor is the center of the world.

As you follow the stairs down to the lower part of the church, you will see a vast number of crosses etched into the walls. At the bottom is the Armenian's **Chapel of St. Helena**, whose dome we noted from above on the terrace of the Ethiopian compound. The contemporary floor mosaic is an Armenian Genocide memorial.

Farther down, there is the **Chapel of the Finding of the Cross**, where Queen Helena discovered the True Cross. Remember that she actually found three crosses—one that had been used to crucify Jesus, the other two used for a couple of thieves.

How did she know which was which? According to one tradition, at least, it is said that the queen touched each cross to a dead baby, and it was the True Cross that restored the child to life.

Be sure to look at the stones which are in the cave. Archaeologists now believe that the stones from this very quarry were the ones that were wheeled into the Old City and used to build the Temple Mount and perhaps to build Herod's Temple.

Just south of the church is the **Mosque of Omar**, where the Caliph came to pray when his armies conquered Jerusalem. It is said that the Byzantine patriarch at the time invited him to pray at the Church of the Holy Sepulchre, but the Caliph did not want to dignify it or Christianity and so chose this spot. The minaret went up in 1417.

Leaving the Church of the Holy Sepulchre plaza, to the southeast you will see a sleek and elegant tower that makes up part of the **Church of the Redeemer**.

Built on the ruins of a Crusader Church, this German Lutheran building was dedicated on the occasion of Kaiser Wilhelm II's visit to Jerusalem. The view from the belfry is about the best you'll get in the Old City and the occasional concert here is another draw.

Opposite the church is what is known as the **Muristan Quarter**. The name is Persian for hospital and this is where the hospitals and hospices were in Crusader and, some say, Byzantine times. During Roman rule it was the site of a forum; today it is a rather unremarkable little bazaar.

The **Eastern Orthodox Church of St. James** is northwest of the Church of the Holy Sepulchre. The nearby **Greek Orthodox Patriarchate**, on the road by that name, is an entire complex that includes, most notably, a library with fragments of the Dead Sea Scrolls, and a **museum** that displays several archaeological finds from the Old City.

Technically, the **Christian Quarter**, as this entire area is called, starts at the **New Gate**, which is new by Jerusalem standards, having been opened in 1887.

Should you overdose on churches, as any tourist is inclined to do in this particular city, you might well note that

A third-century pilgrim's drawing. Right, the 14th Station of the Cross—Jesus' tomb.

MOUNT ZION

Nobody knows exactly where the real Mt. Zion is. What is today called Mt. Zion was in Temple times simply the Upper City of Jerusalem, where the affluent families in town had their digs. This particular hill probably got its name when it was left outside the walls of the Roman city of Aelia Capitolina. Legend has it that Suleiman the Magnificent had his architects beheaded for following the Roman example in excluding this place from the confines of the Turkish city walls.

Whatever its history, Mt. Zion acquired a certain symbolic significance as the heart of the Jewish homeland and gave its name to the political movement that eventually recaptured Jerusalem and all of Israel.

The place of start is **Zion Gate** at the end of the Armenian Quarter. Structurally, the gate was built at a right angle so the onrushing invader would be vulnerable at the turn. Also you will note the slats above the gate, from which hot oil can be poured on the enemy. The entire portal is pock-marked with bullet holes made by the Israeli forces during an unsuccessful attempt to penetrate it in the 1948 War of Independence.

Head straight from the gate to the second path, and turn right. Just up ahead is the **Diaspora Yeshivah**, a very weird place where Jewish Orthodoxy meets sixties hippies and which gets savagely satirized in the Phillip Roth novel *The Counterlife*. Just adjacent to it is **King David's Tomb**, though many believe he was actually buried in the City of David. Nevertheless, an enormous number of Jewish pilgrims come here to pray. The tomb served much the way the Wailing Wall does today during Jordanian rule when the Old City was off limits. In the back is **Chamber of the Holocaust**, a memorial to the Jews slaughtered in Europe, where desecrated Torah scrolls and

yellow stars of shame are on display.

Upstairs from David's Tomb is the **Cenaculum**, a sparse room with vaulting arches where Jesus presumably ate the Passover seder better known as the Last Supper. This is where Jesus also instructed his disciples on the basic points of Christianity and where the apostles—in that Pentecostalist miracle—began speaking in tongues.

Turn right as you leave the Hall of the Last Supper, then follow a short jog to the left, you will find the **Church of the Dormition**, completed by the German Benedictines in 1910. Recognized on the Jerusalem skyline for its black cone roof, this is where Mary fell into an eternal sleep (or dormition) after the crucifixion. The acoustics in the basilica are splendid for the many classical music concerts presented here.

Nearby in the **Old Protestant Cemetery** lie many British archaeologists, diplomats, and missionaries who shaped Jerusalem during the British Mandate and the end of Turkish rule.

Left, the Dormition Abbey on Mt. Zion. Right, blowing the shofar at the Tomb of King David.

MOUNT OF OLIVES

Once the Mount of Olives was covered with olive trees, but the Romans chopped them down to assemble the war machines they used to destroy Jerusalem in 70 A.D. In ancient times, Jewish pilgrims brought red heifers here for purification on their way to making sacrifices at the Temple. Today, the Mount of Olives is revered by all: Moslems live up here, Jews are buried here and the story of Jesus is told in the shrines which draw the tourists to this hill daily.

The popular starting point for any tour is at the top, just beneath the **Intercontinental Hotel**—a place that outrages Jews because it was built on the holy Jewish grave sites during Jordanian rule. This is where you can get the obligatory camel shot and a view that is without parallel in the city especially at dawn and dusk.

Even though Jesus walked up this mountain the evening of the Last Supper, it is customary and physically less demanding for visitors to follow another route in the opposite direction.

Take the road to your right to the Carmelite Sisters' cloister, the **Church of the Pater Noster**. Here is where the Lord's Prayer is handsomely calligraphied in 63 different languages on the courtyard walls.

Also on the property are the ruins of the Byzantine **Eleona Church** that marks the secret cave where Queen Helena said Jesus taught his controversial doctrine at a safe distance from both the Romans and Jews.

Outside the Pater Noster on the right is the **Chapel of Ascension,** the traditional site where Jesus rose to heaven 40 days after his resurrection. On this, the highest point on the mountain, the crusaders rebuilt an earlier Byzantine edifice and for a time the Moslems converted it into a mosque. Inside, the supposed footprint of Jesus is pre-

Preceding pages: ancient olive trees in the Garden of Gethsamane. Jewish cemetary, Mt. of Olives and right, golden domes of the Russian Orthodox Church.

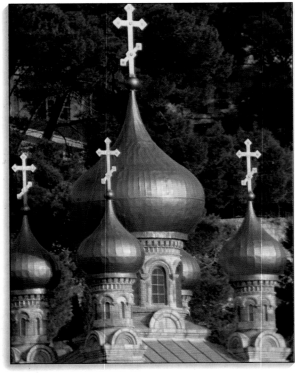

served. On the Christian Feast of the Ascension, most sects gather here. The Russian Orthodox Church, however, believes Jesus rose from the place marked by their steepled **Church of the Ascension** and **Russian Monastery** very close by.

Now backtrack to the hotel and take the path leading down the mountain along the famous **Jewish cemetery** where one can still be buried at the cost of as much as 50 grand per plot. The price is dear because Jewish tradition says that when the Messiah comes to Jerusalem, he will sweep across the Mount of Olives, gather the dead here and enter the Old City through the **Gates of Mercy.**

Actually the Jews and Christians agree the Messiah will appear through these **Golden Gates**, as they're also known. You can see the gates just across the Kidron Valley. You might also notice in the valley the Moslem cemetery strategically positioned in front of the gates just in case the Mes-

siah comes and resurrects the dead. On your left as you descend the hill, are the **Tombs of the Prophets**, caves where Haggai and Malachi rest.

Nearby is an orange sign that calls your attention to a **Mass Grave,** where the heroic last defenders of the Jewish Quarter in 1948 were moved after Israel regained the city and the Mount of Olives in 1967. Many of the other graves you see were desecrated during Jordanian rule; tombstones were carted away and used to build everything from homes to latrines.

Ancient burial grounds: Was this ground used for burial in the time of Solomon, perhaps even Abraham? Take the path to your right, you will discover an ancient **Jewish Necropolis** that has led some archaeologists to this conclusion.

In ancient times, the dead were wrapped in shrouds and then placed in small niches for 11 months, after which time their bones were put in boxes called ossuaries which were as wide as

Easter procession starts on the Mt. of Olives.

a scull bone as long as the thigh bone.

Continue along this side path to the Franciscan **Basilica of Dominus Flevit**, an architectural gem designed by the Italian architect Antonio Barluzzi in 1956 and built on the ruins of a Crusader church.

The chapel is supposed to be shaped like a tear because it marks the place where Jesus cried over the future destruction of Jerusalem. One can almost imagine Jesus gazing on the Temple as he wept. You shouldn't miss the view of the Mount from inside the chapel as it is one of the best in the city.

Further down the mountain is the Russian Church of Mary Magdalene, which distinguishes the Jerusalem skyline with its golden onion-shaped domes. The church was built by the czar in grand Russian style in the late 19th century. It is said that the crypt inside contains some of the hearts of the royal Romanov family which was brutally murdered in the Russian Bolshevik Revolution.

Route of Jesus: Next you come to **Gethsemane**, the garden where Jesus tarried after the Last Supper. For whatever it's worth, the olive trees themselves have been carbon dated and are as old as the savior. Unfortunately because so many pilgrims have ripped off whole tree branches to bring back home with them, the garden itself has been roped off.

If you follow the path through, you arrive at the **Church of All Nations,** which was also designed by Barluzzi (in 1926) and built on the ruins of a Crusader Church.

The Crusader Church was itself built on the ruins of a Byzantine one. Barluzzi used stained glass and purple alabaster and put stars on the ceiling to simulate the nighttime. For it was said to be evening here when Jesus arrived to ask God why he had to suffer and die. The front of the church is beautiful, save those weird creatures on the roof. Did Barluzzi really think that reindeer lived in Jerusalem?

Camels are a common sight.

Below the garden, at the bottom of the mountain, you finally come to **Mary's Tomb,** a candle-lit cave controlled by the Greek Orthodox and Armenian churches. It was preserved during Moslem times as a mosque because the Islamic tradition also venerates Mary. Notice once again the way to the tomb was hacked away by greedy little pilgrims over the centuries. Is there not a town in Europe that doesn't claim to have a piece of the cave at its municipal museum?

Some say that Mary's parents are buried on the right of the cave's entrance, Joseph on the left.

The bridge leading back up to the Old City is known as the **Bridge of Blood** because it was here that Israeli soldiers lost their way one night in the Six Day War and were sitting ducks before the Jordanian army.

Kidron Valley: Before going this direction, you may want to follow the upper portion of the Kidron Valley, also known as the Valley of Jehosaphat, to three more intriguing grave sites. Shaped like a stocking cap is **Absalom's Pillar,** which probably marks the grave of someone very rich and important, but who lived at least 1,000 years after the time of David's rebellious son.

Someone in the Middle Ages had found an important grave, saw that it was near the City of David, and pointed to Absalom's name in the Bible. This is how arbitrarily many places were so dedicated in Jerusalem.

Next to the pillar are the **Tomb of Zachariah** and the **Tomb of Hezir,** part of the same 1st-century cemetery. According to Jewish law they needed to be placed outside the walls of the city.

The Kidron Valley here is now a garbage dump. However above you on the left is the boisterous Arab town called **Silwan.**

Solomon, it is said, gave the town to his wife, Pharaoh's daughter, by political treaty as a wedding present so that she could worship idols upon it.

Tomb of Zechariah in the Kidron Valley.

109

EAST JERUSALEM

The Israelis may believe they "reunified" Jerusalem in 1967, but in truth the city remains bitterly divided. Arab East Jerusalem has its own food, music, and pace of life; its own banks, buses, utility companies, and newspapers. It is largely made up of middle-class Christian Arabs, many of whom understandably complain about the sky-high municipal taxes they must pay every year, given that Israeli Jerusalem provides them with few services. Although Arabs go daily into West Jerusalem—to work, to shop, to travel—Jews scarcely ever venture into East Jerusalem.

For the traveler, however, East Jerusalem should not be missed. One can hardly understand the nature of the current struggles without a visit. The best time to visit is on Saturday, when West Jerusalem closes down. (The Moslem day of rest is Friday.)

For sightseeing, remember, if the Via Dolorosa is an endless row of churches, East Jerusalem is Sarcophagous City. Just north of the city walls, it must have been one of the most popular places in ancient times to bury important and influential people.

The road from Damascus to Jerusalem ends at the **Damascus Gate**, far and away the most impressive port of entry to the Old City. It serves as the hub of Jerusalem's Arab community, leading toward the Moslem Quarter in the Old City and facing Palestinian East Jerusalem outside it. The area in front of the gate is a favorite meeting place. It contains a refiguration of an ancient Moslem drinking fountain, what is known as a **sabil**. Underneath the gate is the **Roman Square Museum**, which highlights the city in Roman times.

Across the way is the **East Jerusalem Bus Station**, where you can catch a bus to Arab towns on the West Bank. Above the bus station is the **Garden Tomb**, which the Protestants believe to be the true place where Jesus was laid to rest. In 1867, when the British General Gordon visited Jerusalem, he concluded that Jesus couldn't have been entombed in the traditionally accepted site, the Church of the Holy Sepulchure. Number one, the place didn't feel right to him. Number two, he knew that according to Jewish custom, Jesus' grave had to be outside the city walls, and—at least at the time of Gordon's visit—the Holy Sepulchre was inside the Old City. During his trip, Gordon lodged in East Jerusalem, and one morning, looking out of his hotel window, he spied a piece of land that looked like a scull, which is how **Golgotha** is described in the gospels. To him, it was a revelation. When a grotto was indeed found on this spot, the Protestants were certain they'd located the real Calvary.

Next to the bus station is **Jeremiah's Grotto,** supposedly the spot where this prophet composed his Lamentations on

Preceding pages: Sheep-herding on the West Bank. Left, smoking a water pipe in East Jerusalem. Right, entertainment at the American Colony Hotel.

113

the fall of Jerusalem. Back across **Suleiman Street** is the **Cave of Zedekiah,** where mean, foolish King Zedekiah fled from the Babylonian invaders, all the way to Jericho. (Whereupon his pursuers caught him, forced him to watch his family murdered, and then made him poke his own eyes out.)

Follow Suleiman Street west to the **Rockefeller Museum,** a white building with the commanding octagonal tower. It's perched on the hill the Crusaders used as a launch point for their invasion of Jerusalem in 1099.

In 1967, the Israeli Defense Forces made similar use of it to retake the Old City. The museum itself was financed by archaeology buffs in the Rockefeller family and was built during the British Mandate.

Heading back toward the bus station, turn right at **Salah ed-Din,** and follow it past the **Albright Institute** and **St. George's Cathedral** to the major intersection with **Shechem**. Here you may enter the **Tomb of the Kings.** This is

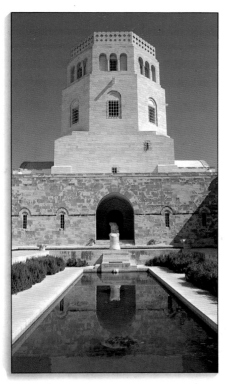

the burial place of Queen Helena of Adiabene (in Mesopotamia) who, along with her children, converted to Judaism and traveled to Jerusalem in 45. She became a heroin when, during a famine, she procured necessary foodstuffs from foreign lands.

Continue down Shechem to the **American Colony Hotel,** a grand Moslem mansion with a peaceful courtyard that has been a haven for foreign dignitaries all century long. The American Colony was founded here in 1881 by the Spaffords of Chicago. After their four daughters drowned in a tragic boating accident, they moved here and dedicated their lives to helping the poor. Several tours of East Jerusalem start from here and the hotel nightclub bar offers entertainment from jazz musicians to belly dancers. The best restaurants in the area to try are **Philadelphia, Dallas,** and **Sea Dolphin,** the last of which is an especially popular place co-owned by an Arab and a Jew.

If you continue north, before you come to the Arab neighborhood of **Sheik Jarrah,** you may follow a narrow road (Othman Ben-Afan) to the right to the **Tomb of Simon the Just,** which marks the burial place of the venerable High Priest of the Jews at the time of Alexander the Great.

Alexander stormed through Asia and Persia, and was on the verge of reducing Jerusalem to rubble, when—according to one esoteric legend—he was appeased by this Simon. Alexander was plagued by dreams of a wise old man with a long gray beard, and when he beheld Simon the Just coming toward him, he was awestruck—for this was the very man.

Alexander agreed to spare Jerusalem, on condition that a statue of himself be erected in front of the Temple. Since statues were proscribed by Jewish law as forms of idol-worship, Simon came up with another idea. His diplomatic suggestion for a more fitting tribute was that each male child born that year be named after him—Alexander.

The **Rockefeller Museum** and right, **Palestinian potter.**

JERUSALEM CUISINE

The Jewish obsession with food is well documented in the Torah. The very first command God gives His people is a dietary or kosher law—he forbade Adam and Eve from eating of the Tree of Knowledge. The Torah then goes on to enumerate a large corpus of kosher laws (such as not eating certain animals or mixing milk with meat), which a large majority of Jews continue to observe to this day. Most restaurants in West Jerusalem serve only kosher food and they display a sign to this effect.

So you should not expect to have coffee and dairy dessert in the same restaurant where you eat a meat dish for dinner. Religious tradition also dictates that people wash before meals and pray after. Most Jerusalem restaurants provide a sink with a pitcher.

What people traditionally associate with "Jewish food" is actually Eastern European—matzo ball soup, gefilte fish, latkes, cholent. The main food Jews and Arabs eat in Jerusalem, however, is largely influenced by the Turks. Turkish cuisine can be sophisticated— a traditional Jerusalem specialty is stuffed vegetables—but is otherwise simple, relying on peasant staples of grains and beans. Although the Middle East has traditionally harvested oranges and olives, only recently—since the Israeli kibbutz system radically changed the face of the land—has there been such a variety of fruits and vegetables available.

A generally accepted kibbutz idea is that during each harvest season the national should try to produce a new fruit. So when Jerusalemites shop at Mahane Yehudah market, they are always delighted to discover the annual treat—whether it be kiwis or strawberries. Jerusalemites take considerable pride in the farming process.

If you love lamb but find it too expensive in other places, in Jerusalem you'll

The Mahane Yehudah Market.

find it's pretty cheap; shashlik is an especially popular dish. Conversely, red meat is prohibitively expensive because there's not enough grass in the land to spare for grazing cattle. Cows here aren't slaughtered for the meat, they're just milked to death. Therefore, the traditional Israeli meat staple is chicken. Some say it's hard to find a meal in Jerusalem that doesn't include either chicken or eggs.

Jerusalemites start their days with a salad and a generous breakfast. Lunch, the biggest meal of the day is taken at 2 p.m., just like in Europe. Siestas are pretty common, especially in the hot summer. By 5 p.m., the cafes are packed with young people. At 8 or 9 p.m., usually a light dinner is served—for example eggs and salads.

All restaurants in West Jerusalem are closed on Sabbath and tourists traditionally check out the many fine restaurants in East Jerusalem on this night. Others try to get themselves invited to a Jewish family's home for an incompa-

rable experience. Sabbath, in short, is a weekly family food feast, and in this respect secular Jews observe the tradition as much as the Orthodox.

On Friday mornings, the man in the family customarily does the shopping, while by early afternoons women start cooking. One must not miss the sweet smells wafting across Jerusalem on the eve of Sabbath.

So too, in the evening one must not miss the sounds rolling down the city's streets of families singing at the dinner table. The meal actually starts with a blessing on the candles, the *challah* (bread) and the wine. The Saturday meal usually consists of extremely well cooked meat and beans—anything that you can put in the oven Friday afternoon and leave there indefinitely.

Jerusalemites are also notorious for their sweet tooths, putting three spoons of sugar in their coffee and wolfing down more pastries per capita than just about any nation in the world. Cafe-hopping is a Jerusalem pastime.

Corner store in the Bukharin Quarter.

THE NEW CITY

For several millennia, Jerusalem consisted of merely a few acres, and even those must have seemed very small, surrounded as they were by a fortress-like wall. Today the city sprawls over an eclectic collection of neighborhoods covering some 40 miles. Together they comprise what is known as the "New City," and by Jerusalem standards they are very new indeed, having sprung up just since the mid-19th century.

At that time, the Jews—many of them recent *Ashkenazi* immigrants from the Pale of Settlement—made up nearly half of Jerusalem's population, then numbering 15,000. And yet they were all crammed into the then filthy, disease-ridden Jewish Quarter, which made up only one-tenth of the area of the Old City.

Still, the idea of moving outside the Old City was unthinkable. There was a pervasive fear of the Bedouin and outlaw tribes lurking in what is today the New City of Jerusalem, but was then considered "wilderness". Nobody wanted to be caught outside the Old City when its gates were locked at the end of the day.

So, in the 1860's when Moses Montefiore, a secular, aristocratic Jew from England, and Yosef Rivlin, a religious Jerusalem-born Jew, began building neighborhoods beyond the gates, they met considerable resistance. Many thought them crazy. It is said that when Rivlin began sleeping outside the Old City, his friends and relatives would dash over to his place each morning expecting to find him dead and his home pillaged.

His "survival" day by day allayed his community's fears. Anxiety or no, Jerusalem simply had to expand—there was no longer enough space in the old Jewish Quarter to accommodate all the new immigrants. By the end of World War I and the start of the British Man-

date, Jerusalem's population was 55,000, and by the end of World War II, it was more that 140,000.

Still, when Jerusalem was "reunified" in June, 1967, after the Six Day War, it was still something of a podunk town. Its most glorious neighborhoods were abandoned and disfigured for having been caught on the border and its growth was stunted by its isolation from the rest of Israel.

When the Israelis resumed control of all of Jerusalem, they began a veritable building boom, putting up whole neighborhoods especially to accommodate the vast numbers of North African and Middle Eastern Jews who'd arrived in Israel since 1948. Since 1967, the city claims to have constructed 27,500 new apartments for Jews, 500 for Arabs.

Given Jerusalem's grand architectural traditions, most of the recent housing structures are miserable failures. It has been said they resemble military garrets more than residences, but perhaps this expresses—even more than editorials in right wing newspapers—how Jerusalemites feel about their condition here.

The saving grace of the architectural landscape is a 1918 decree made by the British High Commissioner. He said that henceforth, no new building could go up in Jerusalem that wasn't made from its indigenous golden white Jerusalem stone. So that even where old meets new, the city bears a striking consistency in tone and texture.

There are several places in the New City to capture a broad view of Jerusalem: the YMCA tower, the Elon Tower, the Hill of Evil Council, and Mt. Scopus—all of which are described later. As you scan the Jerusalem skyline, you will note that most of the skyscrapers—such as the Elon Tower, the Plaza Hotel, the King Solomon Hotel and the Hilton—are in strict violation of the city's building codes against such heights.

For a time in the tourist industry boom following 1967, the municipal

government was handing out exemptions like they were going out of style—all in the name of helping the economy. Citizen outrage has prevailed so that in the future, the mayor assures, no such building will be permitted.

A useful introduction to Jerusalem—a way to gain your bearings—is a special city bus (number 99) called the **Circle Line**, so named because it takes you on a circle of the city. The bus leaves from the Jaffa Gate every hour on the hour, and makes 34 stops at some of the major sites throughout the town.

The other municipal buses, while not catering exclusively to tourists, go everywhere and are cheap. The **Central Bus Station** is on Jaffa Road on the Western rim of city. Remember: taxi drivers will rip you off unless you demand they turn on the meter when you get in.

Getting around: Walking around Jerusalem is no easy trick, though the downtown area of West Jerusalem is fairly compact. The heart of it is formed

by a triangle between **King George Street, Jaffa Road** and the **Ben Yehudah Mall**. This area is offered up in stark contrast to the solemnity of the Old City.

If the latter has captured the foreign traveler's imagination for centuries, the former is capable of showing you a hardy, living city that's grown, quite spectaculary, out of a dying one.

Modern Moses, new neighborhood: An appropriate place to start your tour of the "New City" is at its oldest and most famous landmark, the **Montefiore Windmill,** that conical, four-blade structure that wouldn't know how to turn if a tornado hit it. Built in 1858, it was meant to provide a source of employment for the city's burgeoning Jewish community.

It was never of much use until the 1948 war, when it served as an observation post. The top of the windmill was blown up by the British in what the Jews facetiously described as "Operation Don Quixote." Today the windmill houses a small museum dedicated to the life of its builder, Sir Moses Montefiore, a visionary Jewish philanthropist from England, and to the neighborhood that sprang up here.

When Montefiore visited Jerusalem in the middle of the last century, he was appalled at the deplorable living conditions of Jews in the Old City. At first he wanted to build a hospital here, but then, with the encouragement of some wealthy benefactors and the permission of the Turkish Sultan, he set about building the first Jewish Quarter outside the city walls.

Finished in 1860, he called it **Mishkenot Sha'ananim,** which literally means "Dwellings of Tranquility." It looked like a long squat rampart, and indeed it was well-sealed to protect its inhabitants. Even so, the Jews were so fearful of the "wilderness" (as this area was regarded) in those days, that it took a solid decade before anyone decided to live there.

Today the Jerusalem Foundation

Shops and galleries of Hutzot Hayotzer.

operates Mishkenot Sha'ananim as a Jewish Artist Colony, a subsidized guest house for such well-known figures as Saul Bellow, Joan Didion, Henry Roth, Arthur Rubinstein, and Isaac Stern.

Below the windmill, is the **Jerusalem Music Center**—a respected recording studio—and the **Mishkenot Sha'ananim Restaurant,** which offers a kosherized version of the French high-cuisine and a splendid view.

In 1892, Montefiore expanded the quarter on the adjacent plot of land, **Yemin Moshe,** which you can see as you follow the European-styled red terra cotta roofs north. Like Mishkenot Sha'ananim, during the partition period Yemin Moshe fell on the Jordanian-Israeli armistice line, or "green line" as it was called, and as a consequence it also fell into terrible disrepair. After "reunification," the indigent Jewish tenants who braved the no-man's land conditions were bought off by the city government and the entire quarter was gentrified. In moved the chic artists and affluent families, as the neighborhood quickly became the most prestigious address in the city.

At the end of Yemin Moshe, follow stairs down to **Hutzot HaYotzer,** or the Arts and Crafts Lane. Here several Jerusalem artisans sell directly from their studios—jewelers, silversmiths, sculptors, and potters. At the end of the lane is a mediocre, but conveniently located Chinese restaurant. Also nearby is the **Mitchell Garden,** a quiet, sunny spot.

Next to it, and directly below Yemin Moshe, is the **Sultan's Pool,** which now serves as a concert park. It was originally designed as a reservoir to store rainwater, stopping the flow down the valley to the Dead Sea. Sultan Suleiman the Magnificent renovated it, and thus it took his name. Today, the Sultan's Pool is where stars such as Bob Dylan appear on stage coming to light up and rock Jerusalem.

Sinner's valley: Curving south and

Getting immunized at a local hospital.

west from Sultan's Pool is the **Valley of Hinnom.** A valley that cuts a wide swath between the New City and the Old City, it has long been recognized as the physical location of hell itself. *Gai Hinnon* (Hebrew) is where the false-god Moloch stood with arms outstretched, demanding child sacrifices. It is said that fire rose from Moloch's belly, which perhaps explains what the Torah means when it says that the foul King Menasseh made his own children pass through fire here. It is from this, finally, that the valley became known as the place where sinners burn—*gehenom,* or simply hell.

As the Valley of Hinnom has become a center for Jerusalem secular culture, Orthodox Jews today might still regard it (albeit with a sardonic smile) as a place where sinners go. There is, of course, the Sultan's Pool, but the real cultural nerve center is the small building just above it, the **Cinemateque.** In this film crazy town, movies are prized on both an aesthetic level and as a

means of escape, and people flock here [sometimes, despite Orthodox Jewish protests on Shabbat] from all over.

Upstairs, the Cinemateque Cafe is where the chic Yerushalmi sip oversweet coffee and eat rich pastries while discussing Fellini and Clint Eastwood. Sit on the patio overlooking the Old City long enough, and you may be deceived into thinking that Jerusalem is really a peaceful place, that it can be just like any other city.

Below the Cinemateque, on the bridge that leads you across the Valley of Hinnom, you can see yet another **sabil,** a Turkish water fountain built by Suleiman. Above the Cinemateque, **Derek Hevron** is the road that takes you to that embattled city. Just on your left is a row of overpriced restaurants, that privilege the view over the food.

Across the street is a unique institution called the **House of Quality.** The government awards various artists with a seal of approval and studio space in this charming old converted eye clinic.

Reflections of the New City—banks and beggars.

If you're in the shopping mood, the gallery downstairs sells their crafts but more worthwhile is a tour around the building—take time to talk to the artists or watch them at work.

The stone structure on the hill behind the House of Quality is the **St. Andrew's Church,** built after World War I to commemorate the Scottish soldiers who died in combat. It was named for the Galilean fisherman who became the patron saint of Scotland. Here you will also find a memorial to King Robert Bruce, whose final request—that his heart be transported to Jerusalem—was not ultimately honored, the organ having been buried in Spain when the courier was killed by Moors en route.

On the other side of the church is the **Railway Station,** which has been in operation since 1892, when the Turks laid tracks between Jaffa and Jerusalem, the first train route in Palestine. Today, however, the bus is far and away the preferred means of transportation in Israel. The late 19th century *khan* down the block once served as a storehouse for cargo coming in by train. It has been converted into the **Khan Theater,** a respected cultural center that serves as home to the Jerusalem Repertory Company. Behind it is the **Poire et Pomme,** a favorite lunch and after-theater haunt.

King David Street: On your right, as you leave the Khan, you will pass the **British Consulate** before you come to **King David Street.** Across the way is the **Liberty Bell Garden,** which offers a range of free athletic and cultural activities throughout the summer—especially notable is the annual book fair. The **Train Theater** here puts on puppet shows.

Continuing along King David, on your left is the headquarters for the **Jerusalem Foundation.** The foundation is a private institution which has poured $100 million into various urban renewal projects. One such effort is the **Bloomfield Garden** on your right. If

Concert at the Sultan's Pool.

you duck into this pleasant park at Abar Sikra, you will come to **Herod's Family Grave**. You will recall that the paranoid-schizophrenic king was from an ancestral line of Edomites, who'd been forcibly circumcised and made to worship the Jewish God.

Herod's wife Miriamne, however, was of the Hasmonean family, descended from Judah the Maccabee. When Herod became afraid—however irrational it was—that the Jewish people might rally around his young sons or some future offspring his wife might bear him, he slaughtered all three of them, and perhaps, feeling some compunction, had them buried in this very cave.

Further down on King David Street is the grand **King David Hotel**, the most prestigious hotel in the Middle East, where Jimmy Carter, Anwar Sadat, and Henry Kissinger stayed when they came to Jerusalem. The impossible prospects for any kind of peace in the region can be surmised by walking into the lobby. Here you will find a host of world leaders and would-be diplomats clucking about and popping aspirin tablets: their "missions" in Jerusalem are (inevitably) frustrating and (ultimately) worthless.

Built in 1931, the hotel served for a time as a British base of command. It was during this period, in 1946, that the Menachem Begin-led Irgun set off a bomb that killed 91 and destroyed the southwest part of the building, evidence of which you can still see today. The top two floors are the most recent additions.

The tower across the street is part of the **YMCA**, built in the early 1930s by the power-tower architecture firm of Shreve, Lamb & Harmon, the same people who wrought the Empire State Building. From the top, it presents a spectacular view of Jerusalem.

The YMCA is a moderately-priced and an exceedingly convenient place to set up your lodgings. The cafeteria is a favorite meeting spot and the **YMCA**

Orthodox Jew and young charge take a walk and right, the Liberty Bell Garden.

Auditorium is the home of the Israel Chamber Orchestra. And weekly choral and chamber music concerts are scheduled here.

All along King David Street are car rental places. During the off-peak season, you can usually do pretty well bargaining, but generally expect these agencies to pass along to you the high rates they have to pay insurance companies. For obvious reasons, Israel is not considered a low risk country. Before you rent a car, you should also realize that gas is incredibly expensive.

On the right side of King David Street is the **Hebrew Union College**, an outpost of the American-based Reform Judaism movement. In recent years, the college has been sponsoring more activities for visitors, desperately trying to compete with their Orthodox counterparts for the souls and minds of wandering young Jews. But the truth is, the Reform movement is not too strong in Israel.

Mamillah: At the intersection of King David and **Mamillah Road** is a paean to those dreaded taxes, the **Taxation Museum**. (Only in Jerusalem!) You can head straight toward the downtown area, or follow Mamillah to the right. This was once one of Jerusalem's biggest commercial centers, though today it has suffered from considerable decay. The massive structure on your left is the **Hospice of St. Vincent de Paul**, and on your right is the **Stern House**. A plaque here marks the spot where the crusading Zionist Theodore Herzl stayed during his brief pilgrimage to Jerusalem in 1898.

Like Montefiore before him, Herzl was not favorably impressed with Jerusalem. "The musty deposits of 2,000 years of inhumanity, intolerance, and foulness lie in your (Jerusalem's) reeking alleys," he wrote. "If Jerusalem is ever ours I would begin by cleaning it up."

If the Mamillah neighborhood underwent improvements after Herzl's visit, it fell completely apart during the parti-

A Shabbat stroll in Independence Park.

tion period (1948-67), a border area cum war zone abandoned by all the old merchants. By the mid-1980s, and after much debate, a revitalization project in the area has begun.

To The "Estate of Seven": Mamillah Road takes you down to the Jaffa Gate and the Old City. If you head back from where you came, King David Street branches off to the left to **Hillel Street**. On your left is a **Moslem Cemetery**, and within it the **Mamillah Pool**, an ancient rainwater cistern. Some speculate that the name derives from the Arabic *mayah min Allah,* meaning "water from God."

As you continue, the cemetery turns into the **Independence Park**, where families take afternoon strolls on Shabbat and where young couples issue their mating calls every other day of the week. This is Jerusalem's largest park, and the place upon which all the Independence Day Celebrations focus.

A legend began here in the Middle Ages about a friendly lion, whose cave was shown to pilgrims of various religions. In this cave the lion gathered and protected the bodies of religious martyrs so that they would not be destroyed or abused by animals or vandals. At a northwest entry to the park are three undulating columns by the renowned Dadaist sculptor Jean Arp.

On the right side of Hillel Street is the **Italian Synagogue,** an elaborate building built in 1719 and moved here from a small town near Venice in 1952. But before you come to the synagogue, there is an ugly and unremarkable building, the **Beit Agron**, which houses the government press office and a oldies-but-goodies film center. Since it has always been considered a cultural center, the Beit Agron was exempt from the municipal prohibition against showing movies on Shabbat. In mid-1987, Orthodox Jews from all over city protested that a few brief remarks before an infantile movie hardly constituted a "cultural event," and demanded that the place be shut down on Shabbat.

Famous cafe Atara on the Midrahov.

132

Behind the Beit Agron is **Rivlin Street**, named for the great 19th-century neighborhood-builder Rabbi Yossef Rivlin. Like his secular counterpart Moses Montefiore, Rivlin was sickened by the yishuv ghetto conditions in the Old City, and he too set about starting a settlement outside it.

By the late 1860s, he was one of seven ambitious young Eastern European Jews who collectively bought a small piece of land here specifically for the purpose of building a new neighborhood. They called it, straightforwardly enough, **Nahalat Shiva**, or The Estate of Seven.

Little is left of the neighborhood today, though one can gather from the narrow old alleyways, such as Rivlin and Salomon Streets, some idea of how it was set up. Tucked away in the neighborhood today are several nightclubs and some of the most extraordinary restaurants in Jerusalem—a French and North African place called **Katy** (at 16 Rivlin) foremost among them.

Zion Square: Follow Solomon Street up to **Zion Square**, where all things and all people meet in downtown Jerusalem. The square earned its name from either the Zion Cinema, which was razed here some time ago, or from the fact that zealous young Zionists would gather here for political rallies before statehood. That seven-story cement and glass monstrosity you see here today is called **Beit Yoel**, and represents one of the few subjects upon which everyone in Jerusalem can agree upon: *Never again!*

Zion Square leads into the **Ben Yehudah Pedestrian Mall**, the lifeline of secular Jewish Jerusalem, where the cafe scene gets into full swing, and where the young especially come to see and to be seen. On Saturday nights, after Shabbat, the place is packed wall to wall with people. Especially popular is the **Cafe Atara**, which dates from the British Mandate period. Besides the restaurants and shops, there are several first-run movie houses and bars.

Cafe scene on Ben Yehudah Mall.

For a pleasant detour away from the mall madness, go back to Zion Square and head up Jaffa Road one block to HaRav Kook Street, and turn left. Tucked away at the end of the block is the **Ticho House**, which operates a couple of small museums and a peaceful cafe overlooking a soothing public garden. The building itself is the recently restored turn-of-century home of Abraham Ticho, Jerusalem's first eye doctor, and (in later years) Anna Ticho, the artist.

Next door is the **Rav Kook House**, the modest dwelling of the first chief Ashkenazi Rabbi of Palestine. At a time when the conventional wisdom among Orthodox Jews was to reject Zionism outright, Kook was a bridge between the two camps.

Even though Zionism was strictly a secular political movement, Kook believed that it was a healthy impulse. He thought that the cultural or national identification of assimilated Jews might later be transformed into a more profound religious observance.

Back on Jaffa Road, on the left side, just before King George Street, is a beloved Jerusalem institution called **Fefferberg's**, which serves the Yiddish-mama's cooking from the old country. The intersection of Jaffa and King George is the busiest in the city. Jaffa Road itself was paved for Kaiser Wilhelm's trip toward the Jaffa Gate in 1898, and it leads north to the glorious **Mahane Yehudah**, the finest outdoor food market in the city. The best time to visit is on Friday morning, when each family sends a representative (usually the man) to buy food for the Shabbat dinner. There are several unassuming, traditional restaurants in the neighborhood—cheaper, too, for being off the beaten tourist track.

South of Mahane Yehudah, in the quaint hillside neighborhood of **Nahla'ot**, is **Pargod**, a veritable jazz cave, where you'll find the widest spectrum of musicians jamming this side of the Mediterranean.

Jerusalem buses go anywhere in the city.

If, at the Jaffa/King George intersection, you turn right, you'll be heading toward Mea She'arim, which we'll describe in more detail later. Here, you can continue your tour of the downtown area by turning right.

King George Street: A few paces up, there is another entrance to the Ben Yehudah Mall. Before it is Richie's Pizza, where young Orthodox Jews hang out, and after it, the **King George Youth Hostel**, which is a sort of hippie central for the foreign traveler.

Still further on your left, where King George meets Histadrut, is **Fink's**, an unassuming joint that's reputedly the best bar in Jerusalem. Celebrities from all over the world discreetly make reservations here months in advance, as word of its goulash soup has reached many a far-flung land.

Across the street, go to the top of the **City Tower** for the panoramic view, not for the Jerusalem Delight Restaurant. In front of the City Tower is an Ottoman entranceway and clock that

have been preserved long after the building on this spot was destroyed. It's a common meeting place and archaeologists of the future will certainly have a lot to ponder.

The American Express Office is up on your left and the **Government Tourist Office**, at 24 King George on your right presents yet another worthwhile repository of maps, schedules, and shopping information. Directly behind the tourist office is the **Bezalel Academy of Art and Design**, established in 1906, with its popular **Artists' House Cafe**.

Continuing on King George, just across from the garden, Jerusalem's largest *shul*, the **Yeshurun Synagogue**. Yeshurun was the name by which Moses addressed the 12 tribes of Israel in verse. Behind it is the **Ratisbone Monastery**, established in 1874, by Alfonso Ratisbone, the founder of the Sisters of Zion.

Further down, the **Hechal Shlomo** is where the powerful Chief Rabbinate of

Clock tower in downtown Jerusalem.

Israel meets. Inside the building, the **Wolfson Museum** presents a collection of Jewish ceremonial objects. Next door, in the **Great Synagogue**, note the 18th century ark covering the Torah scrolls, which has been transported here from Padau, Italy.

Several free tours of the city's neighborhoods originate from the Plaza-Sheraton Hotel across the street. At the corner, the **Terra Sancta College** belongs to the Franciscan order, and was borrowed by Hebrew University when Mt. Scopus was first made inaccessible in 1948. Diagonally opposite is the Conservative Jewish movement's outpost in Jerusalem, and next to it, on Gershon Agron Street, is the Alliance Francais, a French cultural center with a hip cafe.

For many new immigrants—whether from the Soviet Union or Yemen—the most miraculous site is just across the street, "Super Sol," the first full-fledged supermarket to arrive in Jerusalem and the first one they have seen.

Rehavia: In the opposite direction, Ramban Street takes you into the heart of **Rehavia**—"God's expanse". Founded along with other secular neighborhoods during the early days of the British Mandate, it became a magnet for German Jews and some of the great Zionist leaders and intellectuals, who wanted none of the restrictions of the religious enclaves. At #30 Ramban, the Ottoman-style **Ruppin House** was the first home built exclusively by Jewish workers, whom the owner paid in cows.

By the mid-1930s, however, Jewish architects escaping from Nazi Germany began experimenting with more modern styles. Among them, the most talented was Erich Mendelsohn, who designed the bold, minimalist **Schoken Library** at #6 Balfour Street. The pervasive influence of Mendelsohn's style can be seen as well at the **Prime Minister's House** at 9 Somolenskin designed by Richard Kauffmann. Among those who set up their homes in

The Tourjeman-Post between East and West Jerusalem.

Rehavia were Golda Meir, Levi Eshkol, Menachem Ussishkin.

Peculiarly in the midst of all the residential dwellings, there's a large Roman-era crypt on Atasi Street. Called **Jason's Tomb**, it was discovered quite accidentally during recent building construction.

German Colony: South of Rehavia is the **German Colony**, founded in 1873 by the German Templars, most of whom left during World War II. Today the neighborhood is one of the city's most diverse and fashionable. Its tree lined streets do not feel like Jerusalem at all. In the neighborhood, you'll find the **Van Leer Foundation**, the **Israeli Academy of Arts and Sciences**, the **President's Mansion**. Behind them is the **Jerusalem Center For the Performing Arts**, which serves as an unofficial culture center. The Henry Crown Symphony Hall is the home of the Jerusalem Symphony Orchestra, and the Jerusalem Theater hosts a wide range of experimental plays and films.

A good place to go after one of these events is **Jan's**, which may be decorated as a Mid-Eastern opium den, but serves some of the best desserts in town. Close by is the **L.A. Mayer Museum of Islamic Art** and the **Natural History Museum**.

Zahal Square: Make your way back to just outside the southwestern corner of the Old City, where Jaffa Road meets Shlomo Hamelech Street. Before 1948 it was named Allenby Square, for the British general, and since it's been called **Zahal Square** to honor the Israeli Defense Forces. Look up at the bullet-riddled **City Hall**.

As you head back up Jaffa toward Zion Square, you'll pass **Gan Auster**, a charming little garden. Behind it are located two French hospices, **St. Louis** and **Notre Dame de France**.

Further up on the block, the **Bank Leumi**, was originally built to house the Anglo-Palestine Bank, designed by the renowned modernist architect Erich Mendelsohn, as were several other

The Russian Compound.

137

neighborhood buildings. Next door is the city's **Central Post Office**. From here you can veer right into an area known as Little Russia.

The Russian Compound: In the 11th century, a determined and devout Russian abbot personally walked from Kiev to Jerusalem, carrying a silver lamp to the Church of the Holy Sepulchre, and his countrymen have been making regular pilgrimages to the Holy City ever since.

By the middle of the 19th century, an increasing number of Russian peasants, especially women, set about this journey. Like the immigrant Jews of their time, however, they quickly learned upon arrival that Jerusalem could be a most uncomfortable and unsafe place to transplant their roots.

Seeking to protect his population here and perhaps to exert more influence in the Holy Land, Czar Alexander II put together a deal in 1860. He bought some land outside the Christian Quarter of the Old City, and the Turkish sultan tossed in a part of it for free.

The Russians initially called these 32 acres "New Jerusalem," however the neighboring Arabs dubbed it "el-Moscoobiya." Eventually over time it became known simply as the **Russian Compound**.

When construction began in the 1860s, it represented no less radical a project than the neighborhoods of Montefiore or Rivlin, though certainly better funded and more grandiose. The new set-up had the effect of encouraging even more pilgrimages than before, so that by the start of World War I, more than 10,000 were making the trip annually, including the Czar's evil adviser Rasputin.

In Russia, Rasputin gave Christianity a bad name, and after the Bolshevik Revolution in 1917, religion itself was scorned as "the opium of the masses." No longer would Russians be permitted to make the Jerusalem pilgrimage, and the priests and nuns already there were effectively cut off from their country.

Aerial view of Mea She'arim.

138

So their joined a kind of Russian Orthodox Church-in-exile, or the "White Russian Church," as it's more commonly called.

Occupying the highest ground on the compound is the sculptural green-domed cathedral, the **Church of the Holy Trinity**. This is said to be where the Assyrians bivouacked during their unsuccessful attack on the Old City in 701 BCE, and where Titus' legion did the same before its successful raid 770 years later. Not long after the walled-in Russian Compound was built, did rumors arise—in certain anxiety-ridden Ottoman circles—that the Russians were planning to use it as a base for an invasion of the Old City.

Today, the cathedral is controlled by the Soviet "Red Russian Church," though most of the rest of the compound is owned by the Israelis. The White Russians, however, still maintain jurisdiction over churches on the Mount of Olives and in the Old City.

Opposite the cathedral, notice the massive pillar resting horizontally. It has earned the nickname **Finger of Og**, for the giant ruler of Bashan, whom the Jews killed in ancient times. On a less folkloric level, many believe there was a quarry here 2,000 years ago and that this particular pillar had been prepared for Herod's Temple. It must have broken in the process and left here, only to be found during construction of the Russian Compound.

The two buildings next to the pillar were originally used as pilgrims' hostels, but today serve as the city police station and **Supreme Court**.

Behind the cathedral, at the back of the complex is another pilgrim's hostel. Today it is called the **Hall of Heroism**, which in a way tells the curious history of the compound in the aftermath of 1917. Throughout the Mandate period, the British occupied the Russian Compound, making it their administrative headquarters. At the end of their rule, it was heavily secured behind barbed wire, earning it the facetious sobriquet

Mea She'arim dress code is fairly explicit.

PASSAGE PERMITTED
►ONLY◄ NO WOMEN
DRESSED MODESTLY
LONG DRESS
LOWER THAN KNEE LENGTH (NO SLACKS)
LONG SLEEVES
BEYOND ELBOW LENGTH
CLOSED KNECKLINE

RESIDENTS OF THE AREA

והיה מחניך קדוש ולא יראה בך ערות דבר (דברים כ״ג)
המעבר לנשים
★ אך ורק ★
בלבוש צנוע!
שמלה ארוכה
המכסה את הברכים
(לא בלבוש מכנסיים)
שרוולים ארוכים
המכסים את הזרועות
בית צוואר סגור
תושבי האיזור

"Bevingrad" (after the British Foreign Minister Ernest Bevin). This particular building was converted into a prison where members of the Jewish underground were held. After the British evacuation and Israeli independence, it was further converted into a Hall of Heroism, a museum commemorating the very Jewish underground that was jailed here.

Beyond the Russian Compound on Heleni Hamalka Street is a bulky structure with the stylish turret, which was where the rich Russian pilgrims lodged. It was named the **Sergei Building** for the Czar's son, Prince Sergei Romanov. In the courtyard next to the turret, the Ministry of Agriculture operates a low-key **Farm Tool Museum**.

Here also are the headquarters of the **Israel Nature Preservation Society**, where you can sign up for some superb tours of the nearby desert and mountains. For lunch or dinner, check out the nearby **Pie House**; for coffee and desserts, **Home Plus** is worth a try.

Street of the Prophets: Walk north a few blocks to the street of the Prophets, or **Rehov HaNevi'im**, as it's called in Hebrew. At the intersection with **Strauss** is the **Israel Center**, which hosts daily lectures and classes on the Torah and Judaica for English-speaking visitors. (Check the calendar here for other events as well.)

Before reaching the Israel Center you will come to the **Thabor House**, where the eminent 19th-century German archaeologist-architect Conrad Schick once lived. Some say Schick, a Protestant missionary, was largely responsible for drawing the broad outlines of the Orthodox Jewish Mea She'earim.

Today Schick's residence is the home of the **Swedish Theological Seminary**.

Curling off HaNevi'im is **Ethiopians' Street**, named for the **Ethopian Church** herein. As you enter the gates leading to the church courtyard, you will see the Lions of Judah. The Ethiopians believe that King Solo-

Children dress up for Purim.

mon himself presented this symbol to his lover the Queen of Sheba, a native of that African country.

Opposite the church and monastery is the **Ben Yehudah House**. Eliazer Ben Yehudah was an early Zionist leader and the father of modern Hebrew. He transformed a biblical, mainly written language into a modern, everyday, spoken tongue, and invested in the project a wellspring of nationalist aspirations and political imperatives.

When he moved his family from Lithuania to Palestine, he refused to speak to his own wife in their native Yiddish or Russian, and would only respond to her when spoken to in Hebrew. To understand the radical nature of Ben Yehudah's work, remember that the Orthodox Jewish establishment considered the use of the Holy tongue for secular purposes a sacrilege and branded this man who promoted such a thing a heretic.

Heading east along HaNevi'im, you will pass another curious architectural specimen, the 19th-century **German Probst Building**, which now serves as an ORT Vocational School. If you were to continue along for half a mile, you'd end up in East Jerusalem. The only passageway linking Jordanian East Jerusalem and Israeli West Jerusalem during the 1948-67 partition period was the **Mandelbaum Gate** near the intersection with Hel Handasah. The portal itself having been removed, the site is marked today by a plaque.

The Israeli border during the partition period was fortified here at the **Tourjeman-Post**. A battle-worn, bullet-riddled old building, it has recently been restored and transformed into a multi-media museum dedicated to describing the division of the city. The roof top offers a fine vantage point for viewing both sides of the green line, and the multi-media displays make some sense of the confusing military history of the country.

The old world of Mea She'arim: Shortly before reaching the Tourjeman-Post,

The haredim of Mea She'arim.

you will see the street Shivtei Yisrael on your left. At the corner is the **Ministry of Education and Culture**. As the road branches off into **Mea She'arim Street** you pass the **Jerusalem Gate** entering the heart of the **Mea She'arim Quarter**. This is the famed ultra-Orthodox Jewish neighborhood, where modesty in dress is not simply requested, but demanded. Mind the signs: you do not want to roam here in tank-top shirts and bikini bottoms.

Ultra-Orthodox Jews here are called *haredim*, which literally means "the God-fearing." The fur hats, long coats, and earlocks (*peyot*) are carried over from the Eastern European traditions. Women must cover their heads (with scarves and wigs) in strict observance of Jewish law.

The strange language that you hear is Yiddish, an expressive melange of German, Russian, Polish, and Hebrew. These are the people who never accepted Ben Yehudah's proposition that Hebrew should become an everyday spoken language, and so they use it only in their prayers. This seems to be another place in time.

The story of Mea She'arim starts in Lithuania in the later part of the 18th century. There, in a town called Vilna, a rabbi called the Vilna Gaon (widely regarded as one of the greatest Talmudic sages in Jewish history) told his followers that it was not sufficient merely to wait for the coming of the Messiah. He believed that the Messiah would come only after the Jews had physically returned to Jerusalem and resurrected the Holy City once again from its ashes.

It was this very idea that led an increasing number of Eastern European Jewish families to move to Jerusalem over the next century.

One family's descendant, Rabbi Yosef Rivlin, was largely responsible for building the first religious neighborhood outside the Old City, Nahalat Shiva. His work understandably sparked a profound dispute among

Gilo and right, the Sanhedrin Tombs.

those who still followed the teachings of the Vilna Gaon. They came to Jerusalem to rebuild the city but was the land beyond the walls even considered Jerusalem? If not, wasn't it better to dwell in squalor within the city than live comfortably outside it?

Furthermore, pious Jews feared that the desire for brand-new homes represented an urge toward material comfort, which would (inevitably) trigger a downward spiral of spirituality. This very fear was a tender point in the 1870s, when the tendency toward assimilation among world Jewry was very powerful.

Perhaps it was to protect themselves against the encroaching *haskala*, as these secularizing, modernizing, and assimilationist tendencies were called, that the zealous Jews of Jerusalem finally built their own neighborhood. They constructed Mea She'arim to resemble a walled-in fortress, one that effectively isolated them from the outside world and the temptations of their time, but also kept them close to their places of worship.

Established in 1874, Mea She'arim could only be entered through various gates, traditionally said to be 100 in number. Thus the name Mea She'arim, which literally means 100 Gates. So fearful were these Jews of the modern world, that they banned Yosef Rivlin from sermonizing in the very neighborhood he built.

The best way to tour Mea She'arim is simply to roam around it, to peek in the numerous synagogues and yeshivot, to stop in the kosher bakeries and to wander about the markets.

Continuing along Mea She'arim Street, you will come to the **Northern Gate**, also known as Mohammed's Gate for the Moslem man who once guarded it.

On your right, in the beautiful, peaceful courtyard below, are the "Hungarian Homes" of the **Beit Ungarin Quarter**, established in the 1880's by Hungarian Jews.

The well at Nebi Samuel.

Now Mea She'arim Street stretches up to Yehezkel Street. The intersection here has been dubbed **Shabbat Square**, for the massive protests waged by the ultra-Orthodox Jews of Mea She'arim against the municipal government until the latter agreed to stop traffic here on Shabbat.

Assuming you don't drive, Shabbat is the best time to visit Mea She'arim. A peaceful atmosphere prevails as you watch huge family clans strolling joyously down the center of the street. And you may leave with a more sympathetic picture of the *haredim* than perhaps the dim, dark one which you may have arrived with.

Bukharin Quarter: North of Mea She'arim on Yehezkelm you enter the Bukharin Quarter, first established in the late 19th century by affluent Jews from Bukhara, an Asian province in what is today part of the Soviet Union. These Jews—who wore long, silk khaftans and colorful hats—flourished here for many years. Today, there are scarcely any Bukharin families living in the quarter.

Turning left on HaBucharim Street there is a large crafts store called **Kuzari**, which itself occupies an impressive Bukharin building. In addition to working with the local women to preserve artistic traditions, the store sometimes offers historical tours of the neighborhood and is a good place to start your visit.

Migration began in the 1870s when a wealthy owner of a Bukharin tea company named Shlomo Mussaieff became a religious Zionist before the practice was common (especially among the rich) and thereupon moved his family to Jerusalem. The trip, by camel caravan, took nine months. Upon his arrival, it is said, Mussaieff immediately decided his father must come here to die and so turned around to fetch him.

The story of Mussaieff and others spread in Bukhara, and with the advent of rail transportation in the 1880s, a wave of immigration began. The Old

Monastery at the Valley of the Cross.

City was too ghettoized for these bourgeoisie Jews, and so they set about building their own quarter. Mussaieff himself traveled to Vienna, Paris, and Rome to study urban planning and the quarter bears a distinct European influence as a result.

Unlike the rest of Jerusalem, you will note the streets here are straight and wide. Above all, the Bukharin Jews didn't want communal courtyards on the order of Mea She'arim. Instead they insisted on private aristocratic estates. This community in essence became the first Jerusalem suburb.

To reach the **Mussaieff House**, continue on HaBucharim Street to David HaHazan. Although it has fallen into considerable disrepair, one can imagine its former splendor from the elegant exterior designs. Peek in at the expansive courtyard, upon which the Bukharin Jews obviously placed such a high premium.

A few blocks away on Ezra Street, there is another idiosyncratically de-

signed mansion called **The Palace**. It was built for the Chafetz family at the turn of the century in some sort of Italian revival style. Because there was no real Jewish architecture in the Diaspora when Jerusalem was resettled in the 19th and 20th centuries, those who could afford to, contracted foreign architects. This resulted in *ongepotchket*—a Yiddish expression for slapped together without form or sense.

By 1914, there were as many as 1500 Bukharin Jews living in the quarter, but during and after the Russian Revolution, their money was cut off. The once magnificent summer homes were parcelled into multi-family apartments. During the 1920s, many of the early Zionists gathered here before finally settling Rehavia, and after 1948, a large number of North African Jews were billeted here.

Northern neighborhoods: West of the Bukharin Quarter, all the animals that received mention in the Torah are gathered at the unique and tranquil **Biblical**

Soccer at Givat Ram and right, the Calder stabile near Mt. Herzl.

Zoo. East and north of the quarter, Yehezkel turns into Shimon HaTzadik (Simon the Just) Street. This takes you into **Ma'alot Dafna**, which, in its simplicity, is typical of the post-1967 Jewish neighborhoods. Here is **Ohr Someyach Yeshivah**, the largest and most controversial educational institution for assimilated young Jewish boys who are exploring a return to their forefathers' religious observance.

North of Ma'alot Dafna along the street **Shmuel HaNavi** ("Samuel the Prophet") in **Sanhedria** are the **Tombs of the Sanhedrin**. In Temple times, the Sanhedrin was the high court of 71 sages who issued *halachic* (Jewish law) decisions, and tradition claims they were buried here.

Despite the secular State of Israel and the increasingly powerful Chief Rabbinate, most believe that any type of Sanhedrin cannot reconvene until the Messiah comes. In the interim, halachic questions are normally put to the leading rabbis around the world.

East of Sanhedria is **Ramat Eshkol**, the first post-1967 neighborhood, and **Ammunition Hill**. At the latter, trenches and bunkers have been starkly preserved to give some idea of what it was like during perhaps the most decisive battle of the Six Day War.

This was the main Jordanian outpost on the Jerusalem front, and when the Israeli Defense Forces captured it the stage was set for the conquest of the Old City. At the top of the hill, a memorial museum commemorates the Israeli dead. Maps and models illustrate the story of the battle as does a weekly film shown here.

The road Shmuel HaNavi leads north of the city limits to the suburban neighborhood of Ramot, which sprang up in the early 1970s. Check out the experimental housing tract known as **B'nai Beitcha**, which literally means "Build Your Own Home."

The tract has been divided into one-eighth acre plots for single-family dwellings. A mile and a half from

Hebrew letters at the Billy Rose Sculpture Garden spell "love."

146

Ramot is the Arab village of **Nebi Samuel**. Here a mosque marks the place where it is incorrectly believed Samuel was entombed. Even though there's fairly solid evidence that he was buried east of here in **Ramah**, both Jews and Moslems consider this a sacred site.

To The Capital: West of the central part of Jerusalem is a huge valley, where Israel's most important cultural and political sites lie. It's sometimes called the **Valley of the Cross** for the unusual, hulking, fortress-esque structure, the **Monastery of the Cross**. Tradition holds that the wood for Jesus' cross was taken from here. Originally built in the 7th century as a Georgian monastery, today it serves as a Greek Orthodox Church.

The squat, wide, modern building you see on the nearby hill is the **Knesset**, the seat of the Israeli government. When the capital was moved from Tel Aviv to Jerusalem, in an act of defiance against the United Nations (which wanted to make the city an international zone), the national parliament first met in what is today's Government Tourist Office. Meanwhile the Rothschild family sponsored construction of the new building, which was finished in 1966. The legislative body of the Knesset consists of 120 elected officials, and the coalition that makes a majority then selects a cabinet and Prime Minister.

You can watch the Knesset in action, as long as you remember your passport for the visit. Note the mosaic in the lobby by Marc Chagall. The **Menorah** in front of the Knesset, a gift from the British Parliament, displays various scenes in Jewish history. Nearby is the verdant **Wohl Rose Garden**, a choice spot for diplomatic receptions, and within it is a Byzantine-era mosaic moved here from the north.

Across the way is the **Israel Museum**, which in very short order (it only opened in 1965) has become one of the world's great archaeological and his-

Inside the shrine of the Book, where the Dead Sea Scrolls are kept.

torical museums. The futuristic, domed **Shrine of the Book** houses the decidedly ancient Dead Sea Scrolls, and is the gem among gems in the museum complex. As you enter, you will see 15 letters written by brilliant Jewish General Simmon bar-Kochba, who led the revolt against Rome in 132.

The **Dead Sea Scrolls** themselves, which represent the huge collection of 1st century Hebrew documents discovered at the caves of Qumran in 1947, are on display in the main hall. Among them is a copy of the **Book of Isaiah**, the oldest known complete biblical document in existence today.

On your right as you leave the shrine for the main part of the museum is the **Billy Rose Art Garden**, designed by Isamu Noguchi. Displayed here are sculptural works by Rodin, Picasso, Henry Moore and several prominent Israeli artists.

The Israel Museum is known best for its archaeology section, which displays mainly artifacts that have been un-earthed in Israel, and is organized chronologically. The highlight of the Jewish art and ethnography section is a group of Torah scrolls that have been gathered from all over the Diaspora. There's also a section devoted to Moslem art, and a 19th and 20th-century art wing, which is especially strong on the French, with works by Monet, Cezanne, Renoir, Van Gogh, and Klee. Also note the museum's two reconstructed 18th-century synagogues, one Sephardic from Italy and the other Ashkenazi from Germany.

The **Hebrew University** campus at **Givat Ram** was built with considerable haste in 1948 when the Mt. Scopus campus was cut off from the rest of the city. Today the campus is mostly used for its departments in the natural sciences. It also includes a memorial to Israel's war dead and the **National University Library**, said to be the largest in the Middle East.

On the second floor are the **Ardon Stained Glass Windows**, designed by

Hebrew University at Givat Ram.

Mordechai Ardon which depict Isaiah's "vision" of the End of Days. Plans to build a new **Hebrew University Stadium** have sparked a heated debate, opponents fearful that games played on Shabbat will disturb Orthodox neighborhoods like Bayit Vegan.

North of the University, next to the **Hilton Hotel** and across from the **Central Bus Station**, is **Binyenei Ha-'Uma**, a common meeting place and lecture hall. This is also where the dramatic and drawn-out 1987 trial of the alleged Nazi war criminal John Demjanjuk was held.

A visit to Herod's Temple: If you're interested in gaining some perspective on what Jerusalem may have looked like in ancient times, be certain to stop at the **Holyland Hotel**, just south of the Orthodox enclave of **Bayit Vegan**. (The Circle Line drops you off right in front.) Ever since the Second Temple was destroyed, Jews have been struggling to reconstruct it in their collective imagination. Maimonides himself made a series of drawings based on Talmudic sources.

What makes the late Avi Yonah's huge and detailed model of the Second Temple so miraculous is that when he finished it in 1969 it was just as the Israeli government was beginning to unleash archaeologists to sort through the rubble of the reunified Jerusalem. What they found during the next two decades largely confirms the accuracy of Yonah's vision.

The model, while large, is built on a scale of 1:50. To imagine how large the Temple was, consider that it was twice the size of the Dôme of the Rock that now sits in its place.

The walls around the Old City represented here were about 70 percent greater in circumference than the ones you see today. You can see that the City of David and Mt. Zion were within these walls. At the location of today's Jaffa Gate, is where Herod originally built his palace. A reconstructed model is on view by the three larger towers.

Model of ancient Jerusalem at the Holyland Hotel.

YAD VASHEM

If Jews have a genius survival—passing down their traditions for more than two millennia of wandering—it is in the face of so many nations in history that have tried to wipe them off the face of the earth—from the Babylonians to the Romans, and the Crusaders to the Spanish Inquisitors. In this century, we have witnessed surely the most systematic of these massacres—the "Final Solution," in which the Nazis annihilated six million Jews in Europe.

The horrible irony of this genocide is that three years after the defeat of Hitler, came the culmination of the Zionist movement—the creation of the State of Israel. It might have been a safe haven for so many who died, as it became for the refugees and survivors of the Holocaust. Some critics of Israel have suggested that the state itself was merely a product of Western guilt over the Holocaust, though this was only one of many factors.

Still, the state has made it possible to preserve the memory of the Nazi atrocities with a fitting memorial to the Holocaust in Jerusalem. It is called Yad Vashem, taking its name from the Book of Isaiah and meaning "an everlasting memorial." It is customary for Israeli soldiers and school children and foreign statesmen (such as Jimmy Carter and Anwar Sadat) to visit Yad Vashem. The most frequent tourists who stop here are Germans trying to wrestle with the burden of history. In general, it is not an easy place to visit.

At the entrance to Yad Vashem, the narrow path leading toward the museum is called **The Avenue of the Righteous Among the Nations**. Each of the 6,000 trees planted here honors a Gentile who risked his or her life for Jews during the Holocaust. One such tree commemorates Raoul Wallenberg, a Swedish diplomat who has come to represent the archetypal "righteous

gentile." Wallenberg first met Jewish refugees from Nazi Germany when he was working at a bank in Palestine in 1936. Descriptions of their persecution made a lasting impression on him and in June, 1944, when he was working at the Swedish embassy in Budapest, Hungary, he immediately began to help Jews, bringing them food and medicines. He also rented 32 apartment buildings in the city to house some

13,000 Jews, and declared them to be under the protection of the Swedish government. When the Soviet Army invaded the city in 1945, all foreign diplomat fled the city except for Wallenberg. When he beseeched the Russians for provisions for the Jews, he was carted off to the Soviet Union. By most accounts he is dead, though some believe he is still alive in Siberia.

At the end of the path you reach the museum with a famous sculpture by Naftali Bezem at the entrance. The first panel depicts the Holocaust; the second, Jewish resistance; the third, the return to the land of Israel; and the fourth, rebirth as a nation.

The museum itself takes you step-by-step through the story of the Holocaust through photographs, documents and various artifacts.

Adjacent to the museum is the **Hall of Names**, which preserves three and a half million names of those who perished in the Holocaust. The names of the others are missing because whole

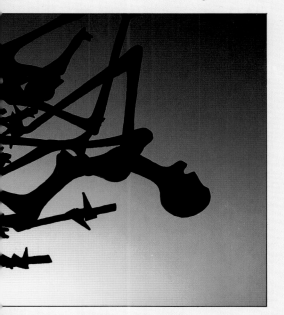

communities were wiped out, leaving no way of tracing some individuals. The Nazi solution was to obliterate every trace of Jews. Today the task is to recover as many names as possible.

The two sculptures outside this building were created by Nathan Rapaport, a Holocaust survivor. In addition, there's an **Art Museum**, which houses many works of art created by the Jews during the Holocaust. These works, completed under extreme duress and prohibited by the Nazis, are evidence of the unshakeable spirit of those who knew they would die to leave some

expression of their experience for future generations.

The **Hall of Remembrance** is the long building with walls made of large stones. Inside, the mosaic floor is inscribed with the names of the 22 largest Nazi concentration and death camps. The ashes of martyrs have been gathered together and brought to Israel from these camps. They have been placed in the vault you see in front of the Eternal Light.

The surrounding area here is called the **Janusz Korczak Park** for the Polish teacher who refused to abandon his students and thus was gassed in a concentration camp with them. The 65-foot (20 meter) tall edifice here is called the Pillar of Heroism.

Nearby you can enter the **Children's Memorial**, which just opened in 1987. It is perhaps the most haunting memorial of all: here you walk through dark corridors of mirrors and candles and hear an endless list of names of some of the one and a half million children who perished in the Holocaust.

The **Central Archives for Holocaust Studies** houses the most comprehensive collection of Holocaust research in the world, containing more than 50 million documents and including some 30,000 eyewitness testimonies of survivors, photographs, films and other artifacts. The library contains more than 75,000 books in 50 languages. Research here has served as the basis for evidence against Nazi war criminals, such as Adolf Eichman.

After Hitler fell, Eichman and many other Nazis leaders assumed false identities and went into hiding all over the world. In 1961, Eichman, the head of Jewish Affairs for the Gestapo, was kidnapped in Argentina by Israeli secret servicemen and was brought to Jerusalem, where he was tried, convicted, and executed.

The Temple itself sits opposite and you can see the heavily gold-coated panels. It is said that at sunrise the Temple would shine as though it were on fire and anyone who gazed at it directly risked becoming blind. The gold spikes were purposely placed there to stop birds from sitting on and befouling the sacred shrine.

The greenish gate is known as Nikanor's Gate because (so the Talmud tells us) Nikanor, a fabulously rich merchant from Alexandria, donated them. They were originally wrought out of copper in Egypt, and covered with gold, silver, and jewels. In shipping them across the Mediterranean, one of the gates fell overboard during a storm. When Nikanor reached Palestine, he bewailed this loss until the gate miraculously appeared on shore. Unfortunately, the gate appeared without its lavish adornments.

Finally, Herzl's home: West of Bayit Vegan, at the intersection of Sdrot Herzl and Hazikaron, is a huge red

installation, an "Homage to Jerusalem" by Alexander Calder. There's a road here that takes you several miles to Ein Kerem and one that stretches back a few hundred yards to the Holocaust Memorial, Yad Vashem .

The entire hill is called Mt. Herzl, or **Har Herzl** as it's known in Hebrew. The **Herzl Museum** across from the Calder work commemorates the Viennese journalist who was the founder of modern Zionism. It traces his careers in law and journalism through photographs and his papers. His comfortable Vienna office is also preserved.

Herzl was an entirely assimilated Jew, whose vestigial tribal instincts were finally aroused during his reporting on the Dreyfus Trail in Paris in 1891. It was here that he realized a modern social anti-Semitism was gaining, and would never be eliminated. His interest was not in perpetuating the Jewish culture or faith, but rather in developing a strategy whereby the Jewish people might simply survive.

Preceding pages: The Holocaust retold at Yad Vashem. Left, modern industry arrives at Jerusalem.

And so it was that he began crusading for a Jewish state. He met with the Turkish Sultan, Kaiser Wilhelm, and other world leaders; he organized in 1897 the first Zionist manifestos the Jewish State and Altneuland. Although he ideally saw the Jews resettling Palestine, he considered for a time purchasing land for a Jewish home in Uganda and South America.

Herzl died in 1904 at the age of 44, a broken hearted man, his dream some decades away. His last wishes were that his body be interred in the Jewish homeland, wherever that land might be. In 1949, after Israel was established, his remains were brought "home," and a simple grave here marks his name in the cemetery behind the museum.

Near the museum is the **Tomb of Vladimir Jabotinsky**, a controversial and brilliant Russian Jew who broke ranks with the Zionists establishment by demanding, well before 1948, the immediate creation of a Jewish state and separate armed forces.

Those who died during the War of Independence in and near Jerusalem are buried in the adjacent **Military Cemetery**. Close to the entrance is a pool commemorating those who drowned in the Mediterranean. Around the corner the home of former Prime Minister Menachem Begin is still guarded by Israeli soldiers, but the former Prime Minister rarely comes out. It is said he is in deep mourning over the death of his wife and the war that he wrought in Lebanon.

Embracing Mountains: If Jerusalem is strategically well-positioned, this is due in no small part to the mountains which surround it on all sides. The Hill of Evil Council is where Jesus said he believed he was the son of God, and his elders ripped his robe and called him blasphemous. Christians also regard this as the spot where Judas Iscariot got his 30 pieces of silver. The Jews called the place **Givat Haananiah** because a high priest by this name was buried here during the time of the Second Temple.

Hadassah Hospital.

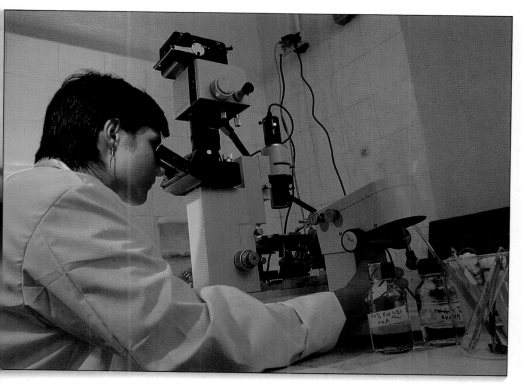

The view from the **Haas Promenade**, the recently renovated walkway of Mt. Moriah—the Temple Mount—is nearly perfect. So much so that one can imagine Abraham coming to this overlook (as some Jews say he did) and seeing in the near distance the place where God intended him to sacrifice Isaac. When Abraham released the asses here, his son then wondered what they would put on the altar. "God will provide the sacrifice," Abraham said.

The white building with the blue flag is the **United Nations Headquarters**. It formerly served as the residence for the "High Commissioner" during the British Mandate. In 1967, the Jordanians crossed the armistice line into this neutral UN zone and occupied the building. It was understood they had joined Egypt in the war against Israel.

South of the Haas Promenade is **Kibbutz Ramat Rachel**, which marks the southern most point of Jerusalem. To the north is the beautiful, if wistfully named **Peace Forest**, and the industrial neighborhood of **Talpiot**. A burgeoning artist's colony is developing loft space here as well.

Further north still is the Arab neighborhood of **Abu Tor**, a name that was actually given long ago to the entire hill. It means "father of the bull" because the hill was the prize for a brave Moslem bull rider who helped defeat the Crusaders in battle in 1187. Abu Tor, the neighborhood, had the misfortune of being "partitioned" between Israel and Jordan from 1948 to 1967. As such, it was virtually a continual battle zone, as you can see from the bullet holes in house after house.

Jerusalem has always been most vulnerable to invasion from the northeast over Mt. Scopus. When the Roman Titus scooped out the holy city from this very spot in 70 A.D., he must have licked his pagan chops and prepared his Roman troops to storm the Temple. Surely the Crusaders felt the same sort of exhilaration here in 1099.

After the dust settled in the 1948 war,

View from Haas Promenade on the Hill of Evil Council.

Israel maintained control of Mt. Scopus itself, even though it was virtually an island in Jordanian territory, cut off from the rest of Jewish Jerusalem. Following an armistice agreement an Israeli convoy, under United Nations protection, was allowed to shuttle up the mountain, a barely tenable arrangement that continued until Jerusalem was reunited in 1967.

Today, Mt. Scopus is known primarily as the site of the country's greatest school, **Hebrew University**. Dedicated in 1925, under the guidance of future Israeli President Chaim Weizmann, Jewish scholars gathered from all over the Diaspora to teach here and at the time, it represented one of the single greatest achievements of the Zionist movement. Since 1967, there have been massive renovations on campus, and the school is bursting with foreign students. Check the calendar for various lectures and concerts, or come up to enjoy yet another splendid view of Jerusalem.

The University amphitheater, at the rear of the campus, with its breathtaking view of the barren **Judean Hills**, reminds you that you are on the fulcrum of two worlds. The renowned **Hadassah Hospital** here was built in 1939. After the Arab Legion massacred a group of scientists and staffers in 1948, however, a new facility was built post haste at Ein Kerem.

The road from Mt. Scopus heads south along the ridge to the **Augusta Victoria**, a large structure built by the Germans as a hospice, now used as a hospital. A bit further down on your right is the new **Brigham Young University** campus. Its construction was bitterly opposed, primarily by Orthodox Jews, who feared that Mormonism was a proselytizing religion. The administration of Mayor Teddy Kollek permitted it anyway in accordance with the principle of cultural and religious tolerance. Finally, the road leads to an Arab village called **E-Tur**, and connects up with the Mount of Olives.

Looking down from Mt. Scopus.

EIN KEREM

Ein Kerem is calm, lush, rural and not too touristy, a welcome reprieve from pressure-packed Jerusalem central. Follow the road from Mt. Herzl a couple of miles into the valley, full of olive trees and rich in vineyards. The valley was populated mostly by Arabs until 1948, but now, aside from the Christian clergymen, it's a predominantly affluent Jewish settlement. This is prime real estate space for local artists and one can well understand the source of their inspiration here.

Ein Kerem is a good place to stroll for an afternoon or hear some music at night. If you feel like staying longer, there are a few hotels, and the **Youth Hostel** on top of the ridge is one of the best kept secrets in Jerusalem. The restaurants are delightful, especially the **Goulash Inn**, a little bit of Hungary in the middle of the Judean hills.

The most important site in Ein Kerem is the **Church of St. John the Baptist**, a Franciscan edifice (1674) on top of ruins from Crusader and Byzantine times. Tradition has it that John was born in the **grotto** down the stairs in the back of the church.

If you walk back to the center of town, you will pass a pleasant cafe on your left before coming to the **Spring of the Vineyard** (or Spring of the Virgin), from which the townlet gets its name and from where it is said that Mary once drank. Follow the road to the right up to the impressive **Church of the Visitation**, built in 1956 by the Italian architect Antonio Barluzzi (who also designed two other churches on the Mount of Olives).

According to Christian tradition, John the Baptist's parents, Zacharias and Elizabeth, had their home here. It was on a visit to Elizabeth that the Virgin Mary received from the Angel Gabriel the Annunciation of the future birth of Jesus.

Continue up the hill to the **Russian Church**, with the resonant red turret. Note another church here was never finished, a casualty of the Russian Revolution. Nearby you can see the **Sisters of Zion Convent**.

On the hill above Ein Kerem, and just a short drive or bus ride away, is the **Hadassah Hospital**, a remarkable medical facility, but even better known for the **Chagall Windows**. The first Hadassah Hospital on Mt. Scopus could no longer function after the 1948 War, and not long thereafter construction began here. In the small synagogue to the left of the main entrance are the stained glass windows made by the Russian Jewish artist Marc Chagall. Each of the 12 represents one of the 12 tribes of Israel, the symbols in various ways corresponding to the blessings Jacob gave his sons. Note the bullet holes made by Arab shelling during the Six Day War. About two miles from the Hadassah Hospital is the **John F. Kennedy Memorial.**

Preceding pages: Ammunition Hill—scene of fighting in the Six-Day War. Left, lush Ein Kerem. Right, the Church of Visitation.

TEL AVIV—JAFFA

The road leading from Tel Aviv to Jerusalem was literally the latter's lifeline during the 1948 War of Independence. It was by this route that the Israeli Haganah hauled supplies and ammunition to the border, and to make this trip in those days was to become a sitting duck for the Arab snipers in the hills. Today, the trip down from the Jerusalem mountains to the coastal town of Tel-Aviv is an easy 43 mile drive. But to many, it is a journey across the world: from sacred religious center to secular mecca, from politically unstable border town to fun, sun-baked Mediterranean metropolis.

In recent years, thousands of Jerusalem families have dug up their roots and made this trip a permanent one. To be sure, they have been lured by better jobs and less expensive housing. But, which is even more striking, they have been lured by the drastically different lifestyle. Whereas Jerusalem is built on stone, upon which every footstep is scrutinized for its political or religious signification, Tel Aviv is built on sand, and you can continually remake of it whatever you wish.

At the moment, with 1.6 million people living in the Tel Aviv metro area (85 percent of them secular), representing more than a third of the population of Israel, this is clearly the country's economic nerve center. It is also its reluctant diplomatic capital since most foreign countries refuse to locate their embassies in Jerusalem.

As hot an arid as the climate may be, it is a place that breathes relief from all the battles everywhere else in the land. The sparkling beachfront crouching behind all those deluxe hotels is a national playground; by night, the party shifts to the pubs, clubs, and cinemas that line Dizengoff. Unlike Jerusalem, they stay open well into the night, *especially* on Shabbat. Compared to most

cities its size, Tel Aviv is a relatively safe, clean place, but some regard it as a modern-day Sodom.

The truth is while scarcely religious, Tel Aviv is nevertheless somewhat miraculous. It sprang up from of the earth outside of the ancient port of **Jaffa** (whose sites we'll discuss at the end of this section), the first strictly Hebrew city in the world.

In 1887, about 20 affluent Jewish families, searching for calm outside the clamorous, Arab-dominated Jaffa, founded a suburb of sorts just north of there. They called it **Neve Zedek**, and it was an early stomping ground of the Nobel Prize winning Hebrew writer S.Y. Agnon. A century later, it has become a artsy, chic, gentrified enclave, especially with the recent opening of the experimental **Neve Tzedek Theater**. As you head uptown from here, at Lilenbulum and Pines Streets is the **Eden Cinema**, Israel's first movie theater, built in 1914.

About that skyscraper: In 1907, fed up with the deplorable living conditions in Jaffa and anxious to build a strictly Jewish/Hebrew city, 60 families gathered on the beach and raffled off a nice swath of land north of Neve Zedek. They named the place "Tel Aviv", chosen for its Zionist resonance. The name also is the Hebrew translation of the title of Theodore Herzl's utopian book *Altneuland* (Old-New-Land).

The first main thoroughfare was named for Herzl— **Herzl Street**—and the first high school at the top of this street. **Herzlia Gymnasium** was built in grand fashion, and when finished, it was the first school where all subjects were taught in Hebrew.

Sadly, however, this architectural and historical landmark was razed in 1959 to make room for that hideous monstrosity that dwarfs the Tel Aviv skyline, the **Shalom Tower**. At 35 stories high, it has the dubious reputation for being the tallest skyscraper in all of the Middle East. Still, the view from the **observatory** here is extraordinary: on a

Preceding pages: "Fun Day" in Tel Aviv; city skyline; ancient port of Jaffa. Below, Agam Fountain.

clear day, you can see Jerusalem. Also you'll find here a four-floor shopping center, a cramped amusement park, and a **Wax Museum**, which houses the modern-day Golems. Near the Shalom Tower is the **Yemenite Quarter**, featuring interesting **Arab Stone Houses** and a **Yemenite Market**.

Rothschild Boulevard: Just a block from the Shalom Tower on Herzl Street starts the grand **Rothschild Boulevard**, named for the famous family of Jewish financiers, who poured a chunk of their vast wealth into the early settlement of Israel, and it takes you into the heart of the modern city.

In the mid-1930s, refugees from the Bauhaus School in Germany came to make Tel Aviv the first *wholly* modern city, a place that would revolutionize the face of the urban center. These "International Style" architects began building like crazy, one white box after another. So much so that Tel Aviv earned the sobriquet, "The White City." The buildings have not aged well and

many have fallen into disrepair, and to live up to its nickname, the town desperately needs a fresh coat of paint.

On the southern part of Rothschild is the **Haganah Museum**, which displays weapons used by the Haganah, Israel's underground defence force, during the War of Independence. It is in the home of Eliahu Golomb, one of the head commanders. At **Allenby Road**, turn west toward the sea. You will pass the **Great Synagogue** and through **Magen David Circle** until you come to the bustling **Carmel Market**, a great place to shop for fruits and vegetables or soak up the local scene.

Still further on Allenby is **Bialik Street**, named for Israel's first "national" poet Chaim Nachman Bialik; his home, **Beit Bialik**, at the end of the block. It was to this neighborhood that the vast influx of Russian immigrants (turned away from America) came in the mid-1920s. Also on this block is the **Rubin Museum** which houses a collection of paintings and drawings by Is-

The curvaceous Asia House and the IBM Building.

raeli artist Reuven Rupin. Finally, you come to the **Museum for the History of Tel Aviv—Jaffa**, a building that served as the City Hall until 1968. Next to the museum is a staircase that leads to **Gan Meir**, a charming garden on one of the more charming streets.

If you make your way back to Rothschild and start north you will arrive at Habima Square. The delightful circular building is the home of the renowned **Habima Theater**, founded at the dawn of nationalism by a group of Jewish actors who fled Russia after the revolution. Many productions offer simultaneous translations so that tourists can follow the Hebrew. Next to the theater is the **Mann Auditorium**, where you can see another national jewel, the **Israel Philharmonic Orchestra** (long conducted by Zubin Mehta). Get your tickets early, as tickets fetch a mighty price on the scalper's market. Behind these buildings is the **Helena Rubinstein Museum for Modern Art**, and aesthetes gather at the **Apropos Cafe** in the little park across the way to discuss the latest exhibitions.

From here head north up **Ibn Givrol Boulevard** and west across **King Saul Street** to the **Tel Aviv Museum**. The museum has several galleries, most notable for their collection of Israeli artists, though with modest holdings from the Impressionist and post-Impressionist periods. The museum attracts large crowds when it hosts cinematic retrospectives and other cultural events in its auditorium.

Further down on King Saul Street are among the city's more recent architectural success stories. The **Asia House**, designed by Mordecai Ben-Horin, is an undulating, sensual edifice that does far more than the Bauhaus buildings in creating a distinct Tel Aviv feeling. That cyclindrical object next door is **IBM Building**. Across the way is the **German Templar Colony**, founded in 1870 and abandoned in 1939, at the height of Hitler's war against the Jews.

In the 1960s Tel Aviv reached so far north that it crossed **Yarqon River**. The Yarqon flows west from the mountains until it spills into the sea, and (the bible tells) it served as the geographical boundary between the tribes of Ephriam and Dan. Across the river is the the **Diaspora Museum**, one of the most interesting museums of its kind in Israel and the world. The museum is on the campus of **Tel Aviv University**.

Another worthwhile place to visit north of the river is **Tel Qasila**, a rich archaeological site that is now part of the **Ha'aretz Museum**, which is actually a whole complex of museums including folklore, glass, ceramic, copper, and neumismatic; there is a planetarium as well.

Night life: In the evening, the center of Tel Aviv and its most frequented meeting place is **Dizengoff Square**, site of the unusual water fountain/sculpture by the Israeli artist Agam. Here you'll find the multiplex cinemas that lure the secular Jews from Jerusalem, the best

Swinging Tel Aviv: beaches by day; cafes by night.

THE DIASPORA MUSEUM

Modern skeptics of organized Judaism are wont to argue that if the religion were true, we should be able to witness God's hand in today's affairs the way ancient Jews supposedly experienced it in their times. Why, these skeptics ask, do we no longer see burning bushes, or parting seas or credible prophets? To this, one may occasionally hear the response: "The story of the Jewish Diaspora, the very survival of the Jewish people for several millennia of wandering in many a far-flung land, is perhaps the most miraculous of all." Now the skeptic comes back: "It all depends on how you define a miracle." To which the religious Jew finally says: "When Moses saw a bush that was on fire but would not consume itself, the miracle wasn't only the bush, but the fact that Moses *noticed* it." Understood this way, it would appear that the aim of the Diaspora Museum in Tel Aviv is to spark the flame of awareness in visitors to noticing the miracle of the survival of the Jewish people in their exile.

Founded in 1979, the Diaspora Museum (or Beth Hatefusoth, as it is called in Hebrew) is designed unlike any other museum. It doesn't display valuable objects or art, but utilizes a multi-media presentation to tell the story of the Jewish people. The main exhibit is organized around several themes of Jewish life in the Diaspora: Family Life, Community Life, Religious Life, Culture, Relations with Non-Jews and the Return To Zion.

The word "Diaspora" comes from the Greek for dispersion or scattering. The Hebrew word for it is *Galut*. The first scattering of the Jews occurred in the 8th century BCE, when the Assyrians wiped out Samaria and 10 of the 12 tribes of the Israelite people.

Nobody knows what happened to the "Ten Lost Tribes," as they are called, though some speculate that the Jews of

Family traces its lineage at the computer study center.

Ethiopia or India or China represent one such lost tribe. In 586 BCE, the Babylonians killed many Jews who belonged to the remaining two tribes and sent the rest to exile in Babylon (modern-day Iraq). Others fled to Egypt and established a huge and prosperous community in the port city of Alexandria.

Jews continued to settle in the Mediterranean and Northern Africa. With the rise of Islam, initially many Jews were massacred, but as time went on Judaism was generally tolerated under Moslem rule.

After the Christians vanquished the Moslems from Spain, the government demanded that Jews convert to Christianity or die. Those who paid lip service to conversion, while maintaining Jewish customs in private, were called *Marranos* (literally "pigs"); those who were found out in the Spanish Inquisition were burned at the stake. The Jews who could, fled from the Iberian peninsula to Northern Europe Protestant nations, such as Holland, England, and Germany. Others set out for America; some even speculate that Christopher Columbus himself was a *Marrano*.

The French Revolution and the Enlightenment gave Jews political rights in Western Europe. No longer facing massacres, many of these Jews began to lose their Judaism through assimilation. This was especially true of the German Jews and the Russians Jews who emigrated to America.

By the dawn of the 20th century, it was apparent to many that "emancipation" had been a failure and some Diaspora Jews began to hook up again with their tradition by returning to the Land of Israel.

The miracle of the Diaspora Jewry wasn't merely surviving the tortures and massacres mentioned above, but the fact that it preserved the heritage and tradition of the Israelite people who've been wandering since the time they received the Torah in the desert at Mt. Sinai.

Diaspora Museum, story of a miracle.

falafel stands in the city. Two blocks away is the **Dizengoff Center**, the modern mall, which came to Israel in the early 1980s to the great fascination and pleasure of the shopping-crazy, film-buff, food-mad Tel Avivis.

Dizengoff Street is one long see-and-be-seen party strip. The Jewish intellectual patter in many foreign languages starts at **Stiematzky**, the Israeli book store, and moves to several of the more quiet and refined cafes, such as **Cafe Afarsemon**. The young Israelis and tourists converge on the rock & roll pubs, such as the **Cafe Cherry**.

If you turn west on Ben Gurion Street, you will come to **David Ben Gurion's House**. This was his permanent residence until the latter part of his life when he settled on the Kibbutz Sde Boker. Despite the 20,000 volume library, it's a modest dwelling in the heart of a city that the first Prime Minister never really cared for very much.

If you head further west, you'll get to the beachfront, studded with hotels, but delightful nonetheless for the **Tel Aviv Promenade**. Several embassies are also located down here, including the hideously ugly American consulate.

Most of the big hotels on the beachfront are overpriced, but the smaller ones, mainly for young travelers, are dirt cheap. While prostitutes down by the beach have led some religious Jews to complain, generally the waterfront is sparkling clean.

Old Jaffa: If you were to walk south on the beach, you'd come to the source of Tel Aviv, the ancient port of Jaffa. And if you stand on the port and gaze out at the Mediterranean, you can see a group of rocks, the most prominent of which is very important in Greek legend. It is known as **Andromeda's Rock** because it is reputed to be the place where that mythic lady was once manacled by Poseidon. She was awaiting sacrifice when her beloved Perseus, wearing the winged sandals of Hermes, swooped down, slew the Sea Monster, and saved her. If there were ever any

Jaffa—where Jonah departed, Zionists arrived.

opportunity to verify deatils of this account, however, they may well have been destroyed during a recent renovation of the pier.

This very port also figures prominently in the story of Jonah, the reluctant prophet. Imagining that he could escape God's orders, Jonah hopped a ship from Jaffa to the land of Tarshish, got caught in a storm, and was swallowed whole by a whale.

In addition, this was the port where the cedars of Lebanon arrived on floats before being sent to Jerusalem for the building of the temples. It is said the Hasmonean King Jonathan reconquered Jaffa in the 2nd century BCE, before it came successively under the rule of the Greeks, Romans, Crusaders, Saracens and Turks.

In the late 19th century, near the end of Turkish rule and before Tel Aviv sprouted up, Jaffa assumed far more significance than it does today. With 8,000 Arabs and 2,000 Jews, it was the largest city along the Mediterannean coast betweeen Port Said in the south and Beirut in the north. It was the primary seaport and trade center for all of Palestine during that time.

Still it was a dingy town when many of the earliest Zionists washed up on its shores from Eastern Europe. The new immigrants were thoroughly disappointed, even shocked. When David Ben-Gurion, Israel's first Prime Minister, then 20, left his home in Czarist-ruled Poland for Palestine, he was repulsed by Jaffa. This was not the Zionist dream that had possessed him. Even though he was exhausted after an arduous, three-week trip, he refused to spend the night there and set off by foot to Petach Tikvah.

Jaffa today: If you are coming to Jaffa from downtown Tel Aviv (walking along the beach is impractical) ask the bus driver to drop you off at the **Clock Tower** on Yefet Street and start your tour here. Each of the stained-glass windows on the tower tells a part of Jaffa's history.

St. Peter's Church: Napoleon slept here.

The **Armenian Hostel** across the way practically served as a check-off point for Zionists on their way from the Diaspora to start settlements in the new old land. The **Mahmoudia Mosque** just ahead was built in 1812.

The nearby **Jaffa Flea Market** is more low-key and authentic than anything in Jerusalem. It's a fine place to browse for ancient relics and modern trash. The restored section of Jaffa is the other way. The **Jaffa Museum** offers a solid collection of archaeological exhibits, but not nearly so interesting to look at as the building in which they are housed: the headquarters of some former 18th-century Ottoman governor.

The **Franciscan Monastery of St. Peter** is the large maze edifice at the top of the hill that defines the Jaffa skyline. And St. Peter himself casts a long shadow over Jaffa lore. When the disciple Tabitha fell ill and died, St. Peter proclaimed, "Tabitha arise!", and she did. Thereafter, St. Peter spent much time in Jaffa, lodging at the **House of**

Simon the Tanner. Tradition places this site where a tiny mosque now stands near the monastery. In the courtyard is the **St. Louis Monastery**, so named for the French King, who led a Crusade here in 1147. Another Gallic ruler, the Napoleon, is said to have rested his imperialistic bones here after conquering Jaffa some 750 years later.

The minaret is part of the **Jama El-Baher Mosque**. Next door is Jaffa's first Jewish house, built in 1820. Nearby, behind the museum, is a Turkish mansion *cum* bath house *cum* nightclub and restaurant called **El-Hamam**. Atop the hill, past the park, follow the narrow alleyways through a maze of artists' studios, galleries and shops. The art isn't cheap but the browsing is fine. On Pasteur Street, that huge, ugly building is a modern mall—an anachronistic juxtaposition here. Inside, you will find **Israel Experience** tourist center, which runs multi-media and sound and light shows.

Back at the center of the town square, called **Kikar Kedumin**, a number of Jaffa excavations are on display. Across the way, are some of the town's most hoppin' night haunts. Peaceful by day, Jaffa absorbs much of Tel Aviv's bustle and commotion in the evening.

The suburbs: Ringed around Tel Aviv/Jaffa like ripples from the sea are the city's bedroom suburbs. Among the noteworthy are **B'nai Brak** and **Petach Tikvah**. The former was established by *frum* (pious) Jews from Poland in 1924, and is one of the best known *chareidi* enclaves outside of Jerusalem. The latter was founded by secular Jews in 1878, and is considered the first Zionist settlement. Today it is a modern industrial city, but at the turn of the century it was known for its beautiful orange groves. Ben Gurion walked there the first night after landing at Jaffa. He wrote: "My heart overflowed with happiness as I had entered the relm of joy...I am in a Hebrew village in the Land of Isreal, in a Hebrew village called Petach Tikva."

Left, nightlife in the town square. Right, artists abound in Jaffa.

DAY TRIPS

Israel is so small as to seem to anyone who lives there for long, downright claustrophobic. Jews walk around with deep-seated anxieties about their vulnerability to outside invasion; Palestinians are increasingly frustrated with what they perceive as police state rule and reasonably wonder where in this tiny, embattled stretch of real estate they can possibly secure a homeland.

For the tourist, however, Israel's size, at least when things are relatively calm, is a blessing: compact and accessible. Jerusalem sits at the nation's crossroads, and using it as your base, you are only a couple of hours from its farthest borders, the Golan Heights in the North and the port of Eilat in the South. Given the time, you are probably better off arranging overnight trips to the green Galilee or the dusty Negev desert, the mystical town of Zfat, and ports of Haifa or Eilat. But just about every other place in the country can be a daytime excursion. Rental cars are expensive, but the national bus service is fairly reliable and the Ministry of Tourism runs several bus tours of the sites outside of Jerusalem. You can pick them up from Citadel of David four mornings a week.

Biblical village: Just six miles south of Jerusalem is the popular Christian pilgrimage site of Bethlehem, today an Arab town. As you enter the village from Jerusalem, you'll come upon **Rachel's Tomb**, a Jewish and Moslem holy site endowed with special meaning—it is one of the few in the land that commemorates a religious woman.

It is believed that King David was born in Bethlehem, and you can visit **David's Well**, just off **Manger Street**. Further on, you'll come to Manger Square, the center of town, from which most formal and impromptu tours begin. If you have ever heard the famed Bethlehem Midnight Mass on Christ-

mas Eve, you will probably be pleased to see the **St. Catherine's Church**, from which it is broadcast. However the plaza itself is built around the **Church of Nativity**, presumably where Jesus was born. Constantine the Great originally constructed a church on this site in 325, but it has been knocked down and rebuilt several times since. If you follow the stairs down, you will come to the **Cave of the Nativity**, where there's a faded 12th-century mosaic and the decidedly glistening **Star of the Nativity**. Note the Latin inscription: It says, "Here Jesus Christ was born of the Virgin Mary."

Mary is said to have placed her newborn child next to the cave in what is today called the **Chapel of the Manger** and nursed him on the site of the **Milk Grotto**. The story goes that she dripped some milk on the floor in the process, hence the white color.

Herodian: A few miles down the road heading southeast of Bethlehem brings you to **Herodian**. The Jewish historian

Josephus described this, Herod's famed artificial mountain, as having the shape of a breast, and it's one to which this strange king retreated and clung when he was feeling especially paranoid in Jerusalem. Upon it, he constructed an impressive palace, which was later converted into a synagogue by the Jews during the War against the Romans. It is said that Herod is buried here, but even if you have no desire to check out his grave, you will not want to miss the breath-taking view from the mountaintop: Like Herod, you can feel like the squire of all you survey. This includes the **Dead Sea**, due East, the lowest point on the face of the earth.

Float away: You may want to make a separate trip to the Dead Sea. They say the mud here has curative powers and many tourists come for the sole purpose of packing it on their faces. Others come to bathe in the hot springs. The Dead Sea itself is so salty that you can literally float on the surface. The Emperor Vespasian is said to have tossed his slaves into the sea just to test its bouyancy, and throngs of tourists are volunteering themselves for this experiment today. (But don't try it if you have any cuts or sores or you'll be in for quite a sting.)

Ein Fesh'ha is one such bathing spring. An ascetic sect known as the *Essenes* once grew its food here. A few miles north is a reconstructed Essene village known as the **Qumran Ruins**. These Essenes, a small rival to the Pharisees and Saducces in Temple times, were zealous and anti-materialistic, and some scholars now believe Jesus belonged to or was greatly influenced by them.

The speculation is based on one of the most startling archaeological finds of the century in the cliffs you see above Qumran. In 1947 a poor Bedouin shepherd was searching for a stray goat and tossed a stone at a cave on the side of a cliffs. When he heard a piece of pottery break, he investigated and later led archaeologists to a storehouse of bibli-

Preceding pages: The awesome mount of Massada; view from the Church of Nativity. Left, Sorek Caves. Right, Herodian, Herod's monument to himself.

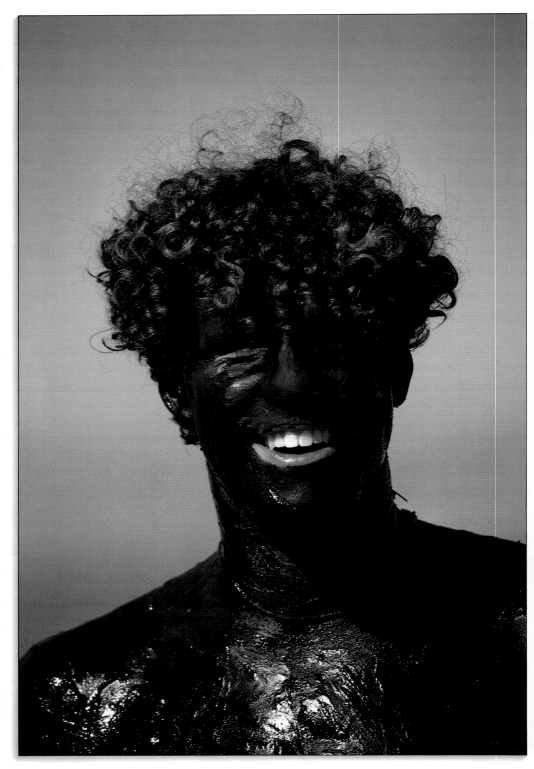

cal and historical texts known ever since as "The Dead Sea Scrolls," kept and collected by these Essenes.

If you follow the Dead Sea coast south about 25 miles, you will come to **Ein Gedi**, an oasis town famous for its date trees and a surprisingly green nature reserve. Go roaming in the wadis here and if you hike up high enough, you'll feel like you're walking on the moon. Seeing seashells lodged in rocks, one senses that this arid, desert landscape was once covered by the Dead Sea, too. (Don't forget your canteen as water is scarce in the area.)

Another 15 miles south and you arrive at **Massada**, the most fabulous and, with the possible exception of the Wailing Wall, the most culturally resonant sight in all of Israel. In 66 A.D., the Jewish War against the Romans began at Massada when zealots seized the garison here. In 73 A.D., three years after the Jerusalem Temple was destroyed, the last heroic Jewish resistence against the Romans was halted, bringing an end to the war.

The Jewish community at Massada (according to historian Josephus) was no more than 1,000 strong, and the mountain was surrounded by 15 times as many Roman soldiers. Sensing their imminent defeat and fearing that they would be killed, their wives raped, their children forced to convert and sold into slavery, the Jewish men organized a mass suicide. First they killed their families and then themselves. It is said that the last ten men drew lots so that one slew the nine others and finally took his own life.

Excavations in the 1960s turned up evidence that supports Josephus' account, and the ruins of Herod's palace. If you're fit and have the time, the **Snake Path** offers an exhilarating climb up; for those short of breath and time, take the **cablecar**.

Jericho: If you visit the **West Bank**, which is the large occupied territory that Israel took from Jordan in 1967, be sure to find out from the Ministry of Tourism which areas may be unsafe. Up until the Palestinian uprisings of late 1987, a beautiful and well-touristed spot was the town of Jericho, reputed to be one of the oldest cities in the world, settled 10,000 years ago. This is where Joshua fought the famous battle "...and the walls came tumbling down."

The ancient city is called **Tel a-Sultan**, just next to the **Spring of Elisha**, the water source that explains the city's origin. A mile and a half north of Jericho is the **Hisham Palace**, a rich archaeological site offering ornate examples of Umayyad Dynasty architecture. North of Jerusalem—Jericho Road—is **Wadi Kelt**, another good place to take a hike.

For the kids: This last side trip about 15 miles west of Ein Kerem is the **Sorek Cave**, a good place to bring children. Discovered by accident in 1968, it is the largest cave in Israel. Tours of the cave are available on which you can observe some of its interesting stalactite and stalagmite combinations.

Left, a Dead Sea facial. Right, relaxing at earth's lowest point.

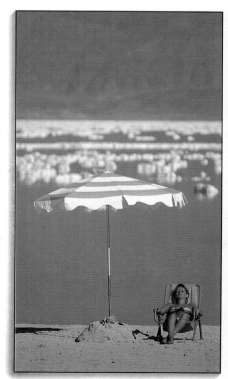

TRAVEL TIPS

DESTINATION JERUSALEM

GETTING THERE

By Air: Ben-Gurion International Airport is situated in Lydda (Lod in Hebrew) near the Mediterranean coast, 20 km (12 miles) southeast of Tel Aviv, 50 km (31 miles) west of Jerusalem and 110 km (68 miles) southeast of Haifa, and is the main hub for international air traffic. Its facilities include a Government Tourist Office, which is open around the clock to provide information and help arrange accommodation, tel: (03) 971485. It also has a bank and post office, both open 24 hours except for holidays and *Shabbat*, plus a cafeteria, shopping area and First Aid post. The El Al Lost & Found department, also open 24 hours, can be reached at tel: (03) 976934. Information about arriving and departing flights is given on a recording, tel: (03) 381111. General airport information is available 24 hours at tel: (03) 972484.

Transport from the airport

By bus: An **El Al airport bus** leaves Ben-Gurion Airport Terminal in Tel Aviv (some 20 minutes away) approximately every hour, from 6 a.m. to 10 p.m. and, in accordance with the arrival of planes, at other hours. **Egged buses** leave for **Tel Aviv** every 15 minutes from 5 a.m. to 11:10 p.m.; for **Jerusalem** (about one hour away) about every 20 minutes from 7:15 a.m. to 6 p.m.; for **Haifa** (one and-a-half hours) from 7 a.m. to 6 p.m. about every 20 minutes.

United Tours Bus no. 222 travels between the airport and the Railway Station, Rehov Arlosorov, Tel Aviv, every hour all the year round. The service operates from 4 p.m. to 12:00 p.m. The bus stops at the Palace, Diplomat, Sheraton and Dan Hotels. For further details contact (03) 298181, 253411.

By taxi: *Sherut* taxis (Nesher), in which each passenger pays for his own seat, travel to Jerusalem in less than an hour. Ordinary taxis are available to almost any point in the country. The fare is fixed and the tourist may ask to be shown the official pricelist. Cost for taxi service to Tel Aviv is about $10—$15, or $22—$30 to Jerusalem. *Sherut* service is considerably less expensive. The United Tours bus to Tel Aviv costs approximately $1 to the railroad terminal, or $1.30 to the city.

Car rentals: Car rental firms which have facilities at the airport are Avis, Hertz, Eurocar, Inter-Rent, Budget Rent-a-car, Kopel and Thrifty.

Airlines: Sixteen international airlines operate scheduled flights to Israel's Ben-Gurion International Airport at Lod: El Al Israel Airlines, Air France, Air Sinai, Alitalia, Austrian Airlines, British Airways, Cyprus Airways, K.L.M., Lufthansa, Olympic Airways, Sabena, SAS, South African Airways, Swissair, Tarom and TWA. In addition, charter flights operate from several European countries, the U.S.A. and Canada, terminating either at Lod or Eilat.

Pan Am, a second U.S. airline, has also been flying to Israel since 1986.

Approximate flying times to:

Amsterdam-
4 hrs. 15 mins.
Athens-
1 hr. 50 mins.
Boston-
10 hrs. 5 mins.
Brussels-
4 hrs. 5 mins.
Bucharest-
2 hrs. 30 mins.
Cairo-
1 hr. 20 mins.
Chicago-
12 hrs. 5 mins.
Cologne-
3 hrs. 55 mins.
Copenhagen-
4 hrs. 30 mins.
Eilat-
35 mins.
Frankfurt-
3 hrs. 55 mins.
Geneva-
3 hrs. 45 mins.
Istanbul-
1 hr. 50 mins.
Johannesburg-
8 hrs. 50 mins.
Lisbon-
5 hrs. exactly
London-
4 hrs. 35 mins.

Los Angeles-
15 hrs. 50 mins.
Madrid-
4 hrs. 45 mins.
Marseilles-
3 hrs. 45 mins.
Miami-
13 hrs. 20 mins.
Montreal-
9 hrs. 55 mins.
Munich-
3 hrs. 30 mins.
Nairobi-
4 hrs. 55 mins.
New York-
10 hrs. 30 mins.
Paris-
4 hrs. 10 mins.
Rome-
3 hrs. 5 mins.
Vienna-
3 hrs. 15 mins.
Zurich-
3 hrs. 40 mins.

By Sea: Israel's main ports are Haifa and Ashdod. The Stability line and Sol line offer regular sailings from Europe to Haifa port, and many Mediterranean cruises include Israel in their itinerary. Official ports of entry for foreign yachts and boats in addition to these two cities also include Eilat and the Tel Aviv Marina.

By Land

From Jordan: **Allenby Bridge**, near Jericho, some 40 km (25 miles) from Jerusalem, is the crossing-point between Israel and Jordan. Visitors entering Israel via the Allenby Bridge, may re-enter Jordan by the same route. However, tourists crossing from Israel into Jordan via the Allenby Bridge, are prohibited by the Jordanian Government from re-entering Israel.

The visa requirements are the same as any other point of entry into Israel. Those who need an Israeli visa in advance should make sure to obtain it before going to Jordan as it is not possible to obtain an Israeli visa in any Arab country (except Egypt) and it cannot be obtained upon arrival at the Bridge. When crossing from Israel to Jordan the tourist must possess a Jordanian visa and a Jordanian permit to cross the Bridge, and pay a transit tax. This is levied in the form of a revenue stamp which can be purchased at any post office in Israel as well as at the Bridge. Private vehicles (including bicycles) may not cross the Bridge. Cameras must be empty of film.

The Bridge is open Sundays to Thursdays, 8 a.m. to 1 p.m. and on Fridays and eves of holidays, 8 a.m. to 11 a.m. It is closed on Saturdays and Jewish holidays. At Allenby Bridge a Tourist Information Office is open at the same time as the Bridge. Other facilities include: currency exchange, post office, public telephones, cafeteria, toilets, porters and *sherut* (service) taxis to Jerusalem, Jericho, Bethlehem, Hebron, Ramallah and Gaza.

From Egypt: Point of entry open between Israel and Egypt are Nizzana, Rafiah and Taba, open 363 days a year (exceptions are *Yom Kippur* and the first day of *Id el Adha*).
Nizzana, which is the main point of entry, is about 60 km (37 miles) southwest of Beersheba, and is open between 8 a.m. and 4 p.m.
Rafiah, 50 km (31 miles) southwest of Ashkelon, is open longer, between 8:30 a.m. and 5 p.m.
Taba, just south of Eilat, is open from 7 a.m. to 9 p.m. Tourists who cross from Taba to Egypt do **not** need a visa in advance, but can obtain one on presentation of a passport. The Egyptian visa, valid up to seven days, is free-of-charge, but there is a $5 tax. Travel is permitted to the tourist sites in Southern Sinai only, and visitors must return to Israel via Taba. The AL-17 entry form into Israel is required.

With the exception of those entering Southern Sinai (through Taba) an Egyptian visa must be obtained in advance. In addition to your valid passport, the AL-17 entry form must be presented. Private vehicles may be driven into Egypt, and documentations must be obtained from the automobile and touring clubs in your country. Rented cars are **not** permitted to cross. The Egged Bus Co-op has regular buses from Tel Aviv to Cairo, with routes planned from Eilat to Sharm el Sheikh and the International Airport Ras el Naqb. Southern Sinai may also be entered by sea through Sharm el Sheikh only. Free visas are obtainable in advance for a 48-hour stay, from the Egyptian Consulate in Eilat.

TRAVEL ADVISORIES

Passports: Tourists are required to hold passports

valid for Israel. Stateless persons require a valid travel document with a return visa to the country of issue.

Visas

Entry visa: An entry visa is required, except where stated below. This visa is valid for a stay of three months from the date of arrival. American tourists do not need a visa to enter Israel, only a valid U.S. passport.

Citizens of the following countries also do not require a transit or visitor's visa for entry into Israel: Austria, Bahamas, Barbados, Belgium, Bolivia, Colombia, Costa Rica, Denmark, Dominican Republic, Dutch Antilles, Ecuador, El Salvador, Fiji, Finland, France, Greece, Guatemala, Republic of Haiti, Holland, Hong Kong, Iceland, Jamaica, Japan, Lichstenstein, Luxembourg, Maldive Islands, Mauritius, Mexico, Norway, Paraguay, Surinam, Swaziland, Sweden, Switzerland, Trinidad and Tobago, the United Kingdom (including Northern Ireland, the Channel Islands and Isle of Man).

Citizens of the following countries receive the visa free-of-charge **at the port of entry:** Argentina, Australia, Brazil, Canada, Central African Republic, Chile, Germany (Federal Republic of) and citizens of Italy, New Zealand, San Marino, South Africa, Spain and Uruguay, born **after** January 1, 1928. Citizens of the Republic of Ireland (Aire) also receive the visa at the port of entry but are required to pay the requisite fee.

Citizens of the following countries receive the visa free-of-charge but must **apply for it**, **before departure**, to any Israel Diplomatic or Consular Mission: Cyprus, Germany (Federal Republic of), born **before** January 1, 1928—for an unlimited number of visits during the validity of the passport in use—and Yugoslavia.

The citizens of countries not mentioned above must submit the visa application for approval to the nearest Israel Diplomatic or Consular Mission and pay the prescribed fee.

Transit Visa: A transit visa, valid for five days, is also available from any Israel Diplomatic or Consular Mission. It can be extended, upon arrival, for a further 10 days, by applying to any district office of the Ministry of the Interior in Israel.

Landing-for-the-Day Card: If you visit Israel on a cruise ship, you will be given a Landing-for-the-Day card, which permits you to remain in the country for as long as your ship is in port, and there is no need to apply for a visitor's visa.

This applies only to people wishing to enter Israel for travel purposes. Anyone wishing to enter for work, study or permanent settlement must apply while still abroad to an Israel Diplomatic or Consular Mission for the appropriate visa.

Extension of stay: Tourists who wish to stay in the country for longer than three months must obtain an extension of stay. This applies to citizens of those countries which are exempt from entry visas and generally requires the stamping of your passport. The extension may be obtained through any district office of the Ministry of Interior.

The addresses of the main offices are:

Jerusalem
Generali Building
Rehov Shlomzion Hamalka
Tel: (02) 228211

Tel Aviv
Shalom Meyer Tower
Visa Department
9 Rehov Ahad Ha'am
Tel: (03) 651941, 657758

Haifa
Government Building
(opp. Municipality)
11 Hassan Shukuri
Tel: (04) 667781

Visa Fees: The visa fees for those who are required to pay for the Israel visa are as follows: Individual tourist visa and transit visa $3. The fee for the extension of a visitor's (tourist) visa, transit or temporary resident's visa is $3 for a year, or part thereof, for citizens of all countries. Only those from Belgium, Holland and Luxemburg, are exempt from this payment.

For further information contact:

The Ministry of the Interior, Immigration and Registration Department, 24 Rehov Hillel, Jerusalem, Tel: (02) 226261.

Entry and Exit Formalities

Form AL 17: All visitors to Israel, are required to fill in the **AL17** entry form.

Visitors continuing to Arab countries (except Egypt) may have the entry stamp put on this form instead of in their passports.

Exit Fees: Visitors leaving Israel from Ben-Gurion International Airport, Lod, are required to pay an airport tax. The tax is frequently increased to keep it equivalent to $10.

Passengers to Egypt pay a tax approximately equivalent to $8. Passengers departing Israel at the Jerusalem and Eilat airports pay a tax of approximately $5.50.

Visitors departing via the land crossing point to Egypt at Nitzana pay a tax approximately equivalent to $2. The tax is paid at the Bank Leumi branch at the terminal. Visitors departing via Rafiah pay a tax roughly equivalent to $8. This tax can be paid at any branch of Bank Hapoalim made out to the Israel Airport Authority, account number 566-05-39710.

These exit fees are charged to all people leaving Israel at the above-mentioned exit points, with the exception of children under the age of two.

Health: There are no vaccination requirements for tourists entering Israel, except if arriving from infected areas. Tourists who are already in Israel and wish to obtain vaccination against cholera and yellow fever before they leave can do so at any of the district or sub-district offices of the Ministry of Health.

Customs: Every adult tourist may bring with him into the country, without payment of duty the following articles, provided that they are for personal use (gift parcels sent unaccompanied—by post or any other means—are liable to full import duties and Value Added Tax):

Eau de Cologne or perfume not exceeding 1/4 liter (0.44 pint); wine up to 2 liters and other alcoholic drinks not exceeding 1 liter; tobacco or cigars not exceeding 250 grams or 250 cigarettes; gifts up to $125 in value c.i.f. (including assorted foodstuffs not exceeding 3 kg or 6 1/2 lbs in weight, on condition that no single type of food exceeds 1 kg).

The following articles may be brought in duty-free on condition that they are taken out on departure and that they are portable and actually in use:

Typewriter; cameras (1 ordinary camera with 10 plates or 10 rolls of film and one movie camera below 16 mm with 10 reels of cine film); tape recorder with 750 yards (700 m) of recording tape or 2 cassettes; record-player; battery-operated radio; binoculars; jewelry; baby carriages; musical instruments; camping equipment; sports requisites (1 set for fishing, skates, 2 tennis rackets); bicycle without engine.

The Ben-Gurion Airport has the red-green customs clearance system. Tourists bringing in goods mentioned above may choose the green channel and leave the Airport. Tourists bringing in other goods, even if they are exempt from duty, must use the red channel.

The following articles brought in with the tourist are subject to declaration and deposits of duties and taxes and the red channel must be taken:

Professional instruments (which can be held in the hand during operation) up to a value of $1,650 c.i.f.; boat (rowing, sailing or motor) and a caravan trailer; scuba-diving gear—portable and appreciably used; records—in resonable quantity.

A televison for the personal use of the tourist may be brought in free of import duty and taxes **provided it is portable and used**. It is, however, liable to a deposit on the duty.

Customs Deposits: The customs authorities are entitled to demand deposits or guarantees on any article brought in by the tourist or sent separately. This is usually enforced only for professional equipment or expensive items. The guarantee or deposit is returned to the tourist when he leaves the country and takes the articles out with him. Since the formalities take some time, it is advisable to make all arrangements a day or two before departure, and preferably at the port of entry of the goods, so that the return of the guarantee can be carried out more easily.

Further information from: The Department of Customs and Excise, 32 Rehov Agron, P.O.B. 320, 91000 Jerusalem, Tel: (02) 245951.

Departure From Israel

Confirming Reservations: You must confirm your scheduled departure with your airline at least 72 hours in advance. To save inconvenience, check the departure time to make sure that it has not been changed.

Procedures On Departure: Departing passengers should arrive at the airport two hours prior to their flight departure time and prepare the following documents: a valid passport, flight tickets and the equivalent of $10 for the airport tax, which every passenger over the age of two must pay. (Israeli currency preferred).

Baggage Services: If you are flying El Al, you can check in your luggage at their office in Haifa, Jerusalem and Tel Aviv the **evening before** departure (except on Friday, holy days and the eve of holy days). It will be taken straight to your plane and you need only arrive at the airport one hour before departure.

The following El Al offices are open for check-in services:

Tel Aviv Railway Station
North Tel Aviv
Tel: (03) 217198
From 4 p.m. to midnight.

12 Rehov Hillel
Jerusalem
Tel: (02) 23333
From 6.45 to 11.00 p.m.

80 Derech Haatzmaut
Haifa
Tel: (04) 641166
From 6.45 to 10.00 p.m.

Security Checks: These are for your protection. Be prepared to unlock your luggage and submit yourself and your carry-on bags to a careful—but courteous—examination. To avoid spoiling any precious records of your visit, make sure to empty your camera of film.

Getting to the Airport

From Tel Aviv: By United Tours Bus no. 222 from Railway Station; Rehov Arlosorov to Ben-Gurion Airport every hour all the year round from 4 a.m. to 12.00 p.m. For details call (03) 298181, 253411. By Egged Buses, every 15 minutes, from 6.15 a.m. to 11.30 p.m.

From Jerusalem: By Egged Buses, from 6.15 a.m. to 7.00 p.m., approximately every 20 minutes. By Nesher *sherut* taxi: book in advance at 21 Rehov Hamelech George. Tel: (02) 227227.

From Haifa: By Egged Buses, from 7 a.m. to 6 p.m., approximately every 45 minutes. By Aviv *sherut* taxi service, at 6, Rehov Nordau, Tel: (04) 666333, approximately every hour from 6 a.m. to 5 p.m.

Getting to the Land Exits

To Jordan (Allenby Bridge)

From Jerusalem: By *sherut* taxi service from Damascus Gate.

From Jericho, Bethlehem, Hebron, Ramallah and Gaza: By *sherut* taxi service from the center of each town. Tourists who wish to leave by other means of transportation must coordinate their departure with the Tourism Staff Officer, Judea and Samaria, Tel: (02) 955318 or with the Allenby Bridge Tourist Information Office, Tel: (02) 922531.

To Egyptian Border Points

From Jerusalem: By *sherut* taxi service from Damascus Gate.

From Tel Aviv: By *sherut* service from Central Bus Station.

In addition to these shuttles, practically every tourist agency in Israel offers inexpensive round-trip bus service in air-conditioned buses which leave daily except on *Shabbat* (Saturdays).

Both El Al and Air Sinai also offer several flights to Cairo per week, which although much more expensive, cut the travel time down from 10 hours to less than 55 minutes.

The Egyptian government requires that you exchange a

certain number of dollars into Egyptian currency to enter the country. Often these regulations can be waived if you are part of a tourist package, which includes accommodation and round-trip transportation.

Visas for Egypt cost approximately $15 and can be obtained from the Egyptian Consulate in Tel Aviv, at 54 Rehov Basel, Tel Aviv, 62744, tel: (03) 224151.

Rented cars are **not** permitted to cross the border. As with the airport, all visitors leaving through the land borders are expected to pay a transit tax.

Foreign Currency: Tourists may bring an unlimited amount of foreign currency into Israel, whether in cash, traveler's checks, letters of credit or State of Israel bonds. They may also bring in an unlimited amount of Israel shekels but are allowed to take out only a minimum amount. No declarations of foreign currency are required.

Tourists who have exchanged foreign currency (dollars) into Israeli currency (shekel), may re-exchange their money into dollars by presenting the **receipt of the transaction** up to a maximum of $500.

This may be done at any bank in Israel during the course of your visit. However, upon departure from Israel, only a maximum of $100 may be exchanged at Ben-Gurion International Airport, after having gone through customs and passport control.

Refund of V.A.T.: After clearing the customs, apply to Bank Leumi B.N. in the exit hall. A refund of V.A.T. (Value Added Tax) of 15 percent is made at the point of your departure from Israel. However, you must make sure that:

1. The total net sum (after the 15 percent reduction) on one invoice is not less than $50. The following items are **not** included in this scheme: tobacco products, electrical appliances and accessories, cameras, film and photographic equipment.

2. The purchased items are packed in a plastic bag with at least one transparent side.

3. The original invoice (white) is placed inside the bag in such a manner that the entries on it can be read.

4. The bag is sealed or glued shut.

5. The bag must remain sealed during your entire stay in Israel.

6. Upon departure, pres-ent the sealed bag with the purchased goods to the Customs Official for approval of refund.

After checking and placing the stamp of approval on the invoice, the Official will direct you to the bank counter where the refund will be made in U.S. dollars.

Export of Antiquities: It is forbidden to export antiquities from Israel unless a written export permit has been obtained from the Department of Antiquities and Museums of the Ministry of Education and Culture, Jerusalem. This applies also to antiquities which accompany tourists leaving the country. Antiquities proven to have been imported after 1900 will be exempted.

Antiquities are defined as objects fashioned by man before 1700. A 10 percent export fee is payable upon the purchase price of every item approved for export.

The articles must be despatched by post, with an accompanying check for the appropriate amount, or taken in person to: The Department of Antiquities and Rockefeller Museum, opposite Herod's Gate. P.O.B. 586, Jerusalem. For personal visits, phone (02) 278627 for an appointment.

INSIDE JERUSALEM

GETTING ACQUAINTED

The State of Israel was proclaimed on May 14, 1948. It is a parliamentary democracy, with a President elected by the 120-member single-chamber *Knesset* (parliament), which itself is elected by universal suf-frage. The Prime Minister heads the Government.

Climate: Israeli summers are long (from April to October), hot and virtually rainless. During these months, the atmosphere in the hill towns such as Jerusalem and Safed is drier and cooler than in other parts of the country. Winters (from November to March), are generally mild but quite cold in hilly areas.

Spells of rain are interspersed with brilliant sunshine. During this period the Tiberias area on the Sea of Galilee, the Dead Sea and Eilat, on the Gulf of Eilat, all have warm, sunny weather.

The weather in Israel al-lows for year-round bathing: from April to October, along the Mediterranean coast and around the Sea of Galilee; and throughout the year, but especially enjoyable in winter, along the Dead Sea shore and the Gulf of Eilat.

Mean Temperatures (Minimum—Maximum)

	January	April	July	October
Jerusalem				
Fahrenheit	42.8—53.0	53.1—69.4	65.7— 83.5	60.4—77.9
Celsius	6.0—11.1	11.7—20.8	19.7— 28.6	15.8—25.5
Tel Aviv				
Fahrenheit	48.9—64.9	54.3—72.1	69.8— 86.4	59.0—83.8
Celsius	9.4— 8.3	12.4—22.3	21.0— 30.2	15.0—28.8
Haifa				
Fahrenheit	45.7—63.3	54.7—77.9	68.2— 85.8	59.9—81.3
Celsius	7.6—17.4	12.6—25.5	20.1— 29.9	15.5—27.4
Tiberias				
Fahrenheit	48.0—64.9	55.8—80.1	73.0— 97.9	65.3—89.2
Celsius	8.9—18.3	13.2—26.7	22.8— 36.6	18.5—31.8
Eilat				
Fahrenheit	49.3—70.3	62.8—87.3	77.5—103.3	68.7—91.9
Celsius	9.6—21.3	17.1—30.7	25.3— 39.6	20.4—33.3

Clothing: Dress in Israel is informal by Western standards. Few people wear jackets and ties in summer except for business. However, even in summer Jerusalem can get quite cool in the evenings. Be sure to bring some conservative clothes, in any case, for visiting religious sites.

A suggested packing list might include the following:

Summer (April—October): Lightweight suit, slacks, shorts and open-necked shirts for men; plenty of light cotton daytime dresses and evening wear for more formal occasions for women; light shoes, sandals and closed shoes for touring; sunglasses, hat, swimsuit and beachwear; a light coat, jacket or sweater for cool evenings in the hills.

Winter (November—March): Warm coat, sweaters, raincoat and hat, walking shoes, overshoes; shirts, slacks, sports jacket and formal suit for men; woollen or heavy suit, blouses, skirts and slacks, long dress or evening skirt for women; lighter clothing and swimsuit for Eilat and the Dead Sea coast.

If you forget anything, don't panic—the shops in Israel have high-quality clothes for all occasions.

Time Zone: Israel is two hours ahead of Greenwich Mean Time, and seven hours ahead of New York's Eastern Standard Time. This means that when it is noon in Tel Aviv, it is:
Noon in
Athens, Cairo.
11.00 a.m. in
Paris, Rome, Madrid.
10 00 a.m. in
London.
7 00 a.m. in

Rio de Janeiro.
5.00 a.m. in
New York, Montreal.
4 00 a.m. in
Chicago.
2 00 a.m. in
Los Angeles.
Midnight in
Honolulu.
8 00 a.m. in
Sydney.
7.00 p.m. in
Tokyo.
5.30 p.m. in
Singapore.
3.30 p.m. in
Bombay.
1.00 p.m. in
Moscow.

Geography: A Middle East crossroads of continents, Israel is bordered by the Mediterranean in the west, the Great Syrian-African Rift in the east and the Red Sea (also part of the Rift) in the south. Lebanon, Syria, Jordan and Egypt are her immediate neighbors.

Israel is a small country, with a total area (including the administered territories) of 21,000 sq. km (8,108 sq. miles)—roughly the size of New Jersey.

The northern and central part of Israel, where most of the population is concentrated, is divided into three distinct longitudinal strips: to the west, the coastal plain with the large cities of Tel Aviv and Haifa; to the east, the Jordan and Arava Valleys with the River Jordan linking the two inland seas—the Sea of Galilee and the Dead Sea; and in the center, the mountain range that includes the hills of Galilee, Samaria and Judea with the capital, Jerusalem.

In the northeast, rise the Golan Heights and the snow-capped Mt. Hermon; and in the south stretches the Negev Desert with Beersheba as the capital and Eilat on the Gulf of Eilat. Altitudes vary from the 1,200 m (3,900 feet) of Mt. Meron in the Upper Galilee, to the -400 meters (-1,300 feet) of the Dead Sea, the lowest spot on earth.

Since 1967, Israel has been in possession of the West Bank, including the hills of Judea and Samaria, and the Gaza Strip. The status of these areas remains unresolved. They are known alternately as the "administered territories" or the "occupied territories" depending on the speaker. The Golan Heights, which Israel won from Syria in 1967, were officially annexed by Israel in 1981.

Population: The population of Israel, including the administered territories, at the end of 1983 was about 4.1 million of which nearly 3.5 million were Jews. The rest comprised Christians, Moslems, Druze and other minorities.

Religions: Israel is home to quite a number of religions, including Jews, Moslems, Samaritans, Protestants, Armenians, Catholics, Copts, Eastern Orthodox, Druze, Bahai and Black Hebrews. All denominations are free to worship in their own ways, maintain their religious and charitable institutions and administer their internal affairs. The inviolability of Holy Places and

centers of worship of all faiths is guaranteed by law.

Each religious body has the statutory right to observe its own weekly rest day and holy days. The Jewish Sabbath (Saturday) and holy days are official holidays in the country.

Calendar: Israel observes a lunar year in accordance with Jewish religious tradition, with the New Year occuring in September/October, with the holiday of *Rosh Hashana*. But the standard Gregorian system is also used.

The work week runs from Sunday to Thursday, and most businesses are open on Friday mornings. From sunset Friday to sunset Saturday, however, everything is shut down in observance of the Jewish Sabbath or *Shabbat*. All banks and public services, including buses and other forms of transportation, are affected. Most of these services resume by Saturday evening.

Moslems and Christians observe their holy days on Fridays and Sundays, respectively.

Banking Hours: Sundays, Tuesdays and Thursdays from 8:30 a.m. to 12:30 p.m. and 4 to 5:30 p.m.; Mondays and Wednesdays from 8:30 a.m. to 12:30 p.m. only. Fridays and eve of holy days from 8:30 a.m. to noon. Branches in the leading hotels usually offer more convenient banking hours.

Electrical Appliances: The voltage in use in Israel is 220 volts A.C., single phase,

50 cycles. Israeli sockets are usually three-pronged, and foreign-made appliances often require an adaptor for the plug. Electric shavers, traveling irons, etc. should be equipped with adaptors to match local voltage or transformers, which can be purchased in Israel.

Weights and Measures:
These are in metric.
1 meter: 1.094 yards
1 kilometer: 0.62 miles
1 dunam (1,000 sq. m.):
  0.25 acres
1 liter: 1.76 pints
4.546 liters: 1 gallon
1 kilogram: 2.2 pounds

Local Currency: After years of fluctuating wildly, the Israeli monetary system has finally stabilized. The currency is the New Israeli Shekel (N.I.S.), the successor to the old Israeli Shekel (I.S.), which was phased out of usage during the fall of 1985. The currency was then devalued by a degree of 1000. Thus the old 1000 I.S. note became one N.I.S., and 100 I.S. became 10 agorot, the equivalent of cents.

Bills are issued in three denominations: five N.I.S. (blue, with portrait of Levi Eshkol), 10 N.I.S. (orange, with portrait of Golda Meir) and 50 N.I.S. (purple, with portrait of Shmuel Agnon). Change comes in denominations of one agora, five agorot, 10 agorot, half shekel (N.I.S.), and one shekel (N.I.S.). Confusingly, the one shekel coin is the smallest of the lot.

Prices are regulated, and exchange rates are the same in all banks.

As of mid-1986, the currency stabilised at approximately 1.5 shekels (N.I.S.) to the U.S. dollar. This experience is a first, and may well change in time.

Credit Cards: The most widely accepted credit cards in Israel are Visa and American Express. Also accepted by many hotels and restaurants are Eurocard and Diners Club.

Travelers Checks: By and large, travelers checks are quite widely accepted.

Etiquette: After receiving some service or purchase, it is polite to say *toda*—"thanks,"or *toda raba*—"thanks very much." Often the response will be *bevakasha*—"please," or *alo davar*—"it's nothing." The standard "hello" or "goodbye" is *shalom.* "How are you?' is *Ma Shlomcha?* to a man or *Ma Shlomayach?* to a woman. "See you" is expressed by *lehitra'ot*.

Tipping in better restaurants is similar to the European standard of 10—15 percent. *Sherut* are not tipped—cab drivers needn't be, but it will be appreciated.

Be extremely sensitive to religious etiquette. Women should dress conservatively (no legs or shoulders exposed, at the very least), and men should wear shirts and pants, when visiting holy sites. When visiting Jewish shrines or memorials it's also standard for men to cover their heads; if you don't have a *kepah* or hat, a cardboard substitute is discreetly provided.

In certain religious Jewish neighborhoods, these conservative rules of dress apply as general practice. While not all Israelis observe it, you should be aware that religious Jews see the Sabbath as a holy day and smoking or other behaviour can be considered offensive in an improper context.

Associations: The following Israeli branches have regular meetings and extend a warm welcome to overseas members: B'nai Brith, Freemasons, Rotary, Soroptomists, Lions, Skal, WIZO and Hadassah.

COMMUNICATIONS

Post Offices: Israel's numerous post offices are identified by a logo of a white stag leaping across a dark blue background. Post boxes are red and carry this logo. They are not abundant, but all hotels usually have a drop-off slot.

It takes 10 days for mail to reach a European destination, and a couple of days longer to the United States.

Stamps can be obtained from most hotels, stationers and souvenir shops as well as from the post offices.

Telegrams can be sent from any post office on weekdays only.

Post offices open from 8 a.m. to 12:30 p.m. and 3:30 to 6 p.m. The main branches in the large cities are open all day.

All post offices are closed on the Sabbath and holy

days, though central telegraph offices are open day and night 365 days a year.

Telephones:
Special Telephone Numbers
Information-14
Time-15
Telephone Repairs-16
Overseas Operator-(03) 622881
Direct Dialling Information-195
Telegrams-171
Auto Alarm
(wake-up calls)-174
Public telephone booths can be found throughout the country. Virtually all of them are operated by tokens (*asimonim*) which can be purchased at post offices and at the reservations desk of some hotels. Long-distance as well as intra-city calls can be made with these tokens. Telephones in pharmacies, shops and restaurants are often available for public use, for local calls only. A call from a phone without a slot machine will cost you more than a call from a public booth.

Long-distance and overseas calls can be booked at your hotel or at a post office. There is also direct dialling to many countries. The local telephone directory is published in Hebrew.

Two warnings: when telephoning abroad by direct dialling, you may have to wait a while for the operator at 18 to come on. Also, many of the public telephones are in poor condition, so having *asimonim* in hand is no guarantee that you will be able to complete a call from a public phone booth.

English-language phone books are available at most post offices and hotels, as is the Golden Pages classified directory.

Media: Having accessibility to news is very important for Israelis, due to their unique geopolitical situation. Listening to the hourly news updates on the radio—in the taxi, on the bus, as well as at home—is a ritualistic part of the daily routine here. There is censorship only in regards to security matters.

The country has over two dozen daily newspapers, the majority of which are printed in English. The English-language daily is the *Jerusalem Post*, which is widely available in all cities. On Fridays, it comes with a weekend supplement which contains listings of all major events, including film, theater, concerts, radio and television. On Mondays, there are excerpts from the *Sunday New York Times*. (There is no Saturday edition).

Radio and Television: Radio programs are broadcast daily in English, Arabic, French, Yiddish, Ladino and other languages. News in English and French is broadcast three times daily. T.V. programs include news, local and foreign entertainment and films.

Kol Israel (Voice of Israel) operates five radio stations, which are on the air some 18 hours a day. Their fare varies from pop music and rock 'n' roll to talk shows, commentary and news broadcasts. There are also Arabic-language and classical music stations.

Israel Television broadcasts educational programs during the day, followed by news and entertainment shows in the evenings. News is usually in Hebrew and Arabic, although many of the other movies and programs are imports from the U.S. or Britain. Jordan Television offers competing entertainment as well. Daily newspapers carry details.

HEALTH & EMERGENCIES

Health: There are no vaccination requirements for tourists entering Israel. Vaccinations against smallpox is required by some countries of travelers returning from abroad. It is advisable, therefore, for visitors to check the health regulations of their own country and, if vaccination is required after a visit to Israel, to obtain it before departure.

Tourists who are already in Israel and wish to obtain vaccination against smallpox, cholera and yellow fever can do so at any district or sub-district office of the Ministry of Health.

Further information from: Ministry of Health, Department of Epidemiology, 38 Rehov Keren Hayesod, Jerusalem, Tel: (02) 638212, or any District Health Office throughout the country.

Emergency Assistance

Police emergencies: In Jerusalem, Tel Aviv and Haifa, phone 100.

Fire emergencies: In these cities, phone 102.

Medical assistance: A high professional standard is obtainable at all times, and most doctors speak English or other foreign languages. For emergency or first aid, call **Magen David Adom**, the equivalent of the Red Cross, (101 in Jerusalem, Tel Aviv and Haifa). Emergency hospitals and pharmacies which are open in the evenings, during weekends and on holy days in the various cities are listed in the daily newspapers.

Visitors temporarily in need of such **medical equipment** as oxygen tanks, wheelchairs, vaporizers, and a host of other items can obtain them on loan, at no charge, at the Yad Sarah Organization for the Free Loan of Medical Equipment, Jerusalem: 49 Rehov Haneviim, (02) 244242, 244047; Tel Aviv: 14a Rehov Ruppin, (03) 238974; Haifa: 4A Rehov Mapu, Ahuza, (04) 245286; Rehovot: 31 Rehov Ezra, in addition to numerous other branches throughout the country.

Dental emergency: Treatments are available during weekends and on holy days, in Jerusalem through the Magen David Adom, and in Tel Aviv at 49 Rehov Bar Kokhba.

Facilities for the Handicapped

At the Airport: Disabled passengers, particularly those confined to wheelchairs, will find sufficient facilities in all sections— widened doorways to the duty-free shops, lowered public phones, widened access in public restrooms, lowered tables in the snack bar, free parking at the terminal entrance and strategically located ramps. There is a specially constructed lift to the planes for the boarding and disembarking of wheelchairs. Ben-Gurion is the only airport in the world with such a facility.

Hire of Wheelchairs:
Folding wheelchairs can be hired—subject to availability—from:

Jerusalem
The Alyn Orthopaedic Hospital for Crippled Children
Rehov Shemaryahu Levin
Kiryat Hayovel
Sundays—Thursdays
9:00 a.m. to 1:00 p.m.
Tel: (02) 412251

Yad Sarah
43 Rehov Hanevi'im
Yad operates over 30 lending stations in Israel.

Dialysis Service for Tourists

Elisha Private Hospital
Mount Carmel
Haifa
Tel: (04) 81419

Security: While Tel Aviv and most Israeli cities are fairly free of crime, you should take common sense precautions. When parking a car, don't leave items on display and doors unlocked. Don't walk alone at night in unknown areas. In places such as Jerusalem, with some inter-racial tensions, take special care not to walk around at night in suspicious areas, or the Arab areas of the Old City.

Though incidents are rare, Israelis are always on the alert for possible bombs. If you see a suspicious or unattended package in a public area, report it to the police. Similarly, do not leave your own bags or luggage unattended in public areas or risk attracting police sappers to the scene.

Traveling in the West Bank or other occupied territories carries its own inherent risks. Always check with a government representative to find out the status of the region before setting out, and arrange for your return transportation in advance.

Political diplomacy will go a long way in easing tensions for you in such places. For example, it is best not to argue the pros and cons of Israeli control of the West Bank, and you would be best off using the Arabic *El Quds* instead of the Hebrew *Yerushalayim* when refering to Jerusalem.

Israeli soldiers and police are numerous, and can always answer questions if necessary. Women are advised not to travel alone where possible.

Spelling: Because there is no standardized spelling of place names, one has "Acre," "Akko" and "Acco"; "Nathanya," "Natanya" and "Netanya"; "Elat," "Elath" and "Eilat"; "Ashqelon" and "Ashkelon"; "S'fat," "Zefat," "Tzfat" and "Safed," etc. As if to confound the visitor, all are used freely.

Tourist Information:
You won't be at a loss for tourist information while in Israel. In fact, you may very well feel inundated by the many weeklies and other literature in your hotel room.

The Israel Government Tourist Office (IGTOs) are the only official purveyors of information, however, and are more than willing to provide you with maps and help recommend restaurants or accommodation, so long as you know what you are looking for. They also will have information about free tours and events.

For specific information about different areas in the country, it is best to contact the local IGTO directly:

Acco
Municipality Building
Tel: (04) 910251

Alleny Bridge
(Israel—Jordan transit point)
Tel: (02) 922531

Arad
Commercial Center
Tel: (057) 98144

Ashkelon
Commercial Center
Afridar
Tel: (051) 32412

Bat Yam
Municipality Building
Information Office
43 Derech Ben Gurion
Tel: (03) 589766

Beersheba
Rehov Nordau
Tel: (057) 36001

Ben-Gurion Airport
Lod
Tel: (03) 971485/7

Bethlehem
Manager Square
Tel: (02) 742591

Eilat
Rechter Commercial Center
Sderot Hatmarim
Tel: (059) 72268, 76737

Hotel Neptune
North Shore
Tel: (059) 74233

Haifa
(Town Branch)
18 Rehov Herzl
Tel: (04) 666521

(Port Branch)
Shed No. 12
Haifa Port (open only ships dock)
Tel: (04) 663988

Jerusalem
24 Rehov Hamelech George
Tel: (02) 241281

Jaffa Gate
Tel: (02) 282295/6

Municipal Information Office
34 Rehov Yafo
Tel: (02) 922121

Nazareth
Rehov Casanoval
Tel: (065) 70555. 73003

Netanya
Kikar HaAtzmaut
Tel: (053) 27286

Rafiah
(Israel—Egypt transit point)

Tel: (04) 37899

Rosh Hanikra
(Israel—Lebanon transit point)
Tel: (04) 927802

Safed
Municipality Building
Central Bus Station
27 Rehov Jerusalem
Tel: (067) 30633

Tel Aviv
7 Rehov Mendele
Tel: (03) 223266/7

Tiberias
8 Rehov Alhadeff
Tel: (067) 20992

In New York, there is an IGTO branch on the 19th floor of the Empire State Building, 350 Fifth Ave., N.Y., NY10118. Offices are also located in Miami Beach, Houston, Chicago, Los Angeles and Toronto.

In Europe, there are IGTOs in London, Paris, Amsterdam, Copenhagen, Stockholm, Zurich, Frankfurt and Milan. There are also offices in Johannesburg, South Africa, and Cairo, Egypt.

Travel Agencies: If you have no fixed agenda, are traveling independently, and want to see more of the country, there are literally hundreds of travel agencies and tour companies that would love to help show you around. The tours range from half-day excursions to round-trip weekends to Egypt or the Sinai, to all-out visits around the country. Most of the travel offices are located near the densest tourist areas—Ben Yehudah Street in Jerusalem—and are, therefore, accessible.

Tour Guides: If you can afford the price, hire a private tour guide, with car, to take you around independently. Israel, in fact, has a special school for tour guides, who need to complete a two-year program to get accredited. When they graduate, these individuals have a sound knowledge of the country's landscape and history, but each guide usually tells the story from his own angle. Many of the best ones have their names passed around by word-of-mouth, the IGTO will also provide recommendations if need be, or at least, steer you in the right direction.

Bar & Bat Mitzvah: For arrangments for *bar mitzvah* and *bat mitzvah* ceremonies at the Western Wall, contact, no later than six weeks prior to the date: Naomi Rosenberg, The Ministry of Tourism, 24 Rehov Hamelech George, Jerusalem, Tel: (02) 237311.

Youth Tours: The Israel Student Tourist Association (ISSTA) arranges low-cost flights to and from Israel and offers young visitors a variety of tours including safaris and work camps. The association also issues and renews International Student Identity Cards. The ISSTA representative at Ben-Gurion Airport answers all queries on *kibbutzim*, archaeological digs, hotels and hostels, buses, taxis, inland flights, discounts and so on.

Its offices are located in Israel's three main cities:

Tel Aviv
109 Rehov Ben Yehudah
Tel: (02): 247164/5

Jerusalem
5 Rehov Elishar
Tel: (02) 225258

Haifa
Hakranot
Rehov Herlz
Tel: (04) 669139

Meet the Israeli: The best way to get to know the people of Israel is to meet them in their homes. Israeli families from all walks of life are happy to extend hospitality to tourists. Arrangements can be made through Tourist Information Offices for tourists to meet those of their own profession and/or Israelis with similar interests.

Recorded Messages: By dialing (03) 223266 tourists can receive information on events in the Tel Aviv area. Tourists can also leave a message should they have any questions, and they will be contacted the next day. This service operates after 6 p.m. Sundays to Thursdays and Fridays after 3 p.m. Jerusalem has a similar service: the tourist may dial (02) 244197 after 6 p.m. Sunday to Thursdays and after 2 p.m. on Fridays. Haifa has a 24-hour telephone service; to hear "What's on in Haifa" call (04) 640840.

ON THE MOVE

TRANSPORT

Buses: Buses are by far the most common means of public transportation for both urban and inter-urban travel. They give regular service and fares are reasonable. When traveling between cities, you can get a round-trip ticket at the bus station at a further discount. The bus fare from Tel Aviv to Jerusalem is approximately $2 one-way, or $3.50 for a round-trip. For long distance trips, especially to Eilat, it is advisable to book a seat a few days in advance. With a few exceptions, buses do not run on the Sabbath, from late afternoon Friday to late afternoon Saturday.

In most areas, bus services start around 5.a.m. The inter-city routes usually run until evening, with the exception of the main routes, Tel Aviv—Jerusalem and Tel Aviv—Haifa, which continue until 11:30 p.m. Bus services within these main cities cease for the day at around midnight.

Most inner-city and city buses are run by the Egged line. In addition, Round-About-Tickets are available at all Egged Tour Offices in Israel for periods of seven, 14, 21 or 30 days. Possession of the ticket allows one unlimited travel anywhere in Israel except for Tel Aviv.

Egged Information Offices:

Haifa
Tel: (04) 515221

Jerusalem
Tel: (02) 551711

Tel Aviv
Tel: (03) 251333

Railways: The Israel Railways run from Haifa and Nahariya in the north and from Tel Aviv to Jerusalem daily. Train fares are considerably lower than bus fares, and seats can be reserved in advance for a small extra charge. Most of the trains are rather old, but all have a buffet car and service, and the trip from Tel Aviv to Jerusalem is particularly lovely, winding through the scenic Sorek valley. There is no train service on the Sabbath, or on Jewish holy days.

Main train stations:

Haifa
Bat Galim
Tel: (04) 531211

Kikar Plumer
Tel: (04) 531211

Jerusalem
Kikar Remex
Tel: (02) 717764

Tel Aviv
Central Station
Rehov Arlosorov
Tel: (03) 254271

South Station
Tel: (03) 254271

Student Discount: On presentation of a student card, a 10 percent discount on all inter-city Egged Bus Company trips and a 25 percent discount on Israel Railways is available.

Taxis and Sherut: Taxis offer a quick and convenient mode of travel in Israel. You can phone for a taxi in any major city or just hail them in the street.

All urban taxis have meters, and it is compulsory for drivers to turn them on. Beware if your driver wants to turn off the meter: he might take you for a ride in more ways than one.

Prices are pre-fixed between cities, and the driver will tell you your fare ahead of time, or show you the official price list if you ask for it. Tipping is not compulsory, but greatly appreciated.

The *sherut* is Israel's own indigenous mode of transportation, operating in and between main cities every day but *Shabbat*, although some private companies or owners operate on *Shabbat*, too. In the *sherut*, individuals share a van or cab, which accommodates up to seven people, at a fixed price usually equivalent to the bus fare for the same route.

Sheruts between cities leave from near the central bus station, and, in Jerusalem, from near Zion Square. In Tel Aviv and some other cities, local *sheruts* follow the main bus routes, making similar stops in quick time.

Rental Cars: Self-drive rented cars are becoming increasingly popular and some of the internationally-known companies will reserve a car for you to collect on arrival at the airport.

The various rent-a-car companies will accept either an international driving licence or a national driving licence issued by a country which recognizes the Israeli licence and printed in English or French. National licences printed in any other language must be accompanied by a certificate of confirmation in Hebrew.

Moped Rental: Otzma B'tnua Mehira B.M. (Power Through Speed Ltd.) is licensed by the Ministry of Transport to rent mopeds. They may be rented by people aged 18 and over who hold a special licence. For further information, contact: Otzma B'Tnua Mehira, 46 Rehov Ha'aliya, Tel Aviv, Tel: (03) 834105.

Road Regulations: Traffic travels on the right side and overtakes on the left side. Priority is given to the driver coming from the right—unless otherwise shown on the international road signs.

Distances on the road signs are always given in kilometers. One kilometer is equal to 0.621 miles. The speed limit is 50 kph (about 30 mph) in built-up areas and 80 kph (about 50 mph) on open roads, except for those authorized. Safety belts are compulsory on all inter-urban journeys.

Touring Club: The Automobile and Touring Club of Israel (MEMS) is affiliated to the Federation Internationale de l'Automobile (F.I.A.) and to the Alliance Internationale de Tourisme (A.I.T.), and as such is linked to every automobile and touring club in the world, providing reciprocal services for all tourists who are members of other clubs. Services include: emergency help, towing and providing legal, technical and touring advice.

Tel Aviv
Head Office
19 Derech Petach Tikva
Tel: (03) 622961

Address for correspondence
P.O.B. 36144
61360 Tel Aviv

Hitch-Hiking: Although hitching is widely practised in Israel, it is not advisable as a means of transport, since most drivers will give rides mainly or only to soldiers.

Table of Road Distances

	Jerusalem		Tel A iv		Haifa	
	Km	mi	Km	Mi	Km	Mi
Jerusalem	—	—	62	39	159	99
Tel Aviv	62	39	—	—	95	59
Haifa	159	99	95	56	—	—
Arad	104	65	158	98	255	158
Ashdod	66	41	42	26	139	86
Beersheba	84	52	113	70	210	130
Eilat	312	194	354	220	451	280
Hebron	35	22	97	60	194	120
Metula	221	137	196	122	120	75
Nablus	63	38	57	35	93	58
Nazareth	157	97	102	63	35	22
Netanya	93	58	29	18	66	41
Rehovot	53	33	24	15	121	75
Rosh Hanikra	201	125	137	82	69	43
Tiberias	157	97	132	82	69	43

NB: Distances indicated are measured along the most convenient routes, which are not always the shortest ones.

Subway: Israel's only subway, the Carmelit, operates in Haifa. The train runs from Central Mt. Carmel to downtown Haifa every ten minutes and makes six stops. The trip takes nine minutes. It operates Sunday to Thursday, from 5:30 a.m. to noon; Friday, from 5:30 a.m. to one hour before the Sabbath; and on Saturday, from sunset to midnight.

Inland Air Travel

Scheduled flights: Arkia Israel Airlines Ltd. operate the following:

From Jerusalem to Tel Aviv, Haifa, Rosh Pinna, Eilat.

From Tel Aviv to Jerusalem, Rosh, Pinna, Eilat.

From Haifa to Jerusalem, Tel Aviv, Eilat.

From Eilat to Jerusalem, Tel Aviv, Haifa.

A number of other companies operate charter flights (three to 10 passengers) to various parts of the country. Further particulars may be obtained from Travel agents or from Government Tourist Information Offices.

El—Rom Airlines operate air services from Beersheba to Tel Aviv, Eilat, Jerusalem and Haifa and from Tel Aviv, Eilat to Mitzpeh Ramon and Sodom.

For further information:

Arkia Israeli Airlines Ltd.
Sde Dov Airport
Tel Aviv
Tel: (03) 424266

El—Rom Airlines Ltd.
97 Rehov Herzl
Beersheba
Tel: (057) 75477

IN TRANSIT

WHERE TO STAY

The range of possible accommodation in Israel is staggering. One night in a hostel, plus modest breakfast, might cost $7—$10, while the same items in a luxury hotel would run 15 times as much.

Other options include holiday villages and *kibbutz* guest houses, or inns, which also vary widely in cost, but are an indigenous form of hostelry, and camping for the ultra-budget-minded. Time-sharing and apartment rentals are also available for the more committed.

Youth Hostels: There are over 30 youth hostels throughout the country, operated by the Israel Youth Hostel Association (IYHA) which is affiliated with the international YHA. They offer dormitory accommodation and most of them provide both meals and self-service kitchen facilities. There is no age limit. Some hostels also provide family accommodation. Individual reservations should be made directly with the hostel.

The IYHA also arranges individual package tours, called "Israel on the Youth Hostel Trail" for 14, 21 or 28 days. These include nights in any of the hostels with dinner and breakfast, unlimited bus travel, a half-day conducted tour, entrance to 31 national parks and numerous museums, a map, and other information materials.

For further information:

Head Office—IYHA
3 Rehov Dorot Rishonim
P.O.B. 1075
91009 Jerusalem
Tel: (02) 240220, 222073

Ein Kerem
P.O.B. 17013
91170 Jerusalem
Tel: (02) 416282

Louise Waterman-Wise
8 Rehov Hapisga
Bayit Vegan
Jerusalem
Tel: (02) 423366, 420990

Moreshet Yahadut
P.O.B. 7880
91009 Jerusalem
Tel: (02) 288611

Ramot Shapira
P.O.B. 7216
Beit Meir, Jerusalem
Tel: (02) 913291

Tel Aviv
32 Rehov Bnei Dan
Tel Aviv
Tel: (03) 455042, 460719

Youth Center
Jerusalem Forest
P.O.B. 3353
91033 Jerusalem
Tel: (02) 416060, 412246, 413065

Kibbutz Inns: Ranging from Kfar Giladi in Northern Galilee to Ein Gedi on the shores of the Dead Sea, Israel's *kibbutz* guest houses offer a host of overnight facilities—including camping in your own tent or caravan with self-catering on the Kinneret, staying at holiday villages on the sea shore or in three-star guest houses in the Judean Hills, Sharon Plains, Mt. Carmel and in the Galilee.

The Galilee also has two four-star guest houses. Israel's guest houses have a friendly and personal atmosphere, the food is fresh and they give you an unique way to see something new and unusual. Guests can meet *kibbutz* members and tour with or without a guide, and to experience that different way of life.

Nof Ginosar***
Kibbutz Ginosar, 14986
Tel: (067) 92161—3
(170 rooms)

Beit Hava**
Shavei Zion
Tel: (04) 92239/2
(85 rooms)

Beit Oren**
Mt. Carmel, 30040
Tel: (04) 222111/2
(67 rooms)

Gesher Haziv**
Western Galilee
Tel: (04) 927711
(48 rooms)

Hafetz Haim**
Kibbutz Hafetz Haim, 76817
Tel: (055) 93888
(57 rooms)

Hagoshrim**
Kibbutz Hagoshrim
MP Upper Galilee
Tel: (067) 45231
(121 rooms)

Kfar Blum*
Kibbutz Kfar Blum
Upper Galilee, 12150
Yel: (067) 43666
(46 rooms)

Kfar Giladi*
Upper Galilee
Tel: (067) 41414/5
(155 rooms)

Kiryat Anavim*
Judean Hills
Tel: (02) 54269
(93 rooms)

Lavi*
Kibbutz Lavi
Lower Galilee, 15267
Tel: (067) 21477
(124 rooms)

Ma'ale Hahamisha*
Judean Hills, 90835
Tel: (02) 542591/7
(121 rooms)

Neve Llan*
Judean Hills
Tel: (02) 541241
(80 rooms)

Nir Etrion*
MP Carmel Beach, 30808
Tel: (04) 942541/3
(74 rooms)

Shefayim*
Kibbutz Shefayim
Tel: (052) 70171, 70612
(110 rooms)

Shoresh*
Judean Hills
Tel: (02) 541171/4
(114 rooms)

For further information, contact:
Kibbutz Inns
90 Rehov Ben Yehuda
61031 Tel Aviv
Tel: (03) 246161

Holiday Villages: Excellent accommodation can be found at Israel's seashore holiday villages. They offer a wide variety of water sports, including swimming, water skiing, skin diving and sailing, as well as riding, tennis, full touring programs and evening entertainment. Predominantly geared to the younger set, with the emphasis on open-air life and informality, most villages are open during summer only.

Ein Gedi HV
MP Dead Sea
Tel: (057) 84757/8
(91 rooms)

Kfar Hamaccabiah Sport Hotel and Convention Center, HV
Rehov Bernstein, Ramat Gan, 52109
P.O.B. 919
Tel: (03) 779031
(103 rooms)

Manof Recreation Village, HV
DN Bikat Beit Kerem
Tel: (04) 914583, 914592
(10 apartments)

Metzoke Dragot, HV
Mitzpe Shalem
MP Jericho Valley
Tel: (057) 84340
(48 rooms)

Mitzpe Rachel
P.O.B. 98, Jerusalem
Tel: (02) 715712
(29 rooms)

Recreation Center, Jerusalem Forest
Yefei Nof Jerusalem Forest
P.O.B. 3353, Jerusalem

Tel: (02) 416060, 412246
(60 rooms)

Camping: Israel is a good country for camping, with camp sites providing an excellent touring base for each region. They offer full sanitary facilities, electricity, a restaurant and/or store, telephone, first-aid facilities, shaded picnic and campfire areas and 24-hour security. They can be reached by bus, but all are open to cars and caravans. Most have tents and cabins as well as a wide range of equipment for hire. All sites have swimming facilities either on the site or within easy reach. For full details contact the Israel Camping Union, P.O.B. 53, 22100 Nahariya, Tel: (04) 923366, 925392.

There is a reception and departure service for campers at Ben-Gurion Airport. By ringing (03) 944524 on arrival, a camping car comes within a very short time to take participants to the reception camping site at Mishmar Hashiva, about 10 km (six miles) from Ben-Gurion Airport. A similar service is available from Mishmar Hashiva to the airport upon departure, if you stay the last night there.

Arriving campers can obtain assistance from the Tourist Information Office in the Arrivals Hall. At the reception camp at Mishmar Hashiva, campers are given maps and folders and are individually advised on touring the country. Reception Site: Mishmar Hashiva, Tel: (03) 984524

Camping sites include Ashkelon, Eilat, Ein Gedi,

the Carmel Coast and Ramat Rachel, south of Jerusalem.

Private Apartments: For longer stay in one place, it can be very economical to rent an apartment, with its own kitchen, bedroom, living room, etc. For families it can mean a cheap way of accommodating the kids; for couples, individuals or groups it can mean a more natural experience of the country, living as the locals do, away from bellhops and room service.

Here, too, options range from the economical to the luxurious. There are several organizations that offer apartment rentals, in single or dispersed buildings.

One company with the greatest resources at its disposal is **Homtel Israel**, which has hundreds of apartments throughout Tel Aviv and Jerusalem, on the Mediterranean coast, on the Sea of Galilee, in Eilat, and other places. They also have offices in the U.S. and Europe. (See the following list).

Jerusalem
3 Ben Sira Street
Jerusalem
Tel: (02) 244-539

Tel Aviv
33 Dizengoff Street
Tel Aviv, 64282
Tel: (03) 289-503

London
Suite 604, Triumph House
189 Regent Street
London, W1R 7WF
Tel: (01) 4372892/3

New York
1170 Broadway, Suite 612

New York, NY10001
Tel: (212) 6869343

Time-Sharing: Time-sharing resorts are available in Tiberias, Eilat and Tel Aviv. Each of these locations are self-contained with sports facilities, swimming pools, restaurants and shops on the grounds.

Christian Hospices: Christians on a pilgrimage to the Holy Land may find board and lodgings, at reasonable prices, in hospices of various denominations all over the country. However, you do not have to be a pilgrim, or even a Christian, to enjoy the hospitality of these gracious, reflective inns.

Accommodation is in single, double, three-, four-, or six-bedrooms or rooms for groups; beds and breakfast, half-board or full board. Additional information from the Israel Tourism Administration, Pilgrimage, Youth and Students Division, 24 Rehov Hamelech George, 94261 Jerusalem, Tel: (02) 237311. Also: the Israel Pilgrimage Committee, P.O.B. 1018; Jerusalem and tourist information offices at home and abroad.

A complete list of Christian Hospices in Israel follows. (See also section entitled Pilgrimages).

Jerusalem

St. Charles Hospice
Order of St. Karl Borromaeus
Roman Catholic (German)
German Colony
P.O.B. 8020

Tel: (02) 637737

Sisters of the Rosary
Roman Catholic
14 Rehov Agron
P.O.B. 54
Tel: (02) 228529

Dom Polski
Order of the Sisters of Saint Elizabeth
Roman Catholic (Polish)
Hakhoma Hashlishit No. 8
Rehov Shivtei Yisrael
P.O.B. 277
Tel: (02) 285916

Filles de la Charité de St. Vincent de Paul
Roman Catholic (French)
Bethany Shiua
P.O.B. 19080
Tel: (02) 282017

Dom Polski
Near Damascus Gate
Old City
Tel: (02) 282017

Franciscaines de Marie "White Sisters"
Roman Catholic (French)
International
9 Derech Shechem
P.O.B. (02) 282633, 288909

St. Georges Hostel
Anglican/Episcopal
Derech Shechem and Rehov Salah Edin
P.O.B. 19018
Tel: (02) 283302

Evangelical Lutheran Hostel
Lutheran (German)
Guest House of the Propst
Old City
P.O.B. 14051
Tel: (02) 2842120

Maison D'Abraham

(Ras El Amuod)
P.O.B. 19680
Tel: (02) 2842120

Sisters of Nigrizia
Roman Catholic
(Italian Sisters)
Bethany Shiva
P.O.B. 19504
Tel: (02) 284724

Sisters of Zion (Ein Kerem)
P.O.B. 17015
Tel: (02) 419609, 415738

St. Andrew's Scots Memorial Hospice
Church of Scotland
(near the railway station)
P.O.B. 14216
Tel: (02) 717701
(Office: Closed Sunday)
Guests (02) 282791

Casa Nova Hospice
Franciscan Roman
Catholic
P.O.B. 1321
Tel: (02) 282791

Christ Church Hospice
Anglican Church (British)
Jaffa Gate
P.O.B. 14307
Tel: (02) 282082
Cables: HOSPITABLE—
JERUSALEM

Ecce Homo Convent
Notre Dame de Sion
Roman Catholic
Via Dolorosa
P.O.B. 19056
Tel: (02) 282445

Fraternite Dominicaine Bethesda
Roman Catholic
Monastére Maronite
22 Rehov St. Mark
P.O.B. 14386
Tel: (02) 285587

Armenian Catholic Church
Catholic
41 Via Dolorosa
3rd Station
P.O.B. 19546
Tel: (02) 284262

Foyer des Pelerins
Greek Catholic
Greek Catholic Patri-
archate
P.O.B. 14130
Tel: (02) 282023

Rumanian Hostel
Rumanian Orthodox
46 Rehov Shivtei Yisrael
Tel: (02) 287355

Foyer St. Joseph
Roman Catholic
Rehov Haneviim
P.O.B. 771
Tel: (02) 226874

St. Joseph House
Syrian Catholic Church
P.O.B. 199
Bethlehem
Tel: (02) 742497

Centre Notre Dame
Catholic Ecumenical
Opposite New Gate
P.O.B. 20531
Tel: (02) 289723/4/5
Tlx: 26526

Hotels: About 300 hotels, recommended to visitors by the Ministry of Tourism, are listed in the booklet: *Israel Tourist Hotels*, published by the Israel Hotel Association and available at any Government Tourist Information Office. They vary from simple establishments to five-star "big name" hotels. There are, in addition, numerous good pensions or boarding houses.

Hotel prices naturally vary according to grade and season but you will find a wide choice of accommodation to suit your tastes, purpose and purse. Hotel rates are quoted in U.S. dollars, and there is a 15 percent service charge.

The following is a list of hotels which are members of the Israel Hotel Association. They are graded in terms of stars—five stars means a hotel is very fancy (and expensive, usually), while two to three stars means it is more reasonably priced.

NYG means a hotel is not yet graded. NYL means a hotel is not listed by the Ministry of Tourism.

Neither of these categories reflect the quality of the hotel (the Imperial in Tel Aviv, for example, and the Menorah in Jerusalem are both pleasant, modern and fairly inexpensive).

Check-out time is noon at the latest; check-in, 2 p.m.

Jerusalem

Inter-Continental*****
Mt. of Olives
Tel: (02) 282551
(200 rooms)

Jerusalem Hilton*****
Givat Ram
Tel: (02) 536151
(420 rooms)

Jerusalem Plaza*****
47 Rehov Hamelech
George
Tel: (02) 228133
(414 rooms)

King David*****
23 Rehov Hamelech
David

Tel: (02) 221111
(258 rooms)

**King Solomon
Sheraton*******
32 Rehov Hamelech
David
Tel: (02) 241433
(150 rooms)

Mount Scopus*****
Sheikh Jarrah
Tel: (02) 284891/2
(65 rooms)

St. George International*****
Rehov Salah Adin
Tel: (02) 282571/2
(150 rooms)

Ambassador****
Derech Nablus
Sheikh Jarrah
Tel: (02) 282515
(118 rooms)

American Colony****
Derech Nablus, 97200
Tel: (02) 282421-3
(102 rooms)

Ariel****
31 Derech Hebron
Tel: (02) 719222
(140 rooms)

Capitol****
17 Rehov Salah Adin
Tel: (02) 282561/2
(54 rooms)

Central****
6 Rehov Pines, 99701
Tel: (02) 223111
(77 rooms)

Jerusalem Panorama
****
Hill of Gethsemane,
97400
Tel: (02) 284886/7
(74 rooms)

Kings****
60 Rehov Hamelech
George,
94262
Tel: (02) 247133
(214 rooms)

Moriah Jerusalem****
39 Rehov Keren Hayesod,
94188
Tel: (02) 232232
(301 rooms)

National Palace****
4 Rehov Az-Zahra
Tel: (02) 282246/8
(108 rooms)

Ritz****
8 Rehov Ibn Khadoun
Tel: (02) 284853/4
(103 rooms)

Shalom****
25 Rehov Shachrai Bayit
Vegan,
91160
Tel: (02) 423111, 422111
(688 rooms)

Alcazar***
6 Rehov Al Mutanbi Wadi
El Joz
East Jerusalem
Tel: (02) 28111, 288628,
288800
(38 rooms)

Christmas***
Rehov Salah Adin
Tel: (02) 282588
(24 rooms)

Commodore***
Mt. of Olives
Tel: (02) 284845
(45 rooms)

Eilon Tower***
34 Rehov Ben Yehudah,
94583
Tel: (02) 233281
(120 rooms)

Gloria***
Jaffa Gate
Tel: (02) 282431/2
(64 rooms)

Holyland East***
6 Rehov Rashid
Tel: (02) 284841/2
(105 rooms)

Jerusalem Tower***
23 Rehov Hillel, 94581
Tel: (02) 222161
(120 rooms)

Jordan House***
Rehov Nur El-Din
Tel: (02) 283430
(25 rooms)

Neve Shoshana***
5 Rehov Beit Hakerem
Tel: (02) 521740, 524294
(27 rooms)

New Metropole***
8 Rehov Salah Adin
Tel: (02) 283846
(25 rooms)

Palace***
Mt. of Olives Rd.
P.O.B. 19143
Tel: (02) 284981, 284523,
283884
(68 rooms)

Pilgrims Palace***
Rehov King Suleiman
Tel: (02) 284831, 283354
(95 rooms)

Ram***
234 Rehov Yafo, 91130
Tel: (02) 535231
(156 rooms)

Reich***
1 Rehov Hagar Beit Hakerem
Tel: (02) 523121
(54 rooms)

Shepherd***
Mt. Scopus
Tel: (02) 282271/2
(52 rooms)

Sonesta Jerusalem***
2 Rehov Wolfson Tel:
(02) 528221
(172 rooms)

Strand***
4 Rehov Ibn Jubeir
P.O.B. 20333
Tel: (02) 280279, 284998
(55 rooms)

Tirat Bat Sheva***
42 Rehov Hamelech
George
Tel: (02) 232121
(70 rooms)

Windmill***
3 Rehov Mendele, 92147
Tel: (02) 663111
(133 rooms)

**Y.M.C.A.—
Aelia Capitolina*****
29 Derech Nablus
Tel: (02) 282375/6
(57 rooms)

Y.W.C.A.***
Wadi Jos
Tel: (02) 282593
(30 rooms)

Astoria**
Mt. of Olives Rd.
Tel: (02) 282965
(23 rooms)

Azzahra**
13 Rehov Azzahra
Tel: (02) 282447
(24 rooms)

City**
Mt. Scopus
Tel: (02) 282472
(22 rooms)

Har Aviv**
16A Rehov Beit Hakerem
Tel: (02) 521515
(14 rooms)

Lawrence**
18 Rehov Salah Adin
Tel: (02) 282585
(30 rooms)

Metropole**
6 Rehov Salah Adin
Tel: (02) 282507
(30 rooms)

Mount of Olives**
Mt. of Olives Rd.
Tel: (02) 284877
(63 rooms)

New Orient House**
10 Rehov Abu Obideah
El Jarrah
Tel: (02) 282437
(22 rooms)

New Regent**
20 Rehov Az-Zahra
Tel: (02) 284540
(24 rooms)

Palatin**
4 Rehov Agrippas
Tel: (02) 231141
(28 rooms)

Park Lane**
Mt. Scopus
Tel: (02) 282208
(20 rooms)

Pilgrims Inn**
Rehov Rashidia
Tel: (02) 284883
(15 rooms)

Rovoli**
3 Rehov Salah Adin,
91194
Tel: (02) 284871
(31 rooms)

Ron**
42A Rehov Yafo
Tel: (03) 223471
(22 rooms)

Vardi-Rosenbaum**
21 Rehov Mekor Haim
Tel: (02) 717796, 716114
(20 rooms)

Vienna East**
Rehov Sheikh Jarrah
Tel: (02) 284826
(39 rooms)

Zion**
4 Rehov Luntz
Tel: (02) 232367
(22 rooms)

Knights Palace**
Rehov Jawalden
Tel: (02) 282537
40 rooms

New Imperial*
Jaffa Gate
Tel: (02) 272400, 282261
(50 rooms)

Savoy*
P.O.B. 19766
Tel: (02) 283366
(17 rooms)

Jerusalem (N.Y.L.)
Derech Nablus
Tel: (02) 283282
(15 rooms)

Jerusalem Laromme
(N.Y.G.)
3 Rehov Ali Ibn Abi Taleb
Tel: (02) 284575, 271352
(74 rooms)

Knesset Tower (N.Y.L.)
Sderot Herzl
Tel: (02) 537368
(174 rooms)

Menorah (N.Y.L.)
24 Rehov David Hame-

lech, 94101
Tel: (02) 223311
(64 rooms)

Mount Zion (N.Y.L.)
15 Rehov Hebron
Tel: (02) 713076/7
(150 rooms)

Ramada Renaissance
(N.Y.G.)
6 Rehov Wolfson
Tel: (02) 528111
(389 rooms)

Victoria (N.Y.G.)
8 Rehov Masudie
Tel: (02) 286220
(54 rooms)

Zohar (N.Y.L.)
47 Rehov Leib Jaffe
Tel: (02) 717557
(116 rooms)

Tel Aviv

Astoria*****
10 Rehov Kaufman,
68012
Tel: (03) 663311
(504 rooms)

Carlton Tel Aviv*****
Rehov Hayarkon
Tel: (03) 291291
(282 rooms)

Dan Tel Aviv*****
99 Rehov Hayarkon
Tel: (03) 241111
(305 rooms)

Plaza Tel Aviv*****
155 Rehov Hayarkon
Tel: (03) 299555
(348 rooms)

Ramada Continental
*****
121 Rehov Hayarkon
Tel: (03) 296444
(340 rooms)

Tel Aviv Hilton*****
Independence Park
Tel: (03) 244222
(614 rooms)

Tel Aviv Sheraton*****
115 Rehov Hayarkon,
63573
Tel: (03) 286222
(360 rooms)

Astor****
105 Rehov Hayarkon,
63903
Tel: (03) 223141
(68 rooms)

Avia****
Ben-Gurion Airport Area,
Yahud, 56000
Tel: (03) 352221-8
(116 rooms)

Basel****
156 Rehov Hayarkon,
63451
Tel: (03) 244161
(138 rooms)

Concorde****
1 Rehov Trumpeldor
Tel: (03) 659241
(92 rooms)

Country Club****
North Tel Aviv
P.O.B. 48200 TA
Tel: (03) 415261
(138 rooms)

Grand Beach****
250 Rehov Hayarkon,
63113
Tel: (03) 241252
(208 rooms)

Park***
75 Rehov Hayarkon
Tel: (03) 651551
(99 rooms)

Ramat Aviv****
151 Derech Haifa, 17210

Tel: (03) 413181
(118 rooms)

Sinai****
11-15 Rehov Trumpeldor,
63803
Tel: (03) 652621
(250 rooms)

Tal****
287 Rehov Hayarkon,
63504
Tel: (03) 455281
(126 rooms) .

Adiv***
5 Rehov Mendele
Tel: (03) 229141
(68 rooms)

Ambassador***
2 Rehov Allenby
Tel: (03) 655118/9
(50 rooms)

Ami***
4 Rehov Am Israel Hai
Tel: (03) 249141-5
(64 rooms)

City***
9 Rehov Mapu, 63577
Tel: (03) 246253
(96 rooms)

Dizangoff Square***
2 Rehov Zamenhof
Tel: (03) 296181
(52 rooms)

Florida***
164 Rehov Hayarkon
Tel: (03) 242184
(52 rooms)

Maxim***
86 Rehov Hayarkon
Tel: (03) 653721
(60 rooms)

Moss***
6 Rehov Nes Ziona
Tel: (03) 651655
(70 rooms)

Ora***
35 Rehov Ben Yehudah, 63807
Tel: (03) 650941
(54 rooms)

Shalon***
216 Rehov Hayarkon
Tel: (03) 243277, 249444, 243037
(42 rooms)

Wishnitz***
16 Rehov Damesek Bnei-Brak
Tel: (03) 777141/3
(102 rooms)

Armon Hayarkon**
268 Rehov Hayarkon
Tel: (03) 455271/3
(24 rooms)

Excelsior**
88A Rehov Hayarkon
Tel: (03) 655486
(24 rooms)

Wagshal**
Bnei Brak
Tel: (03) 784536
(18 rooms)

Bell*
12 Rehov Allenby
Tel: (03) 654291, 657011
(23 rooms)

Europa*
42 Rehov Allenby
Tel: (03) 655036
(Nine rooms)

Migdal David*
8 Rehov Allenby
Tel: (03) 656392
(22 rooms)

Nes Ziona*
10 Rehov Nachlat Binyamin
Tel: (03) 621612
(18 rooms)

Nordau*
27 Rehov Nachlat Binyamin
Tel: (03) 621612
(18 rooms)

Riveria*
52 Rehov Hayarkon
Tel: (03) 653883, 656870
(30 rooms)

Tamar*
8 Rehov Gnessin
Tel: (03) 286997
(10 rooms)

Habakuk Exclusive
Apartment Hotel
7 Rehov Habakuk
Tel: (03) 440011, 443110
(18 suites)

Imperial (N.Y.G.)
66 Rehov Hayarkon, 63902
Tel: (03) 657002, 65672
(48 rooms)

Mandarin (N.Y.G.)
Mandarin Beach
P.O.B. 48170
Tel: (03) 428161
(308 rooms)

Monopol (N.Y.L.)
15 Rehov Allenby
Tel: (03) 655906, 657559
(27 rooms)

Sandi (N.Y.L.)
15 Rehov Allenby
Tel: (03) 655018, 653889
(18 rooms)

Bethlehem

Bethlehem Star***
Rehov Al Baten
Tel: (02) 743249
(54 rooms)

Handel***
Tel: (02) 742494
(40 rooms)

Dead Sea

Moriah Dead Sea Spa Hotel*****
Ein Bokek, Sedom
Tel: (057) 84221
(220 rooms)

Ein Bokek****
MP Dead Sea, 86930
Tel: (057) 84331
(96 rooms)

Galei Zohar****
MP Dead Sea, 86930
Tel: (057) 843311/4
H.O. Tel: (03) 244211
(260 rooms)

Shulamit Gardens****
MP Dead Sea 86930
Tel: (057) 84351
(184 rooms)

Tsell Harim***
MP Dead Sea, 86930
Tel: (057) 84121/2
(160 rooms)

Lot (N.Y.G.)
Ein Bokek, Sedom
Tel: (057) 84321/8
(200 rooms)

Hebron

Eshkolot Hebron
(N.Y.G.)
Kiryat Arba, P.O.B. 40
Tel: (02) 961819. 961245
(45 rooms)

FOOD DIGEST

WHERE TO EAT

Dining is a national pastime in Israel—one engaged in as much and as often as possible. On the street, at the beach, in every public place and certainly in every home, day and night—you'll find Israelis eating.

The Biblical residents of the Land of Canaan were nourished by the fertility and abundance of a land "flowing with milk and honey." Milk was mainly from sheep and goats, and the honey from dates, figs and carobs. Much depended on the sun, the rains and the seasons. Food was simple; feast predictably followed famine.

Times have changed—at least in the culinary sense. Just as Israel is a blend of cultures coming from all over the world, so its cuisine is a weave of flavors and textures, contrasts and similarities. There is no *definite* Israeli fare, just as there is no definitive Israeli. Rather, there is an unique merging of East and West, and the results are a profusion of culinary delights.

The predominant foodstyle, however, reflects the country's geographical location—somewhere between the Middle East and the Mediterranean. Dining out? Don't be led astray by signs that say "oriental" food. No Far Eastern food is intended.

In Israel, "oriental" refers to the Middle East. "Oriental" Jews are those of Sephardic (Spain, Italy, various Arab countries) heritage. Each Jewish ethnic group, whether Moroccan, Libyan, Tunisian, Yeminite, Iraqi or native-born (*Sabra*) Israeli, has its own special dish and holy day fare.

Their food is similar yet distinct from each other. Basic herbs and spices include cumin, fresh and dried coriander, mint, garlic, onion, tumeric, black pepper, and sometimes cardamom and fresh green chili pepper. Dark fruity olive oil brings out tantalising fragrances.

Arabic food is also considered "oriental" and both Arabic and Jewish meals begin the same way—with a variety of savory salads. *Humus*, a ground chickpea concoction seasoned with *tahina* (sesame paste), lemon juice, garlic and cumin—is probably the most popular dip, spread and salad rolled into one. *Tahina* prepared likewise, come next.

Here you'll also find one of the most astounding varieties of eggplant salads you've ever seen; eggplant in *tahina*, fried sliced eggplant, chopped eggplant with vegetables, chopped liver-flavored eggplant and more. Assorted pickled vegetables are considered salads as well.

While the waiters may show some sign of disappointment, you can order the salads as a meal unto itself.

Or you follow them with **kebab** (grilled ground spiced sauce), *shashlik* (grilled sliced lamb or beef with lamb fat), *seniya* (beef or lamb in *tahina* sauce), stuffed chicken or pigeon, chops or fish.

Don't expect pork in either a *kosher* or traditional Muslim restaurant. Both religions prohibit its consumption. Seafood, while forbidden by Jewish and permissible by Muslim law, is widely available. Shrimps and calamari are the predominant varieties.

Do try the fish, particularly in the seaside areas of Tiberias, Tel Aviv, Jaffa and Eilat (there are no fish in the Dead Sea!). Trout, gray and red mullet, sea bass and St. Peter's fish are generally served fried or grilled, sometimes accompanied by a piquant sauce. Authentic North African restaurants will also feature *harimeh*—hot and spicy cooked fish, fragrant with garlic, tomatoes, cumin and hot pepper.

And if you still have room, there's dessert. In Arabic restaurants this may mean *baklava* (filo dough sprinkled with nuts and sweet syrup), and some other rich sweet or fruit. In typical Jewish oriental restaurants it could mean caramel creme custard, chocolate mousse or an egg white confection laced with chocolate syrup and, for some unknown reason, called Bavarian creme. Turkish coffee or tea with fresh mint seals the meal. If you do not wish sugar, inform the waiter in advance.

Yemenite food is characterized by virtually all the same spices as other Sephardic cuisines, but with more of them. Genuine Yemenite restaurants offer exotic soups, including "foot soup," "tail soup" and "udder soup" among others, though more conservative lentil, vegetable, and beef soups are available. All are rich in flavor and aromatic.

Several types of bread are served: *mallawah* (crispy fried, fattening and delicious), *lahuh* (light and pancake-like) and *jahnoon* (slow-baked strudel-like dough with copious amounts of margarine). While *pita* bread is served automatically with any order, others mentioned must be requested for. Eat them with a mixed vegetable salad, humus and/or *ful* (slow-cooked fava beans), *haminados* (slow-cooked brown and creamy-yolked eggs), or by itself with condiments.

Yemenites have their own special mixtures and condiments and believe that they add to health and aid digestion. These are *hilbe* (a bitter-though-interesting fenugreek preparation) thought to be helpful in the treatment of diabetes and *tzhoug* (fresh coriander chopped with hot green or red peppers and spices), considered beneficial for blood circulation. In authentic Yemenite restaurants, these are served along with the meal. You may want to end your repast with coffee with *hawaiig* (a.k.a. Yemenite coffee), a fragrant blend of spices akin to the Indian *garam masala*.

If it's Askenazic or East-ern European Jewish cooking you're after, you can find traditional gefilte fish, chopped liver, *borscht* (beef soup), Hungarian *goulash* (stew) and Russian *peroshki* (baked or fried piquant filled pastries), but these are not considered day-to-day fare and are served only by speciality restaurants.

Due to the influx of the Vietnamese Boat People and former residents of Taiwan, Hong Kong, Thailand and the Philippines, Chinese-style restaurants abound and are much beloved by the native population. Ask the locals for recommendations.

Elegant restaurants are also a part of the local scene, and like their counterparts in other countries, they offer a rich selection of gourmet foods, some authentic to the cuisine they offer, some tailored to local tastes. Thanks to a new generation of young Israeli chefs a new movement is growing, based on an intense desire to create an authentic haute cuisine rooted in classic French cookery and personalized with ingredients indigenous to this country.

The results—dishes like lamb wrapped in bulgar pastry and stuffed with *pate de foie* or sweetbreads stuffed with avocado and served in an avocado sauce—blend the foreign and the familiar.

For a real understanding of the country's cuisine, visit supermarkets, green grocers and open-air markets, and investigate the little out-of-the-way eateries in places like the Old City of Jerusalem, the Yemenite Kerem Hataymanim and Hatikvah quarters in Tel Aviv, the Jaffa port and little villages.

Meals: Most Israelis eat a large breakfast, a main "meat" meal at midday and a light "dairy" meal in the evening. The wide variety of restaurants throughout the country naturally cater to this preference, but are also prepared to suit individual tastes. They range from elegant establishments specializing in cooking from many parts of the world, to simple cafés or pizza stands.

Snacks: Since Israelis are major eaters, snacks play a starring role in the day. Favorite munchies include bagel-shaped, sesame-sprinkled breads (served with *za'atar*—a wild oregano-based spice mixture available only in "ethnic" settings like the Old City of Jerusalem), nuts and sunflower seeds. Pizzas, blintzes, waffles and burgers all come in and out of vogue.

But the ultimate *Sabra* (native Israeli) snack has to be *felafel* (fried chickpea balls served in *pita* bread with a variety of vegetable possibilities). Along the sidewalks of major streets, you can usually find several adjoining *felafel* stands where you're free to repeatedly stuff your pits with all the fixins'—as long as your *pita* holds out.

Tel Aviv's Shuk Betzalel is the most famous of the *felafel* centers. Located just near the Carmel market, it features an entire street of *felafel* vendors, with the largest salad selection this side of the Mediterranean.

Fruits & Vegetables: The country's produce is legendary! Fruits and vegetables arrive at market stall hours after picking, and a trip to the open-air **Mahane Yehudah** in Jerusalem or the **Carmel market** in Tel Aviv, will reveal a sumptuous array of everything from apples to artichokes, *kohlrabi* to celery. Sub-tropical fruits include kiki, mango, persimmon, loquat, passion fruit, cheromoya and papaya. Fresh dates, figs, pomegranates and the world's largest strawberries are seasonal attractions.

Produce is sold by the kilo or gram, and is most reasonably priced at open-air markets. Avoid supermarket produce as they tend to be second rate. Wash everything well before you eat.

Meat And Poultry: Those who prefer fowl will find the chicken and turkey, and in more elegant restaurants, the goose and mullard duck (an Israeli hybrid) excellent choices. While much beef is imported, all fowl is domestically raised.

Dairy Products: In days of old, water was scarce and not very palatable, so milk became a major component of the Biblical diet. Goat's milk was considered the richest and most nourishing. Next came sheep's milk, cow's milk and finally, camels milk.

Today Israel continues the "Land of milk and honey" tradition with a wealth of more familiar cheeses (like Swiss, Camembert, Brie and Gouda), double-rich cottage cheese, and a wide variety of goat and sheep yogurt and cheeses (special types of which are found in some health food stores and the Arab villages).

A visit to the supermarket will reveal uniquely Israeli white cheeses; wrapped in paper or sold in tubs, all marked with labels signifying fat content. Try *Tov Ta' am*, a soft spreadable five percent fat, white cheese wrapped in paper—if you want something low on fat. Or taste *leben* or *eshel*—cultured milk products with approximately the same fat content as yogurt.

Beverages: You **can** drink the water in Israel, though bottled water is also available. Fresh citrus and carrot juices may be found at snack stands, where the standard carbonated diet and regular beverages are also available. "Soda" refers to "soda water," and not a flavored carbonated drink. Diet and regular soft drinks are available in abundance.

Israel has a selection of delicious white and red wines, and dark and regular beers. Domestic liqors are served in bars and restaurants along with more expensive imported beverages.

Kosher Food: The Hebrew word *kosher* means food conforming to Jewish dietary laws. Pork and shellfish are prohibited, and meat and dairy foods cannot be served together. While *kosher* food is the rule in Israel, many restaurants and some hotels—and, of course, Arab establishments—are non-*kosher*.

Holy Day Foods: If there are jelly doughnuts (*sufganiot*) it must be *Chanukah*...the occasion also for *potato latkes* (pancakes). On *Purim* you'll find *oznay haman* (*hamentashen* or filled triangular cookies).

If you're in Israel around holy day time, try to experience some holy day fare. Any self-respecting Israeli will tell you that holy days are especially important occasions and food is involved.

On Passover, it's time for *matzobrie*, coconut macaroons and sponge cake. *Shavuot* is strictly for dairy delights. *Sukkot* and *Tu B' shvat* are celebrated with dried fruits and nuts. Every Friday afternoon, there are special braided *challahs* for the Sabbath. And every Sabbath there is *cholent* (*hamin* if you're Sephardic), a baked bean and meat stew set to bake on Friday for lunch on the Sabbath.

Israel has many worthwhile restaurants; the following is a selection of these. Bon appetit—or as they say in Israel— *be'tayavon* !

Jerusalem

Oriental & Fish

Sea Dolphin
In East Jerusalem
21 A1 Rashadiah Street
Tel: (03) 282788
An almost legendary fish restaurant. Highly popular among Jerusalemites for years. Moderate.

Philadelphia
East Jerusalem
Azzahara Street
Tel: (03) 273735
One of the most famous resturants in the capital. Oriental food. Moderate.

Dallas
East Jerusalem
Azzahara Street
Tel: (03) 284439
Neighbor and rival to Philadelphia.

French & Continental

Katy's Restaurant
16 Rivlin Street
Tel: (02) 234621
Elegant, popular and trendy, with bar. Expensive.

Alla Gondola
14 King George Street
Tel: (02) 225944
Elegant dining with Italian cuisine. Downtown. Moderate.

Cow On The Roof
At the Jerusalem Plaza Hotel
Tel: (02) 228133
Elegant Western dining. By reservations only.

Moroccan

Au Sahara
17 Jaffa Road
Tel: (02) 233239
Reliable Moroccan cuisine and atmosphere, with a variety of North African specialties, downtown. Moderate to expensive.

Dairy & Light Meals

Home Plus
9 Heleni Hamalcha Street
Tel: (02) 222612
Modern interior, pleasant atmosphere near downtown. Pasta and fish dishes, desserts. Moderate.

Anna Ticho House
Off Harav Kook Street
Tel (02) 244186
Garden restaurant/café on first floor of Ticho House Museum. Quiet, youthful atmosphere. The house salad with crushed nuts and cheese is nice. Inexpensive.

La Luna
Off Derekh Hebron
Tel: (02) 718100
The café at the trendy Cinemateque. Chic, busy and young—great view of Mt. Zion. Salads, light meals, desserts.

Chinese

Phoenix
36 Ben Yehudah Street
Good Mandarin fare, spicy food. Popular with Jerusalemites. Moderate.

Hungarian

Europa
42 Jaffa Road
Tel: (02) 228953
Unpretentious atmosphere, central location at Zion Square. Variety of Hungarian specialties including stuffed chicken and goulash. Popular with locals. Moderate.

Vegetarian

Hameshek
14 Shlomzion Hamalcha
Tel: (02) 226278
Soups, salads, quiches, tofu, whole grains, fruit juices, etc. Downtown. Inexpensive to moderate.

Desserts & Coffee

Pie House
5 Hyrkanos Street
More than just a dessert place, this popular Jerusalem hang-out also proffers full meals in its own low-rise house near Zion Square, across the street from Home Plus. Moderate.

Dont Pass Me By
Off Salomon Street
4 Nachlat Shiva
"Don't Pass Me By, Tea and Pie" is its full name, or simply "The Pie Shop." Pies and coffee. Inexpensive.

Chocolate Soup
6 Rivlin Street
Crepes, ice cream confectionary and chocolate soup.

Cafe Atara
Ben Yehudah Street
Coffee and light meals.

Cafe Alno
Another well-liked Ben Yehudah Street institution. Many pleasing pastries.

Rimon Café
Next to Hepner's Deli
off Ben Yehudah
on Luntz Street
A popular hang-out, with a variety of cakes and cookies. Spills out across sidewalk into street on warm days.

Tel Aviv

Dairy & Vegetarian

Eternity
6 Kikar Malchai Yisrael
Tel: (03) 218648
Tofu, ice-cream and snacks. Inexpensive.

TRAVEL TIPS

TRAVEL TIPS

Hasifria (The Library)
6 Kaplan Street
Tel: (03) 216079
Dairy foods in a relaxed and comfortable atmosphere. Musical entertainment evenings. Inexpensive.

Banana
344 Dizengoff Street
Tel: (03) 457491
Tel Aviv's first vegetarian restaurant. Varied menu. Inexpensive to moderate.

Apropos
Off Tarsat Street
Tel: (03) 289289
Chic coffee house/restaurant. Moderate.

Oriental & Fish

Stern Dolphin
189 Dizengoff Street
Tel: (03) 232425
A branch of the Jerusalem Dolphin resaturant, with the same famous menu. A delightful selection of salads, fish, seafood. Moderate.

Shaldag
256 Ben Yehudah Street
Tel: (03) 445465
Friendly with wholesome cuisine. Popular for fish & seafood. Moderate.

Bograchof
On the beach,
near Dan Hotel
Tel: (03) 273822
Casual atmosphere, fun view and decent food. On the beachfront. Inexpensive to moderate.

Yemenite

Ba—Li
8 Ibn Gvirol Street
Inexpensive luncheon-ette-type place with home-cooked Yemenite food. Has all authentic Yemenite breads and soups. Open for lunch and early dinner.

Zion
28 Pedium Street
Tel: (03) 657323
A classic Yemenite restaurant in the Yemenite Quarter. The "exclusive" restaurant is in the back; try the simple workers eatery at the entrance first. Inexpensive to moderate.

Gamliel
38 Hakovshim Street
Tel: (03) 658779
Zion's rival. Also good, same as above. Moderate.

Hungarian

Pirozki
30 Yirmiyahu Street
Tel: (03) 457599
Russian, Hungarian and Jewish specialities, including *blintzes*, *piroshki*, *kreplach* and *borscht*. Inexpensive to moderate.

The Goulash Corner
Hayarkon Street,
at corner of Frischmann
Established place serving the diplomatic crowd, locals and tourists. Good meats, cumin-scented fish, and various oriental salads.

Chinese

The Red Chinese Restaurant
326 Dizengoff Street
Tel: (03) 453423
Pleasant atmosphere, good selection of food, also Thai dishes. In North Tel Aviv. Moderate.

Peking
265 Dizengoff Street
Tel: (03) 453423
Very good food. Moderate to expensive.

Golden Dragon
262 Ben Yehudah Street
Tel: (03) 455070
Like Red Chinese—good food. North Tel Aviv location. Moderate.

Yin Yang
46 Rothschild Blvd.
Tel: (03) 621833
Excellent food, exclusive location but expensive.

French

L'entrecote
195 Ben Yehudah Street
Tel: (03) 230726
Price fixed meal, including salad, fries, and butter-soft steak. Intimate if slightly cramped atmosphere. Moderate.

Casba
32 Yirmiyahu Street
Tel: (03) 442617
Good food, famous for duck.Continental offerings. Piano. Fairly expensive.

Social

Piltz Café
81 Hayarkon Street
Tel: (03) 652778
Pseudo-art deco atmosphere, near hotels, overlooking beach. Continental and local entrees, desserts. Music, often dancing on Thursday, Friday and Saturday evenings. Moderate.

Kumkum
42 Rokach Blvd
Tel; (03) 460164

213

Casual atmosphere, local hangout in Yarkon Park, near sports center, pub/café. Inexpensive to moderate.

Pubs

Bonanza

17 Trumpeldor Street

Tel: (03) 285803
Quiet and relaxed joint, except on Friday afternoons, when regulars come to carouse. Bar and varied menu.

The Stagecoach (Hakirkara)

216 Hayarkon Street

Tel: (03) 241703
Near hotels and waterfront. Live music every evening except Fridays. Drinks, snacks, light meals.

ACTIVITIES

CULTURE & ENTERTAINMENT

Israel has a wealth of cultural and artistic entertainment to divert the visitor. Ticket agencies in each city or town sell tickets for concerts, plays and other events. Calendars of events are available at the Tourist Information Offices.

Concerts: There are several orchestras, of which the most famous is the Israel Philharmonic, playing under the baton of the great conductors of the world and featuring distinguished guest artists. The Jerusalem Symphony Orchestra gives a weekly concert in Jerusalem during winter. There are frequent performances by the Haifa Symphony Orchestra, the Ramat Gan Orchestra and Israel Sinfonietta Beersheba, the Israel Chamber Ensemble and some outstanding trios and quartets.

Theaters: The theater is very popular in Israel and there are many companies performing, in Hebrew, a wide range of classical and contemporary plays, including original works by Israelis. The best known are the Habimah and Cameri Theaters in Tel Aviv and the Haifa Municipal Theater, which take their productions all over the country. Smaller companies often stage productions in English, Yiddish and other languages.

Dances: There are three dance companies in Israel—the Israel Classical Ballet, the Beersheba Dance Company and the Bat-Dor Dance Company. The latter two are modern dance groups. All perform in the three main cities as well as in other towns and in *kibbutzim.*

Cinemas: There are cinemas in all the big towns; most present three performances a day, at about four o'clock in the afternoon and two evening shows.

Art Film Houses

Jerusalem

Israel Museum
Hakirya
Tel: (02) 698211

Cinematheque
Gan Wolfson

Derech Hebron
Tel: (02) 715398, 712192

Jerusalem Theater
30 Rehov Marcus
Tel: (02) 667167

Tel Aviv

Tel Aviv Museum
27-29 Sderot Shaul Hamelech
Tel: (03) 257361

Cinemathque
Municipality Tel Aviv
Kikar Malkhei Israel
Tel: (03) 243311

Nightclubs: They abound in the main cities and resort towns. Many have regular floor shows, while others offer more informal entertainment. Rock, jazz, folk and pop music is the usual fare, together with dancing.

Folklore Evenings: Folklore programs, which portray the spirit of ancient and modern Israel in song and dance, are presented regularly at main hotels in the following towns. For further information contact:

Jerusalem
Tel: (02) 241281, 282295

Tel Aviv
Tel: (03) 223266

Festivals: The Israel Festival of Music and Drama takes place in September each year, with the participation of the country's leading musical and dramatic talent and world-famous visiting companies and artistes. The Festival is centered in Jerusalem, Tel Aviv and the restored Roman theaters in Caesarea and Beit Shean. Performances also take place in other towns and some *kibbutzim*.

The annual Ein Gev Music Festival, presenting classical and folk music, is held during the Passover festival at the Ein Gev *kibbutz* on the Sea of Galilee. Other local festivals are also establishing themselves, the most colorful being the one in Eilat on the Red Sea, where water sports and moonlight pageants are the highlights.

An International Harp Contest takes place every three years, drawing young musicians from all over the world, while the Zimriya, an international choir festival, is another well-established triennial event. Spring in Jerusalem and Tel Aviv, see annual festivals, covering music, drama and dance; the Rubinstein Piano Competition brings talented young artists from all over the world to the country.

Events in Haifa include the International Flower Show (Floris), when hundreds of thousands of flowers from all over the world, typical of their countries of origin, adorn the city. There is also the International Folklore Festival, in which the best folklore groups from all over the world participate in dance and music.

Outdoor Events And Performances: During July and August there are many outdoor events and performances: bands, puppet shows, dance, disco, mime and sports activities. Contact the Ministry of Tourism for the country-wide locations and times of these performances.

Zoos: The Jerusalem Biblical Zoo houses many animals mentioned in the Bible. Other zoos are located in Tel Aviv, Eilat and Haifa.

In Haifa the zoo is located in Gan Ha'em, housing animals indigenous to Mount Carmel and Northern Israel. Tel: (04) 81886.

There is a Safari Park, a 101-hectare (250-acre) wildlife sanctuary in Ramat Gan near Tel Aviv, where hundreds of animals roam freely. At Hai Bar Reserve, north of Eilat, many of the animals mentioned in the Bible can be seen. Visitors to the Safari Park and Hai Bar Reserve may tour in closed vehicles only. In Eilat, there is an underwater observatory to view exotic acquatic life.

Museums

The museums of Israel are a mirror of their country; a land both ancient and modern, a crossroads of civilizations and a "melting pot" of a people returning home from a hundred countries with different cultures and traditions. They are treasure houses of archaeology, folklore and ethnology, of art ancient and modern, of crafts primitive and sophisticated.

Some of the country's museums are unique in the world, such as the Shrine of the Book, repository of the Dead Sea Scrolls and the Museum of the Jewish Diaspora. Some of the principal ones are listed below. For visiting hours of others, see also the Ministry of Tourism brochure, *Museums*.

Jerusalem

Artists House
12 Rehov Shmuel Hanagid
Tel: (02) 232920
Exhibition of local arts and crafts.

Cable Car Museum
Derech Hebron
(near Cinematheque)
Original works of cable car used to transfer the wounded in Old City from Mt. Zion during the War of Independence.

Chamber of the Martyrs
Mount Zion
Memorial to the millions of Nazi victims.

Givat Hatahmoshet
(Ammunition Hill)
Memorial Museum. Ammunition Hill was the scene of the battle for Jerusalem during the Six Day War.

Herzl Memorial Museum
Mount Herzl
Tel: (02) 531108
See the photographs, documents, books and the study in which Herzl wrote

his famous *Altneuland*.

Hechal Shlomo
58 Rehov Hamelech George
Tel: (02) 635212
Museum of Jewish ceremonial exhibits and an Italian synagogue.

The Israel Museum
Hakirya
Tel: (02) 698211
Comprises:

Bezalel National Art Museum
Jewish ceremonial art; ethnography of the Jewish communities and the Arabs of Eretz Israel; European painting and sculpture, 15th-20th centuries; contemporary Israeli art; prints room; art from Asia, Japan, India, Far East, Oceania, Africa and pre-Columbian Americas. Billy Rose Art Garden—modern sculpture. Design pavilion. Library.

Samuel Bronfman Biblical and Archaeological Museum
Archaeological objects and ancient art from prehistoric to Crusader times; coins; neighboring cultures.

Youth Wing
Children's displays. Exhibitions, varied activities and courses. Undoubtedly one of the most advanced of its kind in the world.

Zacks-Abramov Pavillion
New wing for modern art opened in late 1985.

Shrine of the Book
Tel: (02) 633231
The "Dead Sea Scrolls";
Massada scroll fragments; the Bar Kokhba letters and other archaeological finds.

Rockefeller Museum
East Jerusaelm
Tel: (02) 715100
Center for the production, exhibition and marketing of quality products.

Schoken Institute
6 Rehov Balfour
92102 Jerusalem
Tel: (02) 631288
Displays of rare Hebrew and Jewish works.

L.A. Mayer Memorial Institute for Islamic Art
2 Rehov Hapalmach
Tel: (02) 661291
Islamic art of the various periods and lands, including metal work, ceramics, jewelry, carpets, miniatures, textiles, graphics on Islamic lands. Outstanding collection of antique European and Ottoman watches, clocks and music boxes. Archives and library.

Museum of Taxes
32 Rehov Agron
Tel: (02) 245951
History of taxation in Israel and among Jewish communities of the Diaspora.

Ticho House
Rehov Ticho
(near Harav Kook)
Art and literature library, museum shop, coffee shop and examples of Anna Ticho's paintings.

Tel Aviv

Beth Hatefutsoth— Museum of the Jewish
Diaspora
Rehov Klausner
Ramat Aviv
Tel: (03) 425161
Permanent thematic exhibit of Jewish life in the Diaspora, from the destruction of the Second Temple until today, including photographs, models, multimedia presentations, closed circuit television, library and a computer reference bank. Chronosphere exhibit of Jewish Diaspora life. Also temporary exhibits on Jewish communities in the Diaspora. International guest lecturers and study forums.

Ha'aretz Museum
Ramat Aviv
Tel: (03) 415244/8
Some section of the museum are:
The Alphabet Museum
The history of writing, its spread and development: pre-alphabetic, alphabetic, Hebrew alphabetic; copies of important inscriptions. Also a library.

Ceramic Pavilion
History of glass production, methods of styles, especially in Mediterranean lands in antiquity, from Late Bronze Age onwards.

The Kadman Numismatic Pavilion
Greek, Jewish, Near Eastern, Roman, Byzantine, Arab, Crusader, British Mandatory and Israeli coins; banknotes; scales and weights of various periods. Library and reading room.

Man and His Work
Tools and implements for hunting, agricultural indus-

tries, energy, light, writing, measuring, in various materials; eight traditional workshops recreated; steampower in agriculture, oriental market and craftsmen's stoves of last century recreated.

Nehusthan Pavilion

Houses archaeological finds from temples at ancient copper mines at Timna in the Negev, illustrating how the metal was produced during various periods.

Tel Aviv Museum
27-29 Sderot Shaul Hamelech
Tel: (03) 257361;
Helena Rubinstein Pavilion
6 Rehov Tarsat
Tel: (03) 287196
Collections include European and American art from the 17th century until the present; with an emphasis on modern and contemporary art. The collection also includes works by Jewish artists. The collection of Israeli art consists of works from the beginning of the 20th century up to the present time. Temporary exhibitions of modern and contemporary art. Activities include concerts, lectures, gallery talks, cinema, art films and art education.

Acco

The Municipal Museum
Old City
Tel: (04) 910251
Regional archaeology from the Early Bronze Age to the Ottoman period; Persian ceramics; Arabs and Druze ethnology in Eretz

Israel; weapons from Crusader to Turkish times; folk art from Turkish times; the history of the Jewish community through the ages in Acre; library. Housed in an 18th-century bath house—Crusader fortress with a crypt adjacent.

Ein Gedi

Beit Sefer Sade (field school)
Tel: (057) 91008
Exhibition on the flora and fauna of the area.

Holocaust Memorials

The following are memorials to the six million Jews who perished in the Nazi Holocaust:

Jerusalem Area

Yad Vashem, Martyrs' and Heroes' Remembrance Authority
Har Hazikaron
(near Mt. Herzl)
Jerusalem
Tel: (02) 531202
The central museum and monument to the memory of the Holocaust of European Jewry (1933—1945). Exhibition and Hall of Remembrance. Includes archives and library.

Other Galleries: There are score of other museums, small and large, in towns and in *kibbutzim*. They display archaeological finds, ancient glass, coins, folk costumes, natural science collections, as well as contemporary art. In addition, groups of artists have formed "colonies" in the vil-

lage of Ein Hod on Mt. Carmel (near Haifa), at Safed and in Jaffa, with picturesque studios open to the general public.

In Tel Aviv, the gallery scene is centered around Gordon Street, also known as "Gallery Street." In Jerusalem, visiting artists from abroad are housed at the Mishkenot and from time to time give performances or speeches for the public.

The Aika (Ariel Brown) Gallery, in the gritty industrial zone of Talpiot, is where Jerusalem's artists congregate to work. Contemporary art work at 6 Yad Harutzim Street.

Jerusalem also holds a great abundance of public art; the booklet *The City As Museum: Modern Art & Architecture in Jerusalem*, published by the Jerusalem Foundation available in some bookstores, is an exceptional guide.

SPORTS

Israel is an ideal place for sports enthusiasts. There are excellent facilities and you will find opportunities to combine interests such as skin- and scuba-diving, horseback riding, tennis, golf, swimming and skiing with a general tour of the country. The Mediterranean climate also enables the sportsman to enjoy outdoor sports all the year round.

Israel also offers **spectator sports**. **Soccer** is the number one sport with several matches every week. Israelis are especially proud of the Tel Aviv Maccabi **basketball** team, which has won the European championship twice. There are many international matches during winter at stadiums in the Tel Aviv area.

The Mediterranean shoreline and the Sea of Galilee are ideal for **water sports:** swimming, surfing, sailing and water skiing. The Tel Aviv Marina offers yachting as well as sailing. All the large hotels have fine **swimming pools** and there are municipal or private pools all over the country. Skin and aqualung **diving** are especially popular along the Gulf of Eilat; centers at Eilat will rent equipment and provide instruction. **Fishing** equipment, both angling and underwater, can be hired along the Mediterranean and the Red Sea, though the latter is a protected area, with fishing permitted only in certain places.

Tennis courts are available at a number of hotels and the Tennis Center at Ramat Ha-Sharon, near Tel Aviv, is putting Israel on the international tennis circuit. There is a fine 18-hole **golf course** at Caesarea. You can go **horseback riding** in clubs in Arad, Beersheba, Caesarea, Eilat, Netanya, Vered Hagalil and other places. **Bicycles** can be rented in most cities and cycling tours of the country can be arranged. During winter, head to the slopes of Mt. Hermon for **skiing**.

Marches, races and **swimming competitions** are organized by the HaPo'el and Maccabi sports organizations. The highlight of the year is the annual Jerusalem March, a highly organized event, in which thousands of Israelis from all over the country, as well as overseas visitors, both individually, and in groups, make a colorful and highly-spirited pilgrimage to the capital. This event is held during spring, usually in April. A monthly program of events can be obtained from the Israeli National Sports Association, 5 Rehov Warburger, Tel Aviv, Tel: (03) 296387.

Tourists in sports-related professions or those contemplating such careers will be interested in the Wingate Institute for Physical Education and Sports, near Netanya. Under the auspices of the Israeli Ministry of Education and Culture, the Institute consists of the Education Teachers, the School for Sports Coaches and Instructors and the School of Physiotherapy. The Institute also houses the Department of Research and Sports Medicine and the National Archives of Physical Education and Sport.

Golf: Israel's golf course is located on the Mediterranean coast by the ancient seaport of Caesarea. Halfway between Tel Aviv and Haifa (40 minutes by car from either city), the full-sized 18-hole, 72-rating course measuring 6,200 meters is open all year round. A driving range is also available. Professional lessons are given and clubs and other equipment can be rented at the Club's pro-shop. Lockers and changing rooms are at the players' disposal. Restaurant. For further information, contact Caesarea Golf Club, P.O.B. 1010, 30660 Caesarea, Tel: (063) 61174/2.

Squash

Haifa Squash Center
Kfar Zamir, MP Hof Hacarmel
Tel: (04) 539160

Herzliya Squash Center
Tel: (052) 357877

**Ramat Gan
Kfar Hamaccabiah
Sport Center**
Ramat Chen
Tel: (03) 779031/757

Tennis: Tennis is one of Israel's most rapidly growing sports. Courts are available at many hotels and other tennis centers throughout the country. Lessons are offered at several courts.

The Israel Tennis Center, in Ramat Hasharon, just north of Tel Aviv, is the hub of Israeli tennis. Facilities include 16 all-weather, flood-lit courts, training walls and educational facilities. Both national and international tournaments are held in the 5,000-seat Spectator's Stadium.

Israel Tennis Center
Ramat Hasharon
Tel: (03) 481803, 485223

For further information, contact:
Israel Tennis Association
79 Rehov Maze
67137 Tel Aviv
Tel: (03) 613911

Skiing: Israel's only snow skiing resort is located on the north-eastern slopes of the Hermon range, 1,600 to 2,100 meters (5,300 to 6,900 feet) above sea level. The highest peak offers a stunning panoramic view of the Golan Heights. Upper Galilee, the Hulah Valley, the Birket Ram Lake, the Qalat Nimrod Crusader Fortress and the Banyas Spring. The ski resort is 30 km (19 miles) from Kiryat Shmona and 65 km (40 miles) from Tiberias.

The skiing season begins in December or January and ends in mid-April. The heavy and wet snow ranges from two to three meters (six to nine feet) on the highest slope to one meter (three feet) at base level. There may be days when the roads are closed due to heavy snow.

Skiers may phone the ski site between 9 a.m. and 3 p.m. or Moshav Neve Ativ, the holiday village which runs the ski site, throughout the day. The site is open daily from 8:30 a.m. until 3:30 p.m., subject to weather and security conditions. The last ride on the chair-lifts is at 3:30 p.m. A weekday visit is more advisable as the site is less crowded then.

Runs are available for all levels of skiers; the longest run is about two and-a-half km (one and-a-half miles). Other facilities include a shop which rents out ski equipment and sells small ski accessories, a buffet and a cafeteria.

Lodgings relatively close to the site include the *kibbutz* guest houses of Hagoshrim, Kfar Giladi and Kfar Blum, hotels in Metulla and Kiryat Shmona, and the youth hostel of Tel Hai. Other accommodation within traveling distance include the Ayelet Hashachar and Nof Ginosar *kibbutz* guest houses, and hotels in Rosh Pinah, Kare Deshe, Poria and Tiberias.

For further information, contact:

Hermon Ski Site
Tel: (067) 40121

Moshav Neve Ativ
12010, MP Ramat Hagolan
Tel: (067) 41185, 46479/80/81

Israel Ski Club
P.O.B. 211, Givatayim

Riding: Riding schools and stables can be found throughout the country. Horse lovers who are interested in more than just riding can contact the Israel Horse Society, which occasionally sponsors horse shows and concentrates on horse breeding in Israel. For those wishing to explore, there are riding facilities which specialize in trail riding.

Among the larger riding stables are:

Caesarea
Herod's Stables
Dan Caesarea Golf Hotel
Tel: (063) 89065

Eilat
Sunbay Hotel
Lagoon Beach
Tel: (059) 73145

Jerusalem
Havat Amir
Atarot
Tel: (02) 852190

Nahariya
Bacall's Riding School
Sderot Ben Zvi
Tel: (04) 920534

Rishon Le Zion
Havat Hadar Riding Center
P.O.B. 307
Tel: (03) 941088

Tiberias
Vered Hagalil Ranch
Mobile Post Korazim
Tel: (067) 35785

Hang Gliding: The Agur Hang Gliding School in Bat Yam (Tel Aviv Area), offers courses in hang gliding. Course duration is 18 hours or five meetings.

Equipment can be rented from the company upon presentation of an authorized hang gliding certificate. For further inforamtion, contact Mr. Arnon Har Lev, Agur Hang Gliding School anddddub, 124 Rehov Balfour, Bat Yam, Tel: (03) 865262, 804314.

Water Sports

Diving: Israel is truly a diver's paradise. Its mild climate ensures year-round diving in the crystal-clear waters of both the Mediterranean and Red Seas, where hundreds of miles of easily accessible coral reefs and spectacular seascapes await the diving enthusiast. A variety of diving experiences unequalled anywhere in the world include underwater photography, archaeological diving, grotto and cave diving. It should be noted that unless the diver has a two-star license, he must take a special diving course.

In the Mediterranean Sea: The Mediterranean has two good diving seasons: autumn (September to December) and spring (March to May), although there are also fine periods during the summer and winter when diving is possible. Visibility on good days averages 10 meters (33 feet), with calm waters. Tides are never a problem as their average fluctuation is only 40 cm (one and-a-half feet) even on rough days. Water temperatures range from 16°C (61°F) in February to 20°C (84°F) in August.

In the Gulf of Eilat: The Gulf is one of the most unique diving centers in the world, containing an underwater nature reserve with especially exquisite coral.

Diving can be done every day of the year. The area is usually free of large and strong waves: currents and tides are moderate, with variations of up to 80 cm (two and-a-half feet) between high and low tides. These variations do not affect the diver's movement in any way. Visibility is generally excellent, ranging from 15—40 meters (50—130 feet) and even more. Water temperatures range from 21°C (70°F) in February to 27°C (80°F) in August.

Snorkeling: At the Nature Reserve on the Coral Beach, Eilat. Snorkels can be rented. Underwater paths are marked.

Skin and Scuba Diving Courses: The courses for beginners last about five days and cover the theory of diving, lifesaving, physiology, physics and underwater safety. The only qualifications necessary are the ability to swim, a certificate from a doctor confirming fitness to learn diving, and a chest X-ray. Beginners can also go out on individual introductory dives, lasting from one to one and-a-half hours, accompanied always by an instructor.

It is possible to rent all the necessary skin and scuba diving equipment at the following centers:

Tel Aviv

Aquamarine International Diving Club
23 Rehov Hissin
Tel: (03) 284206/7

Andromeda Yachting Club
83 Rehov Salame
Tel: (03) 824725
(Group diving)

Water Sports Center Marina
P.O.B. 16285
Tel: (03) 282972

For further information, contact:

The Federation for Underwater Activities In Israel
P.O.B. 6110
61060 Tel Aviv
Tel: (03) 457432

Water Skiing, Wind Surfing or Board Surfing: These sports are available at

the following centers:

North Beach
Rafi Nelson's Village

Kontiki
11 Rehov Usishkin
Tel: (053) 32954

Tel Aviv
Aquamarine International Diving Club
23 Rehov Hissin
Tel: (03) 284206/7

Swimming: Israel's mild climate allows year-round swimming at all of its coasts—the Mediterranean, the Gulf of Eilat, the Dead Sea and the Sea of Galilee. You will find qualified lifeguards in attendance at all beaches and pools.

Swimming is free at many beaches: Ahziv, Acre, Ashdod, Ashkelon, Eilat, Ein Gedi, Haifa, Herzliya, Nahariya, Netanya, Rishon Lezion, Tiberias and Tel Aziz. Most hotels have swimming pools, to which guests of the hotel have generally free entry, and visitors are allowed in for a fee.

Municipal pools in main cities include:

Tel Aviv
Gordon Swimming Pool
Kikar Atarim, Tel Aviv
Tel: (02) 233241

Jerusalem
Jerusalem Swimming Pool
13 Emek Refaim
Tel: (02) 632092

NATURE

Nature Reserves: There

are over 160 nature reserves in Israel, extending over 60,700 hectares (150,000 acres). Although Israel is a comparatively small country, it has an unbelievable range of different landscapes and natural phenomena.

It is possible to see, side by side, hills of 1,000 meters (3,300 feet) and more, and plains and valleys amongst which is the lowest depression in the world, some 400 meters (1,300 feet) below sealevel; thick maquis and arid and barren zones; huge cliffs reaching a height of several hundred meters, and vast expanses of desert gravel surfaces; narrow canyons and streams; and waterfalls, facing widespread dry riverbeds.

Owing to its geographical location and its particular topographical structure, Israel is a climatic meeting place. There are more than 3,000 different species of plants, 350 species of birds, and 100 species (each) of mammals and reptiles.

The following are some of the principal reserves.

Northern Area

Tel Dan Reserve: There is no other place in Israel with so plentiful a supply of water—about 240 million cubic meters flow annually from the River Dan, the largest of the three sources of the Jordan River, determining the character of this reserve. Here one can find water vegetation of the north, plane trees and Syrian ash, ferns and mosses, together with the giant terebinth. The laurel, known elsewhere as a shrub, appears here as a tall-branching tree.

Southern Area

Ein Gedi: Ein Gedi is an unique oasis, lying between the Dead Sea shore (the lowest place on earth) and the empty, arid Judean desert. The abundance of plant and animal life concentrated here is due to the many freshwater springs and waterfalls. There is tropical water-dependent vegetation that cannot be found anywhere else in Israel. This includes morings, thick-leaved maerua, desert sebestene and salvadora. There is rich fauna, including large herds of ibexes, hyrexes, Black Tristams' Grackles and desert partridges.

Hai Bar Reserve, Totveta: Off the Eilat Highway, in the Southern Rift Valley, lies the unique Hai Bar Biblical Wildlife Reserve. Here animals that were in the past indigenous to the area, or still live under the threat of extinction, are kept under conditions of an open zoo. There are also some animals of desert origin threatened by extinction in North Africa and in desert areas of East Africa. Gatriches, addexes, caracals, wolves, foxes and hyenas are the fauna found here.

Other nature reserves range from Banias and the Hula Valley in the north to Mount Carmel and Nahal Poleg on the coast to the many parks outside Jerusalem in the Judean Hills and around Eilat.

The Nature Reserves Authority has recently commenced the new Visit-All Ticket System for overseas visitors, which enables the visitor to visit 10 possible nature reserves throughout the country and is valid for one month. Tickets are available at: Nature Reserve Authority, 78 Rehov Yirmiyahu, 94467 Jerusalem, Tel: (02) 536271.

National Parks: National parks include nature sites and sites of historical and archaeological interest, such as Hazor, Achziv, Nimrod Fortress, Caesarea, Ashkelon, Megiddo, Herodian, Masada, Qumran, Jericho, Tel Arad and Ein Avdat.

Visitors to sites and parks can buy a multiple entrance ticket at the site or park, permitting them to visit all of the sites or parks within a period of 14 days. For groups, tickets are valid for up to 21 days. It can also be purchased from the National Parks Authority, 4 Rehov Aluf M. Makeleff, Hakirya, 61070 Tel Aviv, Tel: (03) 252281.

Nature Trails: Those searching for the unusual and who wish to tour Israel in a special way, should get in touch with the Society for the Protection of Nature in Israel (SPNI). The Society offers some fascinating tours which combine unique learning experiences in natural settings with touring, hiking and swimming.

These nature trails leave the main roads and penetrate into little-known and relatively unaccessible areas. Experienced guides explain the natural and human history of the region and point out hidden places of beauty and interest. All tours include some walking. Depending on the interests and abilities of the group, this can range from a few hours per day to difficult hikes for experienced trekkers.

There are a number of English-guided trips to all parts of the country suitable for individuals as well as the entire family (children over 12 years old). Their shops also have a selection of publications and accessories regarding natural Israel.

Their main offices are located as follows:

Jerusalem
13 Rehov Helene Hamalka
Tel: (02) 249567

Tel Aviv
4 Rehov Hashfela
Tel: (03) 375063

Haifa
8 Rehov Menachen
Tel: (04) 664136

Desert Tours: Neot Hakikar/Jabaliya runs a variety of tours for those who want to get off-the-beaten track. These include hiking, sailing, cycling, camel riding, mountaineering, camping, trekking and backpacking in all parts of Israel. Research and study tours focusing on special subjects can be tailored to the interests of individual groups.

A special attraction is the Neot Hakikar/Jabaliya desert safaris in the Negev and the Sinai. Transportation is

by 12-seater, four-wheel drive vehicles open at the sides to permit direct vision of the awesome desert scenery. The tours combine driving and hiking with visits to some of the most exciting archaeological sites in the desert. Some nights are spent in organized campsites, some in the home of local villagers and nomads. Camel trekking and challenging rock climbing are a feature of many tours.

For details contact Neot Hakikar/Jabaliya, 36 Rehov Keren Hayesod, 92149 Jerusalem, Tel: (02) 699385, 636494, Tlx: 26261.

Health Resorts

Israel has a number of special health resorts which take advantage of its unique geography and geology. A rare combination of unique therapeutic factors—the mineral-rich Dead Sea, therapeutic mud, sulphur-thermo-mineral springs and a mild, sunny and extremely dry climate—have made certain areas of Israel excellent year-round health resorts, internationally famous since antiquity.

Most of the health resorts are centered in two areas: the Sea of Galilee (-220meters/-660 feet) and the Dead Sea (-400meters/-1,300 feet). Offering a wide range of accommodation and equipped with modern installations, they provide a choice of treatments for a variety of ailments and conditions.

Hamme Zohar (Zohar Hot Springs): Three thera-

peutic centers at Newe Zohar on Dead Sea, for treatment of muscular and joint diseases, traumatic diseases, allergies (especially of breathing passages) and also skin diseases.

Hamme Yesha (Yesha Hot Springs): On Dead Sea, south of Kibbutz En Gedi, for treatment of muscular and joint diseases.

En Boqeq: On the Dead Sea, international center of treatment of psoriasis.

Arad: Desert town in Judean Hills, 620 meters (2,000 feet) above sea level, and about half an hour from the Dead Sea. The cool, dry and pollen-free air, make it an ideal resort for those suffering from asthma, allergies and breathing difficulties.

A special booklet and further information are available at IGTOs abroad and at Health Resorts Authority, 24 Rehov Hamelech George, 94262 Jerusalem, Tel: (02) 231248/9.

Tree Planting: Visitors wishing to plant trees, for a nominal contribution, may do so on their own or as part of tours organized by the Jewish National Fund. Each planter will receive a certificate and a badge to commemorate the event.

Further information from: "Plant a Tree With Your Own Hands," Meir Malca Jewish National Fund, 7 Rehov Shmuel Hanagid, Jerusalem, Tel: (02) 223993 or Visitors Department, Jewish National Fund, 96 Rehov Hayarkon, Tel Aviv, Tel: (03) 234449, 240251.

SPECIAL PROGRAMS

Summer University Courses: The following universities hold special summer courses for students from abroad:

Ben Gurion University, Beersheba
Tel: (057) 64111
Summer course for studying Hebrew.

Hebrew University of Jerusalem
Mr. Weinberg
Department of Summer Courses
Overseas Students Admission Office
Goldsmith Building
Mount Scopus, Jerusalem
Tel: (02) 882604, 882624
Summer vacation program—six-week intensive course in Hebrew or Arabic; three-week intensive course in archaeology; Jewish history; Middle East studies; Israel studies; contemporary Jewry; international relations; folklore; Holocaust; art history; psychology; and environmental studies.

Tel Aviv University
Amos Gilboa
University Campus, Ramat Aviv
Tel: (03) 242111

Volunteer Programs

Kibbutz: The *kibbutz* is a communal or collective settlement governed by the general assembly of its members. All property is jointly owned and work is organized on a cooperative basis. Members receive no salary, but in return for their work, get housing, clothing, food, medical services, education for their children and other social amenities.

Most *kibbutzim* are agricultural but many have added sizeable industrial enterprises. There are over 200 *kibbutzim* in all parts of the country and the number of members range from 90 to over 2,000.

Most *kibbutzim* accept volunteers for varying lengths of time. Volunteers must be between 18 and 32 years. No children or pregnant women are accepted.

For further information contact any Israel Government Tourist Office or the following organizations.

Hakibbutz Ha'artzi
Arie Rudolf & Hedva Ronen
13 Rehov Leonardo da Vinci
64733 Tel Aviv
Tel: (03) 435262

Hakibbutz Hadati
Zipi Romen
Volunteer Department
7 Rehov Dubnov
Tel Aviv
Tel: (03) 257231

Ikhud Hakvutzot Vehakibbutz and Hakibbutz Hemeyuhad
Ben Baor
10 Rehov Dubnov
Tel Aviv
Tel: (03) 250231

or

United Kibbutz Movement
82 Rehov Hayarkon
Tel Aviv
Tel: (03) 651710

It's best to plan ahead of time as far as possible if you are serious about volunteering. In New York, you should direct inquiries to:

The Jewish Agency
Kibbutz Aliyah Desk
515 Park Ave.
New York, NY 10022
Tel: (212) 688-4134

In Europe and elsewhere:

Ichud Habonim-Dror
P.O.B. 154
Waverley 2024
Sydney, N.S.W.
Tel: 389-4993

Kibbutz Representative
1A Accommodation Rd.
London NW11, B.E.P.
Tel: 01-450-9235

Sochnut
17 rue Forunay
Paris 75017
Tel: 766-0313

Ichud Habonim
John Wermeer—
Straat 22
Amsterdam
Tel: 020-719123

Haus des Kibbuzes
D—6000 Frankfurt/Main
Falkensteinerstr. 1
Tel: 0611/556963

Moshav: There are other forms of agricultural settlements—Moshav Ovdim and Moshav Shitufi. Moshav Ovdim is set up on principles of mutual aid and equal opportunity and Moshav Shitufi is based on cooperative economy and ownership, as in the *kibbutz*, but here, each family owns their own house and accepts responsibility for their own domestic arrangements.

For further information contact Liora Fine, Volunteer Department, 19 Rehov Leonardo da Vinci, 64733 Tel Aviv, Tel: (03) 258473.

Others: The Youth Department of the Jewish Agency also helps to place volunteers as workers on *kibbutzim*. The Head Office is located at 49 Rehov Hamelech George, Jerusalem, Tel: (02) 639261.

The Youth Section of the Ministry of Tourism provides maps and other printed information and helps youth visitors to join archaeological digs, many of which are open to student participants from abroad.

Volunteers must be over 17 years and physically fit. They are expected to pay their own fares to and from Israel and take care of their accommodation and other arrangements not connected with their work on the dig.

For further information, contact David Sandovsky, The Ministry of Tourism, Youth and Student Division, 23 Rehov Hillel, Tel: (02) 240141, 240951 write: 24 Rehov Hamelech George, 94262 Jerusalem, P.O.B. 1018, Jerusalem.

Archaeology: Archaeology is one of Israel's best-loved national pastimes, and the opportunities for archaeological exploration here are rich and varied.

There are dozens of major archaeological sites within the country's borders, spanning all time periods of recorded history. The most important sites—such as Caesarea, Ashkelon, Jericho or Masada—are national parks which are regularly open to the public for a small entrance fee. Often these sites include English-language sign posts and have informative brochures to explain the history and design of the site.

More information on the National Parks system is available from the National Parks Authority, 4 Rehov M. Makleff, Hakirya, Tel Aviv 61070, Tel: (03) 252281.

Other sites, however, are more out of the way or unmarked. Quite a few are, in fact, closed to the public without special permission or appointment. For more information on these sites, or to seek permission, contact the Department of Antiquities & Museums.

Numerous museums feature special displays on archaeology, among them the Ha'aretz Museum in (northern) Tel Aviv, and Jerusalem's Israel Museum. Among the presentations at this institution are the controversial Dayan Collection, and the numerous findings housed within the Rockefeller Museum.

Excavations: In any given year there are usually over two dozen separate archaeological sites undergoing excavation, many of which accept volunteers during summer. Among the perennial favorite dig sites are Tel Dan, near *kibbutz* Dan and Banias, in northern Israel, which contains ruins ranging from the Canaanite, to the Israelite, to the Roman, and Tel Dor, on the Carmel Coast near *kibbutz* Nasholim and Caesarea, an erstwhile Phoenician port.

Other sites that have accepted volunteers include Emmaus, Hammat Gadar, Horvat Uza, Sepphoris (two sites), Capernahum, Tel Arad and Timna.

Usually, volunteers must be over 18, although sometimes 16-year- olds are admitted. Applications should be made (early in the year) to individual excavation directors, who are usually connected to different universities in Israel and abroad. These names and addresses, and further information, can be obtained from any IGTO, or Marta Retig, Department of Antiquities & Museums, Ministry of Education & Culture, P.O. Box 586, Jerusalem, Tel: (02) 278502/3.

Dig for a Day: A group called Archaeological Seminars, Inc., nestled in the modern alleyways above the Cardo in the Jewish Quarter of the Old City, specializes in topics regarding Jerusalem archaeology. Their offerings include a variety of three-hour seminars. All cost about $4, and involve multi-media presentations. They also run a program called "Dig For A Day", which allows the visitor the opportunity to excavate at a dig site on a more limited scale. The dig lasts a full morning and costs $15 per person (less for students).

Contact the group at 11 Rehov Shonai Hallachot,

Jewish Quarter, P.O.B. 14002, Jaffa Gate, Jerusalem, Tel: (02) 273515.

There are also numerous daily or weekly guided tours of the Old City, the City of David, or special topics connected to either of these, which are listed at the IGTOs at the Jaffa Gate or 24 King George Street.

There is generally no fee paid but food and accommodation are often provided. Transport to and from the site is generally paid by the volunteer. Persons over 18 can apply. There is a minimum participation time.

The Israel Department of Antiquities and Museums publishes the *Archaeological Excavations Booklet* containing information concerning excavations being conducted as well as precise information for prospective volunteers.

For details contact:

Gershon Di Zahav
P.O.B. 53
22100 Nahariya
Tel: (04) 925392, 923366

"Dig for a Day"
10 Shoney Halachot
Jerusalem
Tel: (02) 273515

Ulpan: Ulpan Akiva is a Hebrew-language school where Hebrew is taught as a licing language in everyday conversation at all levels: reading, writing, speech patterns, drama and idioms. The school is located at the Green Beach Hotel near Netanya and facilities include a swimming pool, tennis and basketball courts and the beach.

Courses are from four to 20 weeks, for families and individuals of 12 years and up. The program consists of: four or five hours of Hebrew study a day, lectures on the Bible, Jewish history, Hebrew literature, current affairs, cultural activities that including folk singing and dancing and meetings with local personalities. Studying side by side with Israelis lets you experience the culture of Israel hands-on. Tours can be arranged to archaeological sites and other places of interest in the area. Courses are run on a residential, full board basis.

For further information, contact Ulpan Akiva, International Hebrew Study Center, Green Beach Hotel, P.O.B. 256, 42100 Netanya, Tel: (053) 52312/3.

Many *kibbutzim* offer courses which cost $50 in return for participants' part-time work on the *kibbutz*. The courses last for five and-a-half months and are open to Jews between the ages of 17 1/2 and 35. Students may arrive at the *kibbutz* a week before the course begins. Participants must be physically fit for work.

For further details, contact Ulpanim's Kibbutzim Department, The Jewish Agency, 12 Rehov Kaplan, Tel Aviv, Tel: (03) 258311.

PILGRIMAGES

While Israel has much to offer each tourist, for the Christian pilgrim, a trip to Israel is more than just a journey. Here the pilgrim

has the unique opportunity of tracing the footsteps of Jesus and the early Christians, the trip becomes a religious experience for him.

Throughout the country, the pilgrim may visit sites significant to the life and teaching of Jesus: Bethlehem, his birthplace; Nazareth, the town of his boyhood; the Sea of Galilee, scene of miracles and his ministerial teaching; Mount Tabor, site of the Transfiguration; the Garden of Gethsemane and Jerusalem, where he spent his last hours before the cruxification in prayer and agony; and Latrun, now the site of a Trappist monastery, where he appeared before his disciples after the Resurrection.

**Places of Interest:
Visiting Hours**

Jerusalem

Armenian Cathedral of St. James
Tel: (02) 282331
Monday—Friday
3 a.m—3:30 p.m.
Saturday—Sunday
2:30 a.m.—3:15 p.m.

Armenian Museum
Closed temporarily.

Bethany St. Lazarus
Tel: (02) 271706
7 a.m.—Noon
2—6 p.m.

Bethphage
Tel: (02) 284352
7 a.m.—5:30 p.m.
(Ring bell)

Cenacle (Last Supper)
8:30 a.m. to sundown

Cenacle Chapel Franciscans
Tel: (02) 713597
7 a.m.—Noon
3 p.m.—sundown
(Ring bell)

Christ Church — Office
Tel: (02) 282082
8 a.m.—10 a.m.
4:30 p.m.—6 p.m.

Christian Information Center
Tel: (02) 287647
8:30 a.m.—12:30 p.m.
3—6 p.m.
(Closed Sunday; 3p.m.—5:30 p.m. in winter)

Dominus Flevit
Tel: (02) 285837
6:45 a.m.—11:30 a.m.
3—5 p.m.

Ein Kare: St. John's
Tel: (02) 413639
5:30 a.m.—Noon
2:30—6 p.m.
(2:30—5:30 p.m. winter)

Ein Karen: Visitation
Tel: (02) 417291
9 a.m.—Noon
3—6 p.m.

Flagellation
Tel: (02) 282936
6 a.m.—Noon
2—6 p.m.
(2—5:30 p.m. winter)

Garden Tomb
Tel: (02) 283402
8 a.m.—1 p.m.
3 p.m.— 5 p.m.
Closed Sunday
(8 a.m.—12.30 p.m. and 2:30—4:30 p.m. winter)

Gethsemane, Church of Agony and Grotto
Tel: (02) 283264

8:30 a.m.—Noon
3 p.m.—sundown
(2 p.m.—sundown in winter)

Holy Sepulchre
Tel: (02) 284215
4 a.m.—8 p.m.
(4 a.m.—7:00 p.m. in winter)

Lithostrotos—Ecce Homo
Tel: (02) 282445
8:30 a.m.—4:30 p.m.
Closed Sunday
(8:30 a.m.—4 p.m. in winter)

Lutheran Church of the Redeemer
Tel: (02) 282543
9 a.m.—1 p.m.
2—5 p.m.
Friday: 9 a.m.—1 p.m.
Sunday for services only.

Monastery of the Holy Cross
Tel: (02) 634442
Irregular hours—phone ahead.

Paternoster Church
Tel: (02) 283143
8:30.—11:45 a.m.
3—4:30 p.m.

Russian Cathedral
Tel: (02) 222565
By appointment.

St. Mary Magdalene
Tel: (02) 282897
Irregular hours—phone ahead.

St. Alexander Excavations
Tel: (02) 284580
9 a.m.—1 p.m.
3—1 p.m.
(Ring bell)

St. Ann's—Bethesda
Tel: (02) 283258
8 a.m.—Noon
2:30—6p.m.
(2—5 p.m. in winter)

St. George's Cathedral
Tel: (02) 282253, 282167
6:45 a.m.—6:30 p.m.

Tomb of Mary (Gethsemane)
6:30 a.m.—Noon
2—6 p.m.

St. Mark's (Syrian Orthodox.)
Tel: (02) 283304
9 a.m.—Noon
3:30—6:00 p.m.
(Ask for key)
(2—5 p.m. in winter)

St. Peter in Gallicantu
Tel: (02) 283332
8:30—11:45 a.m.
2—5 p.m.
Closed Sunday

St. Stephen's Church
Tel: (02) 282213
7:30 a.m.—1:00 p.m.
3— 6 p.m.

Dormition Abbey
Tel: (02) 719927
7 a.m.—12:30 p.m.
2—7 p.m.

Abu Gosh Crusader Church
Tel: (02) 539798
8:30—11 a.m.
2:30—5:00 p.m.

Bethlehem

Bethlehem Nativity Church
6a.m.—6 p.m.

Bethlehem St. Catherine
Tel: (02) 742425

8 a.m.—Noon
2:30—6p.m.

Bethlehem Shepherd's Field
Tel: (02) 742423
8—11:30 a.m.
2—6 p.m.
(2—5 p.m. in winter)

Cana: Wedding Church
Tel: (067) 55211
8 a.m.—Noon
3—6 p.m.
(3—5 p.m. in winter)

Capernaum "City of Jesus"
Tel: (067) 21059
8:30 a.m.—4:30 p.m.

Emmaus—Qubeibeh
Tel: (067) 952495 ext. 4
6:30—11:30 a.m.
2—6 p.m.

Latrun Monastery
Tel: (08) 420065
7:30 a.m.—11:30 a.m.
2:30—5:00 p.m.

Jacob's Well: Nablus
8:30 a.m.—Noon
2:30—5 p.m.

Mar Saba Monastery
(Men only)
Only with permission of the Greek-Orthodox Patriarch

Mount of Beatitudes
Tel: (067) 20878
8 a.m.—Noon
2—4 p.m.

Mount Carmel Stella Maris
Tel: (04) 523460
6 a.m.—Noon
3—6 p.m.
(3—5 p.m. in winter)

Muhraqa: Sacrifice of Elijah
9—11 a.m.
1— 5 p.m.

Nazareth

Nazareth: Basilica of the Annunciation & St. Joseph's
Tel: (067) 72501
8:30—11:45 a.m.
2—6 p.m.
Sunday: 2—6 p.m.
(2—5 p.m. in winter)

Nazareth Synagogue
8:30 a.m.—5:00 p.m.
(Ring bell)

Nazareth St. Gabriel's (Well)
8:30—11:45 a.m.
2.00—6.00 p.m.

Kiryat Yearim
Tel: (02) 539818
8:30—11:30 a.m.
(Ring bell)

St. George's in Wadi Kelt
Visits at any time.

St. Theodosius Monastery
Tel: (02) 742216
8 a.m.—Noon
1—5 p.m.

Tabor Transfiguration
Tel: (067) 67489
8 a.m.—Noon
3—5 p.m.

Tabgha: Primary St. Peter
Tel: (067) 71062
8 a.m.—sundown

Tabgha: Multiplication of the Bread
Tel: (067) 21061

8 a.m.—4p.m.

Temptation Monastery Jericho
8 a.m.—Noon
3—4 p.m.

Good Samaritan Inn in the Judean Desert
8 a. m.—1 p.m.
Closed Friday

Baptismal Sites: An organized baptismal site has been erected at the mouth of the River Jordan, eight km (five miles) south of Tiberias. There are three levels of platforms in the water and descent is by steps or a wheelchair-accessible ramp. There is ample space for groups. The site is open during the day. Entry is free.

Information Offices for Pilgrims

The Israel Pilgrimage Committee: This is an interministerial body which functions closely with representatives of foreign and local trade organizations, as well as Christian bodies. It aims to: establish conditions which will enable Christian pilgrims and visitors who arrive in Israel, singly or in groups, to come into closer contact with the citizens of the country and to be made aware of its achievements and problems; maintain fruitful cooperation with clerical and other Christian bodies in Israel for joint promotional pilgrimage activities; to enable pilgrim groups to summarize their impressions and discuss them in their own language. Israeli personalities in various fields are available to reply to questions concerning the Biblical, cultural, economic and political life of Israel. The panel for this forum can be adapted according to the professional and/or religious composition of each group. The Israel Pilgrimage Com-mittee will offer, free-of-charge, lectures on specific topics like: the remaking of a nation; the conquest of the desert; Israel and the Arabs; the revival of the Hebrew language; biblical archaeology; Judiasm in modern Israel; and films.

For more information contact the Ministry of Tourism, Pilgrimage Division, P.O.B. 1019, Jerusalem, Tel: (02) 247962.

Christian Information Center:
The Center, located inside the Old City's Jaffa Gate, opposite the Citadel, welcomes individuals or groups who, on their arrival in Jerusalem, seek help in planning their tours and visits. Services include: information of Christian and general interest on holy places, Christian hospices, location of churches, times of services, etc; lectures, meetings, exhibitions; a monthly *Associated Christian Press Bulletin*; guide books and maps.

The Christian Information Center, Omar Ibn El-Khattab Square (Jaffa Gate) P.O.B. 14309 Jerusaelm, Tel: (02) 287647.

Franciscan Pilgrims Office:
Located at the Christian Information Center, inside the Old City's Jaffa Gate, opposite the Citadel. The office makes arrangements for Catholic priests who wish to celebrate a Mass. Reservations can be made at the office, free-of-charge, for shrines in Jerusalem, Bethlehem, Bethany, Ein Kerem, Emmaus (Qubeibeh) and Jericho. The office also issues certificates of Christian pilgrimages.

HOLIDAYS

The Sabbath and Jewish Holy Days: The Sabbath, Saturday, Israel's day of rest, and all holy days commence at sundown on the preceding day and end at nightfall. All Jewish shops, businesses, institutions, offices and public places of entertainment (with the exception of a few restaurants and clubs) are closed and most public transport cease. Some shops and all places of entertainment reopen with the termination of the Sabbath or the holy day, and public transport resumes.

The Hebrew calendar, unlike the Gregorian, is a lunar calendar. Jewish holy days, therefore, fall on different dates in the general calendar each year.

Calendar of Jewish Holidays

Holy Day	Hebrew Date	Approx. Gregorian Date
Rosh Hashana	Tishri 1-2	September/October
Yom Kuppur	Tishri 10	September/October
Succot	Tishri 15-21	September/October
Simhat Torah	Tishri 22	September/October
Hanukka	Kislev 25-Tevet 3 or 4	November/December
Tu B'Omer	Shevat 15	January/February
Purim	Adar 14	February/March
Pessah	Nissan 15-21	March/April
Independence Day	Iyar 5	April/May
Lag Ba'Omer	Iyar 18	April/May
Jerusalem Liberation Day	Iyar 28	May/June
Shavu'ot	Sivan 6	May/June
Tisha B'Av	Av 9	July/August

Rosh Hashana and Yom Kippur: *Rosh Hashana* (the Jewish New Year) and *Yom Kippur* (the Day of Atonement) are known as the "Days of Awe." On these days a Jew is called upon to give an account of himself before God. These festivals are purely religious in character, and are observed principally in the synagogue.

Yom Kippur ends the 10-day period of penitence which begins on *Rosh Hashana*. For the observant Jew this is a 25-hour period of complete fasting and prayer. On this day the entire country comes to a standstill. **All public and commercial services shut down** and there is no traffic, either public or private.

There are no organized tours for tourists on this day. Tourists who do not fast are advised to check with their hotels for arrangements about meals.

Succot and Simchat Torah

The *Succot* Festival (Feast of Tabernacles) has a dual significance—religious and agricultural. Observant Jews dwell, or at least eat, in *succot* (booths) erected near their homes to commemorate the Israelites dwelling in the wilderness after the exodus from Egypt. Some hotels and restaurants also build *succot* on their premises.

The agricultural significance of the festival is symbolized by the "four species"—the palm branch, the myrtle, the willow and the citron, over which a special blessing is recited on each day of the festival.

Simchat Torah (Rejoicing of the Law) is on the eighth day of the Feast of Tabernacles and on this day the annual cycle of the reading of the Law (*Torah*) is completed and another cycle begins. This festival is an extremely joyous one and is marked by much singing and dancing in the streets as well as in the synagogues.

Chanukah

Chanukah (Festival of Lights) is an eight-day celebration recalling the successful revolt of the small Jewish community in the land of Israel in the year 167 B.C. against the Syrian Hellenistic empire.

During *Chanukah*, one light is lit on the first night, two on the second night, and so on, in an eight-branched candelabrum, until the eighth night, when the entire candelabrum is aglow. In this way the Jewish people commemorate the miracle of the burning oil in the Holy Temple which occurred after the revolt. When the victorious fighters came to cleanse and rededicate their temple, which had been polluted by idolatry, they found that the supply of ritual oil, sufficient only for one day, miraculously burned for a full eight days—the length of time needed to prepare a new supply of the special oil.

During *Chanukah*, large electric lamps are lit outside public buildings and many shops display the eight-branched candelabrum in their windows. Hotels conduct candle-lighting ceremonies for their guests, after which traditional *Chanukah* fare, such as doughnuts and potato pancakes, is served.

Tu'B'Shvat

(The New Year of the Trees): On this day, which is also considered the awakening of spring, children all over Israel carry tree saplings which they plant in special planting areas, singing traditional *Tu B'Shvat* songs. Fifteen species of fruit are also to be tasted traditionally on this day and a blessing said over them.

Purim

This festival commemorates the events which took place in Shusan in ancient Persia, when the wicked chancellor Haman persuaded Ahasuerus, king of Persia, to kill all Jews in his domain. Through Queen Esther and her uncle Mordechai, the plot was foiled and the Jews were saved.

The festival takes its name from the Hebrew word *purim*, meaning "lots," which Haman cast to determine the day to carry out his terrible plan. On the eve of the festival, the Scroll of Esther, which relates the tale, is read in every synagogue. All through the festival children and adults dress in colorful costumes and masks and eat triangular-shaped pastries, filled with fruit or poppy seeds, aptly known as "Haman's Ears."

Pesach

(Passover): One of the main festivals in the Jewish calendar, joyously commemorating the exodus of the Jews from Egypt and the miracles that preceded it (including the last plague, which struck the first-born sons of the Egyptians but "passed over" the Israelites).

The center of festivity is the home, where the ritual Passover meal (*Seder*) takes place on the eve of the festival, accompanied by the reading of a special text (*Haggadah*) which recounts the historic events of the Passover through ritual questions and answers, blessings and songs.

During the time of Passover (seven days in Israel and eight abroad) only unleavened bread (*matza*) is eaten and there is abstention from all fermented foods. Jewish hotels do not serve bread during this period. It is also a time for pilgrimage to Jerusalem, as are *Shavout* (Pentecost) and *Succot* (Feast of Tabernacles). In the Christian tradition, the Last Supper was a Passover meal, and Easter Sunday is determined as the first Sunday in the Passover period.

Shavout (Pentecost): This ancient holiday is mentioned in the Holy Scriptures as the "Feast of the Giving of the Law" (*Torah*), commemorating the day God gave Moses the Ten Commandments, which he in turn gave to the children of Israel; the "Feast of In-gathering," marking the end of the wheat harvest; and the "Feast of the First Fruits," for in ancient days, first-fruit offerings were brought to the temple in Jerusalem as an expression of gratitude to God.

In Israel, *Shavout* is observed with prayer and public celebrations. School children parade with flower garlands and baskets of fruits on their heads. The entire night preceding the festival is devoted to the study of the Law (*Torah*), and the next day special prayers are recited in the synagogues, which are decorated with flowers, fruit and greenery. It is customary to eat dairy foods and honey during this happy festival.

Tisha B'Av (The ninth of *Av*): Commemorating the destruction of the first and second temples, and other tragedies that befell the Jewish people in later history, *Tisha B'Av* is a traditional day of mourning and fasting.

Christian Holy Days: These holy days are celebrated on different dates by different denominations— Catholic and Protestant (on same dates), Greek-Orthodox and Armenian. (See the following listing).

Christian Holy Days— Protestant, Roman Catholic and Christian Eastern Church

Month/Feast
January
-New Year (Holy Mother of God)
-**Epiphany**
March
-Miracle of the Wine (Cana) St. Joseph
-The Sorrows of Our Lady (Calvary)
-Bethphage
April
-Flagellation
-Gethsemane
-Coenaculum (Mt. Zion)
-Gethsemane (Holy Hour)
-Good Friday
-Holy Saturday
-**Easter Sunday**
-Easter Monday
May
-Invention of the Holy Cross (Holy Sepulchre)
-**Ascension Day**
-**Pentecost Day**
-Visitation (Ein Karem)
-Procession in Jerusalem
June
-Corpus & Sanguis Christi (only in Holy Sepulchre)

-St. John the Baptist (in Ein Karem)
-St. Peter & Paul
August
-**Assumption Day**
September
-Nativity of the Holy Virgin (at St. Anne's)
-Exaltation of the Holy Cross (Calvary)
December
-Immaculate Conception-
-**Christmas Day**

Holy Sepulchre Procession: Daily at noon in the Church of the Holy Sepulchre. **Way of the Cross** (Via Dolorosa): Procession every Friday at 3 p.m. starting from the Antonia. Protestant holy days, are the same as above except that Pentecost is called Whitsunday.

A list of churches and prayer times are available at all tourist offices.

Muslim Holy Days: Friday is a holy day for Moslems and places of worship are closed during prayers on that day, as they are on all holy days. Moslem holy days are decided on in accordance with the appearance of the new moon, thus falling on different dates in the general calendar each year.

The most important are:
-*Id el Adha*, Sacrificial Festival (four days)
-New Year
-Mohammed's Birthday
-Ramadan Feast(1month)
-*Id el Fitr*, conclusion of Ramadan (three days)

Druze Holy Days
-*Id el Adha*, Sacrificial Festival
-*Nabi Shu'eb* and
-*Nabi Sablan*

SHOPPING

Most stores in Israel are open daily from 8 a.m. to 1 p.m. and 4 p.m. to 7 p.m. Shops in the hotels are often open until midnight. On Fridays and the eve of Jewish holy days, the stores close around 2 p.m. Jewish stores are closed on Saturday and on *Yom Kippur*. Moslem shops are closed on Friday, Christian shops, on Sunday.

Merchandise:

Shops in Israel offer a wide variety of merchandise and gifts. These include exclusive jewelry and diamonds; oriental carpets and antiques; fashionable ladies' wear and elegant furs, leather goods; paintings and sculptures; ceramics; silverware and copperware; embroidery, batiks and religious articles.

There are several hundred shops approved by the Ministry of Tourism which display a sign stating "Listed by the Ministry of Tourism" and the Ministry's emblem (two scouts carrying a bunch of grapes on a pole between them)—the symbol of fair-priced merchandise.

In addition, you can find colorful oriental markets and bazaars in the narrow alleyways of the old cities of Jerusalem, Bethlehem, Acco, Nazareth, Hebron and Druze villages. These sell handmade arts and crafts—including olive wood, mother-of-pearl, leather and bamboo items, hand-blown glass, clothing, vegetables and fruit.

Duty-free shops are located at Ben-Gurion and Eilat airports and at most leading hotels. Foreign-made articles such as watches, cameras, perfumes, tobaccos and liqor, as well as many fine Israeli products may be purchased with foreign currency for delivery to the plane or ship prior to departure.

Judaica:

Besides these items, Israel has an unique variety of traditional crafts and Judaica for sale, ranging from religious articles like *menorahs*, *mezzuzot* and spice boxes to wall hangings and statuary, which can be ostentatiously ornate or stunningly minimal.

Centers for buying fine crafts include several locations in Jerusalm, among them the House of Quality, the Khutzot Hayotzer Arts & Crafts Lane, Yochanan Migush Halav Street and the Mea Shearin area.

Bargaining:

In the Old City of Jerusalem and other Arab market places bargaining is a standard practice. Usually you can purchase an item at 23 percent off by starting your side of the haggle at half the quoted price. Avoid haggling if you are not interested in buying or if the item is cheap. Brassware, carvings and fabrics are among the more popular finds here.

Other popular shopping places include the weekly Bedouin market in Beersheba on Thursday mornings, and the Druze markets in the north.

Value Added Tax:

V.A.T. at the rate of 15 percent is charged on all goods and services and is included in the quoted price.

Tourist Reductions:

Tourists who buy fur or leather goods at shops listed by the Ministry of Tourism and pay for them in foreign currency, are exempt from V.A.T. on furs, and receive a 25 percent discount on leather goods, if these are delivered to them at the port of departure.

At selected shops any purchase in foreign currency, exceeding $50, entitles the tourist to a discount of at least five percent at the shop and to a refund of the V.A.T. at the port of departure, upon presentation of the bill and goods. (Not applicable to tobacco, electrical and photographic supplies). Shops participating in this reduction scheme display an appropriate sign.

Tourists are also exempt from V.A.T. on the following services: accommodation and the meals included in hotel bills, regular and charter tours and the meals supplied en route, hire of cars with driver guides, self-drive car hire, flights and tours of inland air companies. (Payment does not have to be made in foreign currency, but your passport must be presented).

LANGUAGE

Hebrew, the revived language of the Bible, and Arabic are the official languages of the country. English is also widely spoken. Road signs are in Hebrew, Arabic and English. Tourist information is usually available in French and German as well. Other languages spoken widely include Spanish, Russian, Polish, Yiddish and Hungarian, among others.

Still, it is a good idea to know some basic Hebrew words and phrases before coming to the country. Here are 60 basic words which may help you find the language a little less daunting:

All-purpose greeting
(literally "peace")
Shalom

good morning
boker tov

good evening
erev tov

yes
ken

no
lo

please
bevakasha

thank you
toda

very much
raba

good
tov

bad

ra

big
gadol

little
katan

more
yoter

less
pahot

I
ani

you (singular—
male/female)
ata/at

(plural—male/female)
atem/aten

we/us
anahnu

them (male/female)
hem/hen

want (male/female)
otseh/rotsa

how much?
kama?

too dear
yakar midai

cheaper
yoter zol

bank
bank

restaurant
mis'ada

post office
do'ar

hotel
malon

shop
hanut

taxi
monit

train
rakevet

bus
autoboos

station/bus stop
tahana

Where is?
eyfo?

right
yemin

left
smol

when?
matai?

white
lavan

black
shahor

red
adom

blue
kahol

right, correct
nahon

wrong
lo nahon

straight
yashar

one *ehad*	eight *shmoney*	cinema *kolno'a*
two *shtayim*	nine *taysha'*	newspaper *'iton*
four *arba'*	ten *'esser*	water *mayim*
five *hamesh*	hundred *elef*	food *okhel*
six *shesh*	many *harbey*	check *heshbon*
seven *sheva'*	stop, wait a minute! *rega!*	

DIPLOMATIC MISSIONS

EMBASSIES AND CONSULATES

Most embassies are closed on Sundays. It is advisable to phone and check for their opening hours.

Embassy of The Republic of Argentina
112 Rehov Hayarkon
2nd Floor
63571 Tel Aviv
Tel: (03) 293411/2

Australian Embassy
185 Rehov Hayarkon
63405 Tel Aviv
Tel: (03) 243152

Embassy of the Republic of Austria
11 Rehov Hermann Cohen
64385 Tel Aviv
Tel: (03) 246186

Embassy of The Kingdom of Belgium
266 Rehov Hayarkon
63504 Tel Aviv
Tel: (03) 454164/5/6

Embassy of The Republic of Bolivia
85 Sderot Ben Gurion
3rd Floor, Apt. 10
64514 Tel Aviv
Tel: (03) 230868

Embassy of The Federative Republic of Brazil
14 Rehov Hei Be'Iyar
Kikar Hamedina
5th Floor
62093 Tel Aviv
Tel: (03) 219292/4

Embassy of The Socialist Republic of The Union of Burma
19 Rehov Yona
52376 Ramat Gan
Tel: (03) 783151

Embassy of Canada
220 Rehov Hayarkon
63405 Tel Aviv
Tel: (03) 228122/5

Embassy of The Republic of Chile
54 Rehov Pinkas
Apt. 45, 11th Floor
62261 Tel Aviv
Tel: (03) 440414/5

Embassy of The Republic of Columbia
52 Rehov Pinkas
6th Floor, Apt. 62
62261 Tel Aviv
Tel: (03) 449616

Embassy of The Republic of Costa Rica
Mercaz Clal
97 Rehov Yafo
7th Floor, Room 714
94342 Jerusalem
Tel: (02) 244418

Royal Danish Emabssy
23 Rehov Beni Moshe

62308 Tel Aviv
Tel: (03) 440405/6

**Embassy of The
Dominican Republic**
Asia House
4 Rehov Zamenhoff
Herzliya B
Tel: (052) 72422

**Embassy of The
Republic of Ecuador**
Asia House
4 Rehov Weizmann
Room 231
64239 Tel Aviv
Tel: (03) 258764

**Embassy of The Arab
Republic of Egypt**
54 Rehov Basel
62744 Tel Aviv
Tel: (03) 224151

**Embassy of The
Republic of El Salvador**
16 Rehov Kovshei
Katamon
Jerusalem
Tel: (02) 633575

Embassy of Finland
Beit Eliahu, 8th Floor
2 Rehov Ibn Gvirol
64077 Tel Aviv
Tel: (03) 250527/8

Embassy of France
112 Tayelet Herbert
Samuel
63572 Tel Aviv
Tel: (03)   245371/3,
249666, 222648

**Embassy of The Federal
Republic of Germany**
16 Rehov Soutine
64684 Tel Aviv
Tel: (03) 243111/5

British Embassy
192 Rehov Hayarkon
63405 Tel Aviv

Tel: (03) 249171/8

**Diplomatic
Representation
of Greece**
35 Sderot Shaul
Hamelech
64297 Tel Aviv
Tel: (03) 259704, 266127

**Embassy of The Repub-
lic of Guatemala**
1 Rehov Bernstein Cohen
Apt. 10
47227 Ramat Hasharon
Tel: (03) 490456

Embassy of Haiti
Asia House
4 Rehov Weizmann
Room 230
64239 Tel Aviv
Tel: (03) 252084

Embassy of Italy
Asia House
4 Rehov Weizmann
64239 Tel Aviv
Tel: (03) 264223/5

Embassy of Japan
Asia House
4 Rehov Weizmann
64239 Tel Aviv
Tel: (03) 257292/4

Embassy of Liberia
119 Sderot Rothschild
Tel Aviv
Tel: (03) 247507, 247191

**Embassy of the United
States of Mexico**
14 Rehov Hei Be'lyar
Kikar Hamedina
62093 Tel Aviv
Tel: (03) 210266/7/8

**Royal Netherlands
Embassy**
Asia House
4 Rehov Weizmann
64239 Tel Aviv

Tel: (03)   257337/9,
257370

**Royal Norwegian
Embassy**
10 Rehov Hei Be;lyar
Kikar Hamedina
62093 Tel Aviv
Tel; (03) 295207/8

**Embassy of The Repub-
lic of Panama**
28 Rehov Hei Be'lyar
Kikar Hamedina
62998 Tel Aviv
Tel: (03) 253158, 256711

**Embassy of The Repub-
lic of Peru**
52 Rehov Pinkas
Apt. 31, 8th Floor
62261 Tel Aviv
Tel: (03) 454065, 457886

**Embassy of The Repub-
lic of the Philippines**
12 Rehov Hei Be'lyar
4th Floor
Kikar Hamedina
62093 Tel Aviv
Tel: (03) 258143

**Embassy of The Socialist
Republic of Romania**
24 Rehov Adam Hachen
64585 Tel Aviv
Tel: (03) 247379, 242482

**Embassy of The Repub-
lic of South Africa**
2 Rehov Kaplan
9th Floor
64734 Tel Aviv
Tel: (03) 256147

Royal Swedish Embassy
Asia House
4 Rehov Weizmann
64239 Tel Aviv
Tel; (03) 258111

Embassy of Switzerland
228 Rehov Hayarkon

63405 Tel Aviv
Tel: (03) 244121/2

Legation of Turkey
34 Rehov Amos
62495 Tel Aviv
Tel: (03) 454155/6

Embassy of The United States of America
71 Rehov Hayarkon
63903 Tel Aviv
Tel: (03) 654338

Embassy of The Oriental Republic of Uruguay
52 Rehov Pinkas
2nd. Floor, Apt. 10
62261 Tel Aviv
Tel: (03) 440411

Embassy of The Republic of Venezuela
Asia House
4 Rehov Weizmann
5th Floor

64239 Tel Aviv
Tel: (03) 222002, 245839

United Nations Truce Supervision Organization
P.O.B. 490
91400 Jerusalem
Tel: (02) 716223/6

ART/PHOTO CREDITS